Student Nationalism in China, 1927–1937

Hoover Institution Publications

JOHN ISRAEL

Student Nationalism in China

1927-1937

951.04
Is7

Published for the
Hoover Institution on War, Revolution, and Peace
by Stanford University Press, Stanford, California, 1966

Stanford University Press
Stanford, California

© 1966 by the Board of Trustees of the
Leland Stanford Junior University

Printed in the United States of America
L.C. 66-15300

To My Father,
Bert Israel,
1908–1954

This book explores an academic wilderness. Its sources, un-indexed and heretofore unexplored, are scattered over three continents, and much information remains hidden in libraries and archives on the Chinese mainland, and in the memories and memoirs of thousands of men there and abroad. Of five narrative chapters, the subject of only one, the December Ninth Movement, has been treated extensively by previous writers. Therefore, I hope that this pioneering effort will not be taken as a "definitive" work.

Obviously I do not subscribe to the notion that the writing of recent history must wait until all the facts are in, or until time has removed the historian from the controversies of the past. Time destroys historical materials as easily as it unearths them, and the heated disputes that still rage over the era of Confucius suggest that perfect objectivity does not necessarily come with the passage of centuries. It may even be asked, as Page Smith has done in *The Historian and History*, whether a totally dispassionate approach is desirable, though, of course, he does not advocate the historian's becoming a political pamphleteer. Following Mr. Smith's advice, I have tried to understand the Chinese student movement not only in the context of the past, but for the light it throws on the present. A broad comparative history of student movements in many countries may soon be possible thanks to the work of a number of men, including Seymour M. Lipset and his students at Berkeley; a conference in December 1966 is expected to produce a volume of essays on student politics in the developing nations. Meanwhile, there is much groundwork to be done, Page Smith's well-founded attack on monographs notwithstanding. We can only hope that the word monograph will be pried loose from the adjective "dull."

The itinerant scholar can never adequately acknowledge his gratitude to those who have helped him along the way. Thanks are due the curators and employees of the libraries that are mentioned in the Abbreviations following the text. In particular, David Tseng of the staff of the Hoover Institution has gone far beyond the demands of official duty to help me and other young scholars reap maximum benefits from the Institution's rich resources. I am especially indebted to the many government and Kuomintang officials in Taiwan who made it possible for me to spend several fruitful months at the libraries of the National War College, the Kuomintang Archives, and the Ministry of Justice's Bureau of Investigation. I trust that my published views on Taiwan's political problems will not be construed as expressions of ingratitude to these individuals or institutions.

Lo Chia-lun, President of the Academia Historica, and Pao Tsun-p'eng, Director of the National Historical Museum, were exceptionally helpful. Kuo T'ing-i, Director of the Institute of Modern History at the Academia Sinica, placed the facilities of the Institute at my disposal. Professor Wu Hsiang-hsiang of National Taiwan University located valuable Japanese-language materials for me in the University library. And I owe a special word of thanks to Professor Li Ting-i, then of National Taiwan University, who unselfishly gave of his time, energy, and understanding. Mr. Winston Hsieh aided me in many ways both in Taiwan and in this country, and Professors Banno Masataka and Ichiko Chuzo of the Toyo Bunko were uncommonly helpful during my brief visit to Japan.

I am also indebted to the dozens of former students, teachers, administrators, officials, missionaries, and journalists who shared their recollections and insights with me, though only a few of their names appear in the footnotes.

The following people read all or part of the manuscript and made useful suggestions: Professors Chow Tse-tsung, Dennis

J. Doolin, John K. Fairbank, Albert Feuerwerker, Jerome B. Grieder, Allen B. Linden, Maurice Meisner, Benjamin I. Schwartz, Lyman P. Van Slyke, Ezra F. Vogel, and Mary C. Wright. Professor Fairbank's contribution was invaluable, for he read the manuscript in its earliest and crudest form, subjected reams of turgid prose to incisive criticism, and guided to completion the dissertation on which this book is based.

Finally, two others have patiently seen this work through its manifold stages. For his painstaking editorial assistance, I am deeply indebted to my stepfather, Dr. James A. Brussel; and for the faithful handling of innumerable tasks, including editing, typing, transcribing, admonishing, and encouraging, I am forever grateful to my wife, Mary Horn Israel.

I would like to thank the Viking Press and Alfred A. Knopf, Inc., respectively, for permission to quote passages from James Bertram's *First Act in China* and Relman Morin's *East Wind Rising*.

This list of acknowledgments would be incomplete without a word of appreciation to the foundations whose generosity made my work possible. The Ford Foundation, which saw me through my undergraduate years, underwrote research and writing through the Foreign Area Fellowship Program then under its administration. The Woodrow Wilson National Fellowship Foundation was initially responsible for my attending graduate school, and the Inter-University Fellowship Program made possible my intensive study of spoken Chinese. The final stages of writing were expedited by a grant from the Hoover Institution.

Most of the names and places mentioned in this book are well known to students of Chinese history. Specialists interested in less familiar ideographs should consult the glossary in my dissertation, "The Chinese Student Movement, 1927–1937," which may be read in the Archives of Harvard University's Widener Library or obtained without special permission via interlibrary loan.

J. I.

Contents

Abbreviations Used in the Text

CCP	Chinese Communist Party
CEC	Central Executive Committee
CNLV	Chinese National Liberation Vanguard
CTM	Committee for Training the Masses, of the Kuomintang Central Executive Committee
CY	(Chinese) Communist Youth Corps
FNSA	All-China Federation of National Salvation Associations
KMT	Kuomintang
NSA	(Chinese) National Student Association
PSNSU	Peiping Student National Salvation Union
RJNSA	Resist Japan National Salvation Association
YMCA	Young Men's Christian Association

Student Nationalism in China, 1927–1937

For two decades Chiang Kai-shek's Kuomintang government faced a bewildering array of problems: Japanese aggression, Communist insurrection, warlord insurgency, economic depression, natural disasters, intraparty dissension, demands from an alienated literate minority, and resentment on the part of the impoverished and illiterate masses. In Chiang's time, as in centuries past, a leader could remain in power only by winning support from one key group, the intellectuals, and by controlling or neutralizing another, the peasants. In the end, Chiang failed on both counts.

Intellectual protest has a long history in China, from the massive literati remonstrances of the first century B.C. to the examination candidates' demonstrations against the humiliating treaty of Shimonoseki in 1895.[1] Student movements after 1919, however, had little in common with this long tradition. The abolition of the Confucian examination system in 1905 had undermined the position of the traditional literati. Their successors lived in the dormitories of several dozen colleges and universities in the principal cities and immersed themselves not in Confucian classics, but in chemistry, sociology, and foreign literature. They wrote in colloquial *pai-hua,* not in classical *wen-yen*; they spoke not of serving their country, but of saving it. Upon graduation some entered the professions; many became teachers, writers, and businessmen; others entered Kuomintang government service after 1925; a radical minority joined the Communists. Many found no employment. By comparison with the scholarly gentry of earlier times, nearly all were, psychologically and socially, displaced persons.

The twentieth-century Chinese student rankled at nearly a century of national humiliation at the hands of overbearing imperialists, at the woes of warlord rule, and at the bankruptcy of old ideologies. Student activity was increasingly important after the crisis of 1895. The boycott of 1905 protesting American immigration policy enlisted student support. Young intellectuals, especially those returning from Japanese high schools and colleges, were a mainstay of the 1911 revolution and played a prominent role in protesting the Twenty-one Demands of 1915. A penchant for political involvement and a stockpile of experienced leadership were the legacies of these years. At the same time, exposure to a wide spectrum of new ideas aroused discontent and led to demands for fresh solutions. Among the Western credos contemplated by Chinese students and intellectuals were Christianity, utopian socialism, anarchism, Wilsonian liberalism, and the worship of science.

By the end of the First World War, students were in a position to play a leading role in China's political struggles. For many of the economic and technological factors that permitted nationwide movements, the students could thank the same imperialist powers whose outrages they were protesting. Eighty years under the Treaty System had provided China with a communications network that linked major cities and reached the outside world. Newspapers spread reports of demonstrations to other students and to the literate public; telegraph lines speeded requests for support to distant campuses; railroads carried scores of student delegates to national conferences and thousands of young demonstrators to the capital. Furthermore, key groups had emerged to join the students in their anti-imperialist crusade. Treaty-port manufacturers and merchants vulnerable to the economic effects of imperialism could be rallied to boycotts. Labor unions were beginning to organize a growing proletariat. An older generation of alienated intellectuals, some of them as radical as the students themselves, stood ready with aid. Finally, by the early 1920's modern political parties had evolved and were prepared both to encourage and to manipulate student protest.

The catalyst that activated these explosive ingredients was the decision of the Versailles powers to sanctify Japan's occupation of Shantung. Historians date the modern Chinese student movement from the demonstration of May 4, 1919, which was staged to protest this injustice and to denounce the pro-Japanese warlords and politicians who had acquiesced in it. The ensuing nationwide indignation culminated in China's refusal to sign the treaty, and more important, made student opinion a power to be reckoned with. The salient features of the student movement in subsequent years—the countrywide unity, the slogans denouncing Japanese imperialists and Chinese traitors, the demonstrations, the use of modern propaganda methods, the crusades to educate and indoctrinate workers and peasants—all can be traced back to May Fourth.

Thus in 1919 a pattern was set for a generation of student uprisings. During the next three decades it became common to see thousands of high school and college youths surging through the streets demanding resistance to imperialist insults or an end to unpopular policies in their own government. Police suppression usually failed to end these disturbances and in fact often won the demonstrators wide support both from fellow students and from the public at large. Sympathy was especially prevalent among writers and journalists. Professors also applauded the students' aims, though not always their means; administrators in government schools were torn between their obligation to enforce the law and their desire to defend students from police oppression. Movements spread rapidly to cities with large collegiate populations. Regional and national student organizations were quickly formed. However, the emergence of these bodies was invariably accompanied by a decline in spontaneous mass participation. Representative organizations tended to become forums for interested minorities of political activists. Student movements that began as expressions of public opinion thus became tools of revolutionary causes.

The nature of student commitment was radically altered between 1919 and 1949. The May Fourth generation was in revolt against all authority: family, school, and state alike seemed decadent, venal, and hopelessly encrusted with worn-out ways of thought. From about 1915 through the early 1920's, the accent was on liberating the individual from the old order. Anti-Confucianism, the family revolution, and the "literary renaissance" were foremost in students' minds. But though the family revolution continued, after the May Fourth demonstration the battleground began to shift from the home to society and the nation. The new student generation acquired new loyalties.[2]

Three events in particular rechanneled the revolt: the birth of the Chinese Communist Party (CCP) in 1921, the reorganization of the Kuomintang (KMT) in 1923, and the May Thirtieth Incident in 1925. The explosive combination of outraged nationalism and skilled political management brought politics to the fore, made national rather than individual salvation the key issue, and intensified the outcry against imperialism and warlordism.

Both Sun Yat-sen and Mao Tse-tung understood the political implications of the May Fourth Movement. Sun encouraged the students' anti-warlord activities and initiated a vigorous and highly successful Kuomintang drive to enlist campus recruits. Mao, fresh from his political baptism as a middle school agitator in Changsha, also realized the importance of intellectual leadership for the workers and peasants.[3] Meanwhile, young disciples of professors Ch'en Tu-hsiu and Li Ta-chao at National Peking University (Peita) were forming socialist groups, and students returning from France were gaining prominence in the CCP, the KMT, and the Young China Party (Chauvinists). Beginning in 1923, Chinese Communists, following Comintern orders, joined the Kuomintang, which was being reorganized along Leninist lines as a result of Sun Yat-sen's entente with Soviet emissaries. In May 1924, the Whampoa Military Academy opened in Canton, under the young Commandant Chiang Kai-shek. A year later, on May 30, 1925, British-led Shanghai police fired into a crowd of students protesting the murder of a Chinese textile worker by a Japanese foreman; thirteen demonstrators were killed and many were injured. More died in the same city on June 23, when English and French machine gunners mowed down parading students, cadets, and workers. On March 18, 1926, bullets fired by troops of the warlord Tuan Ch'i-jui felled more than two hundred youthful Peiping demonstrators. Aroused by these imperialist and warlord outrages and excited by the promise of the KMT-CCP alliance, students flocked to Canton by the hundreds to join the swelling ranks of the crusade to save China. Schoolboys who cast aside their books and ran off to join the Revolutionary Army were in step with the times. Even literature was being molded to serve political ends. Writers of the Creation Society turned away from purely aesthetic pursuits to produce propaganda. Kuo Mo-jo, their leader, and Mao Tun, another promising young writer, became important agitators in the Political Department of the Revolutionary Army Headquarters.[4] When the Northern Expedition set forth from Kwangtung in June 1926, it enjoyed the active support of China's young intelligentsia.

Student political activities ranged from nationwide drives involving tens of thousands of crusaders against imperialists and warlords to "student tides," local disturbances in which a few dozen or a few hundred youths disputed political, ideological, and educational issues with academic authorities. In no case did these actions involve more than an infinitesimal portion of China's millions. College students numbered 44,167 in 1931, roughly .01 per cent of the population. High school (middle school) students were more numerous, yet they constituted only .1 per cent of the population.[5] China's predominantly male students were older than their Western counterparts. In 1932, 75 to 88 per cent of all college students were men, and 69 per cent were in the 21–25 age bracket.[6] They were drawn from an economic elite. Even the relatively low annual tuition, room, and board of the government university was equivalent to perhaps five months' wages of a Shanghai textile worker. The same worker would have had to spend five and a half years' earnings to put his son through four years of missionary college.[7] In short, a family had to have an upper-middle-class income to send a child to a public college and an upper-class income to send him to a missionary institution.

Though the missionary school, with its democratic and Christian orientation, was inclined to breed nineteenth-century liberals rather than twentieth-century radicals, an American missionary school such as Yenching produced free-thinking, socially conscious, politically active undergraduates. Yenching, not Peita, sparked the December Ninth Movement of 1935. A wider gulf separated both government and missionary college students from the thousands of young men and women who had studied abroad. Students returning to China, especially those who had studied in the most modern industrialized nations, were even more alienated than the students in Chinese universities—the skills and values they had learned abroad seldom seemed relevant to Chinese conditions. Having roots in foreign soil, they suffered psychological and sociological problems that those who remained at home avoided. Domestic students, in spite of a modern education under Western-trained teachers, were less ambivalent; China's destiny was their destiny. It is with them that this study is concerned.[8]

Most college students in the 1930's were from families that had been directly affected by China's confrontation with the West. Only one out of five came from an agricultural family. The rest were children of businessmen, officials, teachers, and other professionals.[9] Two-fifths of the fathers in sociologist Olga Lang's still more urbanized sample had attended modern colleges and had felt the full force of the New Culture Movement.[10] This helped to soften the impact of the revolution in the family. Parents who had rebelled against authority in their parents' homes were inclined to be more permissive with their own children.

China's urbanized modern student movement was to a considerable extent a tale of two cities. In 1932, 30 per cent of the nation's college students were in Peiping, 24 per cent in Shanghai.[11] Peiping (known until 1928 and since 1949 as Peking), for centuries the capital and cultural hub of China, was the home of National Peking University, China's first modern government university, birthplace of the May Fourth Movement. Shanghai, which shared the limelight in student politics, was everything that Peiping was not: the most modern city in China; the center of treaty-port commerce, industry, and culture; one of the world's great seaports. Shanghai looked toward London, Tokyo, and New York, rather than toward China's hinterland. The relative security of both the foreign-governed International Settlement and the French Concession helped make Shanghai the nation's publishing center and attracted many of China's most controversial personalities—journalists and other writers, politicians, and professional revolutionists. Thanks to the militancy and numerical strength of her modern proletariat, Shanghai spawned the May Thirtieth Movement of 1925. Little wonder that both in 1919 and in 1936 student leaders chose Shanghai, rather than Peiping, as the headquarters of the National Student Association (NSA).

From time to time, other cities briefly caught the spotlight. Canton, with 9 per cent of the nation's college students, had a magnetic appeal for the political vanguard of Chinese youth from 1924 to 1926, when it served as the headquarters of the revolutionary Kuomintang government. Subsequently Wuhan enjoyed fleeting prominence as capital of the left-wing KMT-CCP coalition. After the Mukden Incident of September 18, 1931, Nanking attracted young petitioners from Peiping, Shanghai, and elsewhere.

We have observed that slightly more than half a million college and middle school students formed an educated elite among nearly half a billion Chinese. But the course of student political activities was plotted by a mere handful of leaders. Although an extraordinary national crisis or an imperialist affront could rally youths by the thousands to demonstrate in the streets and public squares, young scholars usually remained at their desks. Less than 10 per cent led an active political life in school, and perhaps less than 1 per cent (often KMT or CCP cadres) controlled city, provincial, and national organizations.

The student political apparatus was democratic only in structure. By the time of the Northern Expedition, there were in most schools popularly elected associations from which representatives were chosen for city and provincial groups. These in turn sent delegates to the national union in Shanghai. A nine-member executive committee elected by this organization met twice a year and appointed a standing committee that functioned as the regular executive body. The apparatus, similar to that of the KMT and the CCP, operated with only slightly greater democracy. Professional and amateur agitators skilled in propaganda, oratory, and controlling mass meetings (which sometimes replaced representative government) were generally able to dominate the majority of less interested and less adept students.

The pyramid-like representative apparatus erected by numerous elections and sub-elections acted independently of its constituents. Minority control, somewhat characteristic of the local school associations and city unions, was most evident in the national organization. Nevertheless, in the councils of the KMT and in the public eye, this body represented five or six hundred thousand college and middle school students.

Preoccupation with scholarship also helps to explain the movement's uneven development, its tendency to flare up with explosive fury only to suddenly die down. In this respect, a comparison with the peasant movement is illuminating. The farmer-turned-rebel committed himself as the student-demonstrator did not. When the student was arrested, wealthy or influential relatives could generally secure his release; the peasant rebel faced summary execution. Though students were politically sensitive, hence easily aroused, their comparative economic prosperity and their prospects of future careers made them fair-weather friends of political crusades, a fact that Communist organizers understood very well. As a nationwide phenomenon, the student movement responded to irregular, uncontrollable external stimuli and was perpetuated by indirect and impersonal communications media. Long-term continuity was next to impossible.

Though it was erratic, the movement had profound effects, perhaps even more profound than the historical record reveals. The psychoanalyst Robert Jay Lifton has suggested that the study of people between the ages of sixteen and thirty may be a key to understanding the political behavior of China's adults. These years of "late adolescence and early adulthood," he writes, are "the period in which adult identity takes shape," and "the more intense the identity strains and patterns of alienation . . . the greater the possibility of this group's adopting extremist approaches to the resolution of such strain."[12]

One can only speculate on the number of today's Communist leaders who took on their current identity in the student movements of the 1920's and 1930's.

Such psychoanalytic interpretation may be useful, but even without it the record shows that the student movement exerted a disproportionately strong influence on the course of China's history. In a country of illiterates, where political noninvolvement was traditional, the educated, sensitive, and mobile school population was the *vox populi*. The students said those things the censored press dared not print. More than once, student demonstrations influenced the decisions of powerful generals and statesmen; more than once, the country was outraged at the slaying of schoolboys. The May Fourth and May Thirtieth Movements showed students how to enlist the support of teachers, writers, merchants, soldiers, workers, and peasants. In a nation swept by nationalism, it became dangerous to question the students' credo, "Down with the imperialists and their running dogs!"

With the establishment of the capital at Nanking, the Kuomintang was no longer an insurgent force but a legitimate order. The students—volatile, emotional, and unpredictable—had helped bring the party to power. It remained to be seen what the relationship between the KMT and the students would be, whether the new regime would contain, or would be defeated by, the militancy of the students. The answers to these questions were worked out in the complex interplay of nationalism, Communism, and imperialism during the Nanking government's first decade. Two wars bounded the period, which began in Canton with the Kuomintang army embarking on its victorious Northern Expedition against the warlords and ended as the National Government came to grips with the Japanese at the Marco Polo Bridge, beginning the Second Sino-Japanese War. Although the two events marked high points of the KMT's popularity in the schools, the years between them produced significant changes in the quality of the party-student relationship. What these changes were, why they occurred, and how they altered the course of China's history is the subject of this book.

Prelude—The Northern Expedition

Intense excitement gripped the Chinese student world as the Northern Expedition set out from Canton in the summer of 1926. The force of Right, represented by the Kuomintang, was about to expunge the twin villains, Warlordism and Imperialism. Using its newly acquired Leninist techniques, the KMT had mobilized China's students in a nationwide crusade. Many Communists had infiltrated the Kuomintang majority that dominated an estimated 478 provincial and city student associations.[1] But in 1926, it was the exceptional youth who could differentiate between the two parties. Only the Chauvinists and the KMT's "Western Hills" faction opposed what they considered an unnatural alliance between the party of Sun Yat-sen and the agents of Soviet imperialism. For example, in Shanghai these two joined forces to wage pitched battles against Communist students while other young KMT followers vacillated between assisting their right-wing comrades and watching from the sidelines.[2]

The warlords' indifference to campus politics drew fire from the British writer Herbert Owen Chapman, who attributed their leniency toward subversives to a "false analogy" between these "schoolboys" and the traditional scholar class: "Their persons are regarded by all classes of people as almost sacred and their opinions as entitled to peculiar respect, so that they are able to engage in seditious propaganda or even wild rioting for which others would be imprisoned or shot."[3] Egotism, emotionalism, and volubility, said Chapman, were the most striking qualities of the young nationalists.

Few students would have agreed with these generalizations. Far from being free to riot and spread propaganda, they faced brutal, though erratic, counterattacks. Hundreds paid with their lives for their political commitment. They saw themselves as self-sacrificing revolutionaries through whose efforts China was finally rising to overthrow the unequal treaties and the military despotism that were responsible for her woes. They felt that their cry, "Down with the imperialists and the warlords!" reverberated throughout the land only because it voiced the urgent demands of China's millions.

But though students paid a high price for political privilege, they nonetheless benefited from the warlords' indifference to ideas. Young intellectuals read with equal impunity the KMT's *Min-kuo jih-pao* (Daily Republican), the Communists' *Hsiang-tao chou-pao* (Guide Weekly), and the Chauvinists' *Hsing-shih chou-pao* (Awakened Lion), and heard lectures by such agitators as the KMT's Wang Ching-wei, the CCP's Yün Tai-ying, the Chauvinists' Ch'en Ch'i-t'ien, the Comintern agent Mikhail Borodin, and many others who visited campuses to promote revolutionary doctrines. Whampoa Military Academy agents scoured the country for cadet talent, and KMT organs secretly administered entrance examinations to the young volunteers. Recruits flocked to this new mecca on the Pearl River, and Chiang Kai-shek's Soviet-model officers' academy became "a high school for earnest, high-spirited youngsters."[4] Meanwhile, those who stayed behind pressed demands for a voice in school government, for the secularization of missionary schools, and for increased powers for student unions.

This was an exhilarating era, a time of action for China's youth. Looking back to the years when he was a middle school pupil in Shansi, Kuo Jung-sheng (who is now a Young China Party representative in the National Assembly on Taiwan) recalls:

I ardently loved China, but I adhered to no party; I wanted to save China. I participated in the Down-with-Imperialism Movement, . . . the Down-with-the-Warlords Movement, . . . the movement to recover the foreign concessions; I took part in parades, and in the surrounding of the Bureau of Education and . . . the Provincial Government. We kicked out our school principal and . . . the guidance director.[5]

The Northern Expedition started from Kwangtung in June 1926, and quickly fought its way to the Yangtze. Students regarded the smart-looking, well-disciplined Whampoa officers in leather belts and polished boots as symbols of the future, and welcomed them with parades and demonstrations. But not all was well in the revolutionary camp. Internal dissension was tearing at the KMT-CCP alliance, threatening to destroy not only the united front but the Kuomintang itself. In Canton, rival organizations—a radical Young Soldiers' Union and an anti-Communist Society for the Study of Sun-Yat-senism—fought for control of the Whampoa cadets. The Northern Expedition reflected this dichotomy, the left following the Hunan-Hupei route to the Wuhan cities, and the right, led by Chiang Kai-shek, taking a more easterly course through Kiangsi. Each was preceded by a large number of young agitators who solicited popular support for the advancing armies and succeeded in thoroughly demoralizing enemy troops. George Sokolsky wrote:

No enemy of the Kuomintang can fight with his rear assailed; no opposing army can be trusted to encamp in large cities where there are students and workers, for in time the agitators will eat into the very hearts of the soldiers until they have neither the will nor the courage to fight.[6]

The propaganda corps, including disproportionately large numbers of Communists and fellow travelers, scored its most notable victories in the western sector; in the east, its activities were restricted by Chiang.[7]

Wuhan became the seat of the "left Kuomintang" government and the nucleus of Chinese student activity after Wuchang was captured on October 10, 1926. Just as Whampoa had attracted the most determined and idealistic youths in the previous two years, so Wuhan now attracted them for a brief period. Students like Ching, the Shanghai student heroine of Mao Tun's novel *Huan-mieh* (Disillusioned), rushed to support the revolution. Rebellious young men and women left home to enroll in the Central Military and Political School.[8] Students became editors and writers for official organs, street orators, labor union organizers, rural cadres, military propagandists, government officials, and the mainstays of the incessant street demonstrations staged to keep mass enthusiasm at a fever pitch.

By April 1927, when the left wing of the NSA moved its headquarters from Shanghai to Wuhan, the intensity of student activities had reached its limit, and a reaction set in. The movement was weakened by Chiang's Shanghai coup of April 12, the ensuing extermination of leftists, and the growing rift between Kuomintang and Communist elements in Wuhan. In addition, a surfeit of slogans and parades had emotionally enervated Wuhan's young revolutionaries. As Chapman observed, "By the time the hot weather in May began, it was obvious that the Government had overdone this method of propaganda. . . . At last even the schoolboys themselves . . . began to complain that they were spending far more time in processions than in school classes and were tired of it."[9]

Hu Ch'iu-yüan's story illustrates the rise and fall of the Wuhan student movement. Marxist anti-imperialist theories had attracted the fifteen-year-old Wuhan University prodigy to the Communist Youth Corps (CY). Encouraged by a friend in the organization, he spent the 1925–26 school year reading translations of Russian Marxist writings, studying, attending discussions, and participating in demonstrations. When the Wuhan government was formed, he was recognized as a talented lad and was assigned to the magazine *Wu-han p'ing-lun* (Wuhan Critic). He soon found himself attending meetings at Central Party Headquarters with such luminaries as Soong Ch'ing-ling (Sun Yat-sen's widow), Sun Fo (his son), T. V. Soong (his brother-in-law), Yeh Ch'u-ts'ang, and Borodin.

Nevertheless, he quickly became disillusioned with the "revolutionary" government. The city wall, reviled as a symbol of feudalism, had been torn down with great fanfare, but that widely despised anachronism, the *likin* tax, remained in effect. Classes were suspended at Wuhan University as meetings and parades continued ad nauseam. Like Mao Tun's Ching, Hu discovered that his co-revolutionaries were selfish, corrupt, and boorish. He was repelled by the arrogant way they wore their uniforms, by their lust for official position, by their sexual promiscuity, by the rise of a privileged class of revolutionary leaders, and by the ominous beginnings of a reign of terror. Hu and his friend quit CY and returned to academic work. The silent withdrawal of students like Hu was a step toward the downfall of the Wuhan government.[10]

Party Purification

The Party Purification Movement—the eradication of Communist elements from the Kuomintang—began on April 12, 1927, with Chiang Kai-shek's bloody suppression of Shanghai's Communist labor movement. This purge lasted almost a year, spreading to many parts of China (including some not under Nanking control); like all purges, it was indiscriminate in its choice of victims and brutal in its methods of dispatching them. Among the many students who perished was 22-year-old T'ang Chien, Communist chairman of the National Student Association.[11]

In the eyes of China's youth, "party purification" had not cleansed but had soiled the fair banner of the Kuomintang revolution. They deplored the suppression of popular movements; Chiang Kai-shek's alliance with wealthy landlords, "reformed" warlords, and Shanghai's secret societies and moneyed interests; the KMT-CCP rift; and the intraparty struggle for the mantle of Sun Yat-sen. According to the Christian youth leader Y. T. Wu, "The imagination of the students had been raised to the point of exhilaration only to be lowered again by disillusion and disappointment."[12]

Students had long awaited a cause to which they could pledge their absolute allegiance. After the 1911 revolution failed to produce a unified republic, they had suffered through a decade and a half of warlordism, an era in which a shattered nation lay defenseless before foreign enemies while military adventurers ravaged the land. Thus the northern expeditionaries found in the students a revolutionary vanguard of true believers. But suddenly, with the millennium in sight, the grand alliance had disintegrated. No wonder YMCA workers found students "confused and despondent" and asking such questions as "Why do young men like to join the Communist party?" and "Should a young man kill himself when he cannot find any interest in life?"[13]

The bickering left the party's student supporters angry and uncertain. The Shanghai Student Union's message of May 4, 1928, expressed disillusionment: "Dear fellow students! In this stagnant environment, don't we all feel troubled and upset? Yes; we all feel troubled and upset within. . . . "[14] The young vanguard of the Northern Expedition was seeking a new allegiance.

There was little to be gained from the extreme left. Reeling from the sudden collapse of its pro-KMT policies and crippled by Chiang Kai-shek's purge, the Communist Party offered no hope. Students hastily deserted the Communist Youth Corps. CY figures indicate a loss of over half its thirty-five thousand members from July to August 1927.[15] This reflects many factors, including loss of workers and peasants, but hardest hit was CY's core of student cadres.

The Communist Party had always found it difficult to restrain the militants in its Youth Corps.[16] Now, however, party leaders desperately needed a scapegoat for the failure of their abortive alliance with the Kuomintang, and the "petty bourgeois" students filled the bill.[17] When warlord troops exterminated Moscow's ill-conceived Canton Commune in December 1927, the bloody debacle was blamed on "the upper stratum of the . . . organization, which consisted entirely of students."[18] A Chinese delegate reported to the Young Communist International that a majority of the "petty bourgeois and intellectual elements" had deserted to the enemy.[19] The result was a decision to change CY's composition from students to workers and peasants.[20] New entrance requirements made admission more difficult for students than for any other group except renegades from hostile political parties and officers of "reactionary armies."[21]

Prospects in the Kuomintang camp were still dimmer. The loss of the dynamic Communist component had dealt an almost mortal blow to KMT youth groups. Furthermore, many party leaders were having second thoughts about letting students play an active role in politics. Debate over this issue broke out early in 1927. Support for student activism came from Wuhan; opposition eventually coalesced in Nanking. Defending the status quo, longtime party stalwart Yeh Ch'u-ts'ang urged young people to devote eight hours a day to political work.[22] But the respected educator Ts'ai Yüan-p'ei, who had resigned as Peita chancellor in the wake of the May Fourth demonstration, disagreed. He upbraided students who "strike one day, parade the next, and completely forget about study," and suggested that seeming contradictions between learning and patriotism be resolved by the formula "In loving your country, don't forget to study; in studying, don't forget to love your country."[23] This maxim in a slightly revised form —"In saving your country don't forget to study; in studying, don't forget to save your country"—became the favorite slogan for moderates opposed to the Wuhan type of student activity.

Just one month after the publication of Ts'ai's views, his neatly balanced academic aphorisms were swept aside by Chiang Kai-shek's reign of terror. Among the goals of the Party Purification Movement were the destruction of Communism in schools, and the return of students to academic pursuits. Educators who sought to combine patriotism and pedagogy were checked by the official directive: "Put the school environment in order."

Drastic steps were taken to force the pablum of book learning on a younger generation that had already tasted revolution. New administrators, sent to "reorganize" suspected hotbeds of radicalism, discharged teachers and students alike. One Anhwei school lost nearly a sixth of its enrollment.[24] In Hunan and Hupei all schools were closed for six months to clean out Communists.[25] Elsewhere in the Yangtze Valley, loyalty oaths became part of admission requirements. Those who confessed and recanted Communist membership were rewarded with leniency; perjurers were dealt with severely. Although the government enforced rigid security measures— every applicant had to be sponsored by a reputable shop or firm; student bodies were divided into five-man groups collectively responsible for members' behavior—Communist ideology persisted.[26] To silence these thousands of zealots in a war-torn land was no easy task.

Pending the formulation of effective policies, the Kuomintang attempted to channel student dynamism into the anti-Communist drive. On the eighth anniversary of May Fourth, some twenty thousand young Shanghai stalwarts voted anti-Wuhan resolutions at a mass meeting.[27] Special groups were established at provincial and local levels to revamp the youth movement and place it under KMT control.[28] A similar effort was undertaken in the NSA, which had only recently rid itself of Communist influence.[29] To complete this housecleaning, and to prevent infiltration by "reactionary . . . and opportunistic elements," the Kuomintang established a special bureau consisting of representatives from provincial and city student unions. These delegates were to be investigated by a subcommittee responsible to National Party Headquarters.[30]

The Kuomintang's success was reflected in the annual program adopted by the new NSA's Central Executive Committee (CEC) in February 1928, which promised to disseminate Sun-Yat-senism "in order to unify the thought of the entire nation." Chauvinists, Communists, and anarchists were singled out for denunciation. Terms such as "construction," "education," and "tutelage" dotted the pronouncement, bearing out the Nanking government's theme of national reconstruction.[31]

By February 1928, powerful elements within the Kuomintang were prepared to go beyond a program of ideological control in order to strictly limit student political activities. Their hand was strengthened by the return to power of Chiang Kai-shek, following several months in retirement, and by the continued absence of Wang Ching-wei. Hence, the Fourth Plenum of the KMT's Central Executive Committee (February 3–9) abolished the party's Youth Bureau (as well as other bureaus concerned with mass movements) and called student political involvement a "grievous mistake." The solution was to bar primary and secondary pupils from politics and to permit college students to join parties and social movements only as individuals, not as members of school or student organizations. Moreover, their unions were to be refashioned into "student self-governing associations" with functions limited to educational activities.[32]

But the opponents of student activism were not strong

enough to win a total victory. The same meeting that passed
this resolution also established a Committee for Training the
Masses, controlled by party organizers and a group of educators who were involved in a power struggle against Ts'ai
Yüan-p'ei and his supporters in the National Academy. Chairman of this committee was Ch'en Kuo-fu, the leading advocate
of an active KMT-controlled student movement. At least two
of the other four members, Ching Heng-i and Chu Chi-ch'ing,
were former adherents of the Wuhan government who were
at odds with Ts'ai on various issues of education.[33] Nonetheless, the Plenum's formal policy was to discourage student
activism.

The Tsinan Incident

Scarcely had the new policy been announced when it was
dramatically reversed by the Tsinan Incident of May 3, 1928,
a clash between units of the Northern Expedition and Japanese troops allegedly sent to protect Japanese citizens in the
Shantung capital. By late April, Japan's announcement that
troops were being dispatched produced inflammatory reports
in official Chinese news media. China's millions were aroused
to anger and indignation by daily headlines:[34]

MASSES OF CITIZENS PROTEST THE SENDING OF
JAPANESE TROOPS TO SHANTUNG

ENTIRE NATION UNANIMOUSLY WANTS TO BEAT DOWN
JAPANESE IMPERIALISM

UNIVERSAL WRATH AGAINST THE SENDING OF JAPANESE TROOPS:
CONCENTRATE POWER UNDER PARTY LEADERSHIP

Responding swiftly to the KMT's war cries, student associations led a nationwide drive to protest this latest instance of
foreign military intimidation. The campaign naturally centered in Shanghai, since China's other major university city,
Peking, was still under the rule of the warlord Chang Tso-lin.
By May 3, when fighting erupted in Tsinan, the student movement had been remobilized. Encouraged by the ruling party,
students promoted a boycott of enemy goods. In Shanghai the
drive began on May 6, when students were told to "arouse the

inhabitants" of the Chinese section of town.[35] The campaign assumed national proportions on May 24, when the NSA proclaimed a boycott of Japanese products.

However, the movement, backed so enthusiastically by some KMT leaders, caused increasing apprehension within party councils. Wang Ching-wei's Reorganization Clique had been pressing for a reactivated student movement, and other KMT groups feared that these ambitious men would try to ride the patriotic tide to power. Many party leaders were afraid that Communists would subvert the student drive. Ten days before the Tsinan Incident, the commissioner of Shanghai's police warned that Communist disturbances were likely to develop in the wake of demonstrations and boycotts.[36] On May 6, all party branches were ordered to prohibit public observances of that month's revolutionary holidays. Only Shanghai, because of its superior educational level and highly developed mass organizations, would be permitted to carry out "revolutionary construction movements," and even there the KMT issued a warning against "reactionary elements."* Yeh Ch'u-ts'ang, who a year earlier had advocated maximum student political involvement,[37] assured a congress of the impatient Shanghai Student Union that the KMT would deal with the imperialists after it had defeated the warlords and captured Peking. Meanwhile, students were not to allow themselves to become cat's-paws of outside interests.[38]

Yet the Kuomintang was reluctant to take an altogether negative position on this issue. The youthful torrent of righteous indignation had undeniable advantages for Nanking. When the Japanese consul demanded that China ban all anti-Japanese slogans, organizations, and movements, the government replied that it was powerless to interfere so long as these activities were within the law.[39] The patriotic movement, though potentially dangerous to the KMT, was at that moment too convenient a diplomatic weapon to dismantle.

The authorities' ambivalent attitude was reflected in the

---

* "Reactionary" was the Kuomintang's term for Communists as well as a favorite CCP name for the KMT. At this time, Nanking may have been returning the compliment of the Reorganizationists, who used the epithet for Nanking.

columns of the official KMT newspaper, the *Chung-yang jih-pao* (Central Daily News). In its issue of May 5, the paper provided front-page space for a Shanghai Student Union announcement of a three-day strike to disseminate propaganda, but also carried a Garrison Command warning against "illegal actions."[40]

Relations between students and authorities deteriorated during the school strike. The Garrison Command and the Peace Preservation Corps broke up a mass meeting; two youths from the Workers' University were arrested on the streets of Shanghai. Following repeated appeals to students to be patient and law-abiding, the government announced that large quantities of Communist literature had been unearthed, and accused the CCP of using school strikes to foment disorder.[41]

The Shanghai union conceded that students had been beguiled by a handful of *hsüeh-fa* ("school lords"), but defended the strike, pointing out that it had been ordered by the Central Government's education ministry, the National Academy.[42] The union then moved to conciliate the Garrison Command by advising member schools to desist from inflammatory speeches and acts. The Command responded in kind, permitting an anti-Japanese rally for the following day. However, it imposed strict conditions: no parades would be tolerated; each school must carry its official banner; supervisors in every institution would have unquestioned authority over students; and only groups of five or fewer would be permitted to pass through the foreign concessions.[43] The meeting was held without incident. During the week of May 17, Shanghai students capped the patriotic drive by soliciting over $24,000 to support Chinese troops in Shantung.[44]

The Nanking union failed to organize a similar unified, large-scale movement, but a number of schools acted independently. More than a thousand students attended an anti-Japanese meeting at National Central University on May 6. At Nanking Middle School a joint student-faculty assembly was held, and Yü Yu-jen addressed another group at Nanking University. Even cadres of the Central Party Affairs School sent more than five hundred petitioners to KMT Headquarters to demand that the government take various steps against Japan, among them lifting the ban on mass movements and sending the school's students northward to fight the enemy.[45]

Peking youth beseeched the city's warlord rulers to remove the ban against the local student union and to permit agitation against Japan on the condition that no radical elements would be allowed to participate.[46] Missionary schools and other private schools sent delegates to a Yenching University meeting to protest the aggression in Shantung. National Peking University activists issued an anti-Japanese manifesto in the name of the long-outlawed student union. On May 9, the thirteenth anniversary of Japan's infamous Twenty-one Demands, private schools observed National Humiliation Day. Within a week, a 24-hour walkout closed the city's schools. Many schools in Peking and Tientsin declared an early summer vacation owing to "unsettled conditions" and the "severe attitude of the authorities toward the Kuomintang students."[47]

By the end of May, the Tsinan crisis was being resolved by diplomatic means, and the Kuomintang was discouraging further student protests. However, the movement had left its mark on Chinese politics and education. Japan replaced England as the primary target of student anti-imperialist barbs. On May 30, heretofore the occasion for anti-British proclamations, the NSA made the following statement: "The Japanese were the initiators of the May Thirtieth Incident. The British played into their hands, and the shooting that took place in Nanking Road was unpremeditated. However, the massacre of our fellow citizens in Tsinan *was* premeditated by the Japanese."[48] The British had lost forever the distinction of being the most detested foreigners in China.

After the Tsinan Incident, the KMT began a universal program of anti-Japanese education: students were indoctrinated by a curriculum of anti-Japanese history, geography, and even arithmetic.[49] This program, which developed during the next seventeen years, fostered a more intense youthful nationalism than Chiang had bargained for; it intensified political repercussions when he set out to destroy the Communists before turning to fight the foreign aggressor.

Persistent student demands for military instruction had prompted the National Academy to order army training at least three times a week at all schools above the primary level.[50] A detailed curriculum was drafted by Ho Ying-ch'in and approved by the National Educational Congress. Meanwhile, the Shanghai Student Union had taken the initiative by organizing its own unit, drilled by school athletic instructors. On June 10, some 8,000 school trainees, 2,000 first-aid corpsmen, and 2,000 members of a "Children's Army" marched in a Shanghai Student Army review.[51] Authorities tolerated the program, allegedly "as a means of sublimating the 'military ardour' of the students."[52]

However, the contradictions in the Kuomintang's attitude toward the student movement remained unresolved. After working for the dissolution of the anti-Japanese drive, the ruling party had capriciously decided to encourage it, only to back away warily when it seemed likely to get out of hand. No long-term policy was formulated. Bombarded by student demands for the restoration of mass movements, the party could only beg the petitioners to be patient and await further orders.[53]

At the same time, the Kuomintang began to lose its hold over the anti-Japanese boycott, which was being zealously promoted by students all over the country. Frustrated in its attempts to retain control, and realizing that the boycott was an increasing liability in its attempts to ameliorate Sino-Japanese relations, the Kuomintang became openly critical of it.[54]

Having turned against the social revolution in April 1927, the Kuomintang had to base its appeal to the younger generation on its reputation as *the* nationalist party of China. When the Tsinan Incident offered a golden opportunity to capitalize on this asset, the ruling party had seized, but failed to hold, the initiative. The party's indecision led many disillusioned students to look elsewhere for leadership.

The Policy Vacuum

Inconsistencies in the Kuomintang's attitude reflected fundamental intraparty disagreements. As we have seen, there was deep concern in Nanking that Wang Ching-wei's Reorganizationists might seek to ride the youth movement to power. Indeed, the Reorganizationists did insist that a Kuomintang divested of its Communist element could still promote a social revolution among workers, peasants, and students. Eloquent spokesmen for this viewpoint were Ch'en Kung-po, editor of the popular but short-lived periodical *Ko-ming p'ing-lun* (Revolutionary Critic), and ex-Communist Shih Ts'un-t'ung, who wrote for the same publication. Shih strongly criticized student leaders for isolating themselves from the student rank and file and from the toiling masses. Until this weakness was eliminated, he said, the student movement would be an ineffectual elitist operation in the hands of "student politicians" and "student officials" appointed by the "reactionary clique."[55]

Within the Kuomintang's inner circles were men with similar ideas. Their sentiments found expression in the Committee for Training the Masses (CTM) established by the CEC's Fourth Plenum in February 1928. An inaugural address by CTM standing committeeman Ch'en Kuo-fu* strongly suggested that this "mistake" should be perpetuated. Ch'en blamed his party for allowing popular movements to fall into Communist hands by default, and expressed the hope that in the future his committee would provide the KMT with a central body to coordinate mass movement activities.[56]

The committee had a grandiose view of its mission. Its duties, as it saw them, were to complete the revolution and establish a "Three People's Principles nation" which would destroy all vestiges of "feudal thought" among the people and substitute the ideology of Sun Yat-sen. Existing organizations were considered inadequate for this purpose. New ones would have to be established quickly, lest the masses, "just liberated from warlord oppression, suffering from the excesses of their wild state of exuberance, their knowledge and thought tending toward disunity, . . . go off down a hundred different paths and make a muddle of organization." Young radicals in particular would have to rid themselves of "wild ideas that have in the past persistently gone counter to reality."[57]

A more detailed critique came from the CTM's Peiping

* Ch'en Kuo-fu and his brother, Ch'en Li-fu, headed the nascent "Organization Clique," also called the "CC Clique" or "Ch'en Brothers Clique."

office. Party leaders there expressed dismay that student action lacked a central theory, discipline, and leadership; that it was emotional, irrational, and destructive; and that it had been corrupted by individualism, heroism, liberalism, Communism, and anarchism. The only solution was to enlist China's younger generation in the cause of the Three People's Principles by using strict party discipline. The future youth movement would be a tool for fighting imperialism, warlords, political bosses, local riffraff, and oppressive gentry; a force for renovating education, enlightening the masses, and for leading "liberation movements" of peasants, workers, and women; and a medium for military training.[58] Any spare time would presumably be spent in school.

Ch'en Kuo-fu's dreams were shattered by shouts of protest from Kuomintang educators, whose most articulate spokesman was Ts'ai Yüan-p'ei. As president of the National Academy, Ts'ai convened the First National Educational Conference in Nanking on May 15, 1928. The political rationale behind this move was to give educators, rather than party functionaries, a decisive voice in making educational policy, including policy on the student movement.[59] Ts'ai proclaimed that students must be isolated from national politics:

Now the responsibility for eradicating bad government lies with several hundred thousand party troops, and the administration of sixteen provinces is under the direction of Party Headquarters. There are men available for the task. Students should study diligently to equip themselves for great service at a future date.[60]

Delegates to the meeting formulated some general principles, which they forwarded to Central Party Headquarters. They recommended that student political activities be confined within the boundaries of the schools, under supervision of school authorities. The politically oriented student associations would become student self-governing associations; inter-school unions would be forbidden. Students would not be permitted to assume responsibilities at Kuomintang headquarters.[61] Thus, the educators rejected the idea of party-led movements divorced from the schools, as advocated by KMT politicians of the CEC's February Plenum. Instead, they proposed that students remain under school control, isolated from the KMT.

Influential persons allied with Chiang Kai-shek agreed that learning must come before politics, but they were reluctant to draw an ineradicable line between school and party. Hu Han-min, whose alliance with Chiang crystallized in October 1928, warned "immature youth" of the lures of the Communist Youth Corps and cautioned them against political embroil-ment, but insisted that the Three People's Principles be taken as guidelines for study.[62] Chiang's intimate associate, Tai Chi-t'ao, urged his party to concentrate on education, but to permit students of universities and technical schools to join political organizations, provided that the students' motives were "pure."[63]

So delicate was the balance of factions in the high councils of the Kuomintang that the Standing Committee of the party's Central Executive Committee reversed its own position within five weeks. On June 4, the group approved a plan of the CTM calling for a national youth organization and for student leadership of mass movements.[64] The occupation of Peking on June 9 may have helped swing the balance to those who opposed continuation of the youth movement once the North-ern Expedition was concluded. In any event, the revised bill of July 9 abandoned the idea of a national youth organization and called upon students to concentrate on their studies and eschew political struggles.[65]

The CTM was unshaken by this rebuff. Ch'en Kuo-fu was convinced that mass movements under party auspices must continue and that only students had the ability to lead them. Therefore, the CTM drafted a scheme for a national student union that would ultimately be expanded to include young farmers, workers, and merchants. The proposal was placed on the agenda of the CEC's Fifth Plenum, which was scheduled to meet in August. The elaborate structure of the proposed union is shown in Figure 1. The CTM plan ran counter to the ideas of the previous KMT plenum, the Standing Committee, and the National Educational Conference. To complicate mat-ters, a second proposal for student organization emerged from

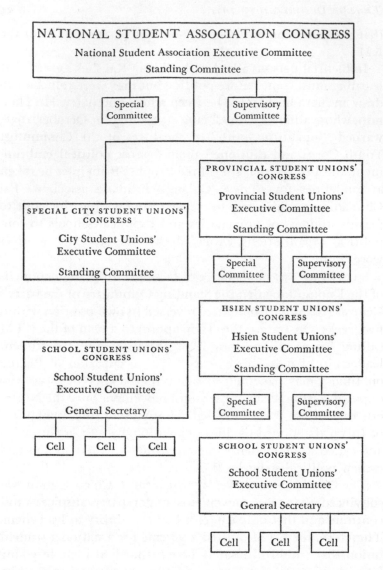

NATIONAL STUDENT ASSOCIATION CONGRESS
National Student Association Executive Committee
Standing Committee

Special Committee

Supervisory Committee

PROVINCIAL STUDENT UNIONS' CONGRESS
Provincial Student Unions' Executive Committee
Standing Committee

SPECIAL CITY STUDENT UNIONS' CONGRESS
City Student Unions' Executive Committee
Standing Committee

Special Committee

Supervisory Committee

HSIEN STUDENT UNIONS' CONGRESS
Hsien Student Unions' Executive Committee
Standing Committee

SCHOOL STUDENT UNIONS' CONGRESS
School Student Unions' Executive Committee
General Secretary

Special Committee

Supervisory Committee

Cell   Cell   Cell

SCHOOL STUDENT UNIONS' CONGRESS
School Student Unions' Executive Committee
General Secretary

Cell   Cell   Cell

Figure 1. Plan for a National Student Association presented by the Committee for Training the Masses to the Fifth Plenum of the Second Central Executive Committee of the KMT. *Source:* KMT, Chung-yang mi-shu ch'u (Central Secretariat), ed., *Chung-kuo kuo-min-tang ti-erh-chieh chung-yang chih-hsing wei-yüan ti-wu-tz'u ch'üan-t'i hui-i chi-lu* (Record of the Fifth Plenum of the Members of the Chinese Kuomintang's Second CEC). Shanghai, 1928.

the National Academy's University Committee. A third suggestion came from the Kwangtung and Kwangsi departments of education in conjunction with Sun Yat-sen University.[66]

The entire problem was finally placed before the CEC's Fifth Plenum, which opened in Nanking on August 1. There members of the National Academy made the student movement a key issue in their struggle to guard education from party control.[67] Ts'ai Yüan-p'ei eloquently presented the case for discontinuing the movement. Contending that students had been enlisted in the revolution only because it would have failed without them, he labeled as folly any plan that would keep them from their studies now that the revolution had succeeded. He maintained that China's major problems were economic and cultural degeneration, for which education, not agitation, was the solution. Ts'ai predicted a national disaster if young people were burdened with heavy political responsibilities, which crushed even older men. Furthermore, he denied that KMT withdrawal from the youth movement would permit rival groups to subvert impressionable minds:

Since our party has the power to control the schools, our doctrines and plans are edited into the textbooks, faculty and students have a chance to enter the party, and district bureaus and district party headquarters are organized in the schools. If there are those among the students who secretly support movements of other groups, educators and students loyal to party principles can always ferret them out; there is no need for special organizations.[68]

Ts'ai concluded that China would incur "a tremendous loss in the academic realm" if the KMT fostered student political groups.[69]

An immediate rebuttal came from the NSA, which sought a "strong national youth organization." NSA spokesmen insisted that since China's older men were too conservative, it was up to the younger generation to destroy the inequities in Chinese society and build a revitalized nation.[70] This argument echoed the recent views of the nonpartisan philosopher Hu Shih (generally an eloquent opponent of student activity). Hu had defended youth's participation in national affairs on the grounds that middle-aged men of learning and experience had not taken the helm.[71]

Though the NSA rejected Ts'ai's views, its leaders also looked askance at Ch'en Kuo-fu's vision of a KMT-controlled youth movement. They contended that such an attempt to impose unanimity would subject students to machinations of "reactionary elements."[72] Though loyal to the Kuomintang, they were not prepared to let the student movement become the tool of the CC clique.

Thus a debate long waged behind the scenes and in party publications erupted at the Fifth Plenum; however, no decision was reached. The conference's Examining Committee blandly observed that the masses had the legal right to organize, but only under party leadership and government supervision. Accordingly, the CTM proposed to the KMT's Central Executive Committee a new plan for a party-controlled National Student Association. The CEC sent the measure for revision to its Standing Committee, which finally buried it by a parliamentary maneuver.[73]

This ended the first phase in the KMT's quest for a new student policy. The problem of what to do with existing national and local associations stayed unsolved. Student leaders remained uninstructed; the legality of their political activities remained undefined; and no solution was in sight.

The Price of Indecision

Contradictions in Kuomintang policies were magnified in the party's relations with leading student organizations. For example, the Shanghai Union, representing the most active and sophisticated students in Chinese politics, was sympathetic to the views of the KMT's Reorganizationist faction. The Union's leaders contended that the Nanking government had fallen far short of Sun Yat-sen's revolutionary ideals, and argued for a powerful student movement to invigorate the new regime. The Union's viewpoint was tersely summarized in a speech by one of its leading members, Hsia T'ien:

The spirit of China's people is perishing; this is especially true in the student world. Why? First of all, because Communist deception has corrupted youth and caused universal disorder. Second, because outside forces, pretending to be revolutionary but actually counterrevolutionary and decadent, have not hesitated to sacrifice the true revolutionary elements and wipe out the student movement. As good Kuomintang members, students must heed Sun Yat-sen's injunction, "In study, don't forget the revolution."[74]

Hsia and his colleagues were vitally interested in the outcome of the Kuomintang's debate over the future role of China's young intelligentsia. Soon after the Fourth Plenum, the Shanghai Union bluntly asked the party if it intended to discontinue the student movement.[75] There is no record of an answer. On May 27, more than a hundred representatives of Shanghai's schools met at the invitation of the city's KMT officials to express opinions on the current anti-Japanese movement. A prominent Kuanghua University student leader urged the Shanghai KMT to support student patriotic endeavors, to oppose the Educational Conference's bill to reorganize student political associations into associations for student government, and to resist attempts by school authorities to suppress the student movement. These and other politely phrased requests were readily accepted by Party Headquarters.[76] In May, at the height of the Kuomintang-inspired anti-Japanese campaign, the Shanghai KMT still enjoyed cordial relations with the students.

By August, the young politicians had become irritated by official charges of Communism in their ranks and by continued KMT procrastination on the subject of the student movement. The Shanghai Union replied to Ts'ai Yüan-p'ei's address before the Fifth Plenum with a thinly veiled attack on the Kuomintang government:

As of today, has the suffering of the nation's people been alleviated? Are youths no longer afflicted with economic ... and religious oppression? Have they an ideal environment in which they can peacefully pursue their studies? From the viewpoint of this association, the result of the revolution has been this: aside from a few who have reaped without tilling and have become rich officials and prospered, the masses remain as before, unliberated; youth also remains unliberated. While this suffering continues, can anyone possibly hope to make us sing the praises of the heavenly king and the enlightened sage, and bury our heads in study?[77]

However, a heated dispute between China's most powerful student organizations enabled authorities to divide and conquer. In the summer of 1928, the Shanghai Union charged that the NSA had intentionally sabotaged the post-Tsinan patriotic movement. It denounced NSA leaders as pro-imperialist and servile to the KMT, and accused them of accepting a $30,000 bribe to send three delegates to the World Youth Peace Conference convened by the "imperialists" in Holland that August. Worst of all, NSA leaders had shown their indifference to the student movement by not even convening the annual congress required by the NSA's constitution. The Shanghai Union thereupon called its own preparatory meeting for the national congress.[78] This conference was torn by confusion and dissension, caused in part by the Kuomintang's disunity; numerous delegates were challenged, and some left in disgust. Although the customary KMT funds were withheld, the meeting nevertheless accomplished its work—the Tenth NSA Congress was ultimately convened.[79]

The Congress opened in Nanking on September 2. Having failed to prevent the meeting, authorities conceded its legitimacy by sending government and party delegates; these men helped keep criticism within bounds. In the words of an informed observer, the assembly was "on the whole, pro-Kuomintang."[80] A student captured the spirit of the occasion when he declared that the youth movement, though spontaneous and independent, should voluntarily accept KMT leadership.[81] Militant but orthodox resolutions denounced "slave education" and "cultural imperialism" and eulogized the Three People's Principles.

However, the final proclamation was bolder. It warned that the path of Sun-Yat-senism was obstructed by "reactionary elements" (foreign imperialists and domestic feudal remnants), and specifically by Communism, anarchism, and Chauvinism. Only if strong mass movements involving peasants, workers, and students were preserved, could the will of the National Father be done. For the sake of solidarity, Wang Ching-wei should be called back from exile, and China should join in a united front with the revolutionary forces of the

world. The resolution denounced those who wished to end
the youth movement, expressed grief that the political environment was conducive to neither learning nor action, and
vowed that students would continue to march in the revolutionary vanguard.[82]

While these noble sentiments were being voiced, however,
students throughout the country were returning to their classrooms. The initial terror of the Party Purification Movement
had dissipated by mid-1928. With the Tsinan affair settled,
and with much of Manchuria and North China unified under
Nanking, public opinion rallied to support the fledgling government. A more positive attitude toward academic pursuits
followed the wave of optimism that swept China's campuses.
Given peace and tranquillity, the school system might become
the cornerstone for a new China.

The new mood was especially evident in the north, recently
liberated from warlord rule. In Peiping and Tientsin schools,
an officially sponsored political rebirth accompanied the unprecedented love of learning. An active branch of the CTM
not only encouraged the revival of student unions but used
them as nuclei for other popular organizations.[83] Thus highly
controversial plans, still under debate in Nanking, were implemented by Ch'en Kuo-fu's followers in this newly pacified territory. Basking in unaccustomed freedom, student cadres cooperated. It appeared that the dissensions of Shanghai would
not be repeated in Peiping.

But harmony was soon disrupted when students were drawn
into another intraparty debate over academic policy. The government, as part of its French-inspired educational reorganization program, had set out to create a Peiping School District
to incorporate all centrally controlled institutions of higher
education in Peiping and Tientsin into a single university.
This administrative innovation provoked bitter opposition in
academic circles. Students, especially those from proud and
famous Peita, joined the protest with demonstrations and
angry telegrams to Nanking. At the outset of the 1928 school
year, impatient young scholars organized a "study movement"
dedicated to abolishing the District Plan and to reopening the

schools, which had remained closed pending settlement of the dispute. Nanking responded with accusations that Communists were exploiting students in the former capital.[84] Controversy raged until the following summer, when the District Plan was finally discarded.

Elsewhere, conflict developed between the central government and missionary school radicals, some of them KMT members. The latter took it upon themselves to uphold the Kuomintang's vow to regain "educational rights" from foreign control. When an attempt was made to reopen St. John's University (the prominent Christian school in Shanghai that had been closed as a result of the May Thirtieth Incident), young agitators rallied under the slogans "Down with slave education!" and "Down with cultural aggression!" in an effort to keep the school closed. The movement was supported by the Tenth Student Congress.[85] Anxious to restore stability to the academic world and to avoid further provocation of Western powers, the government offered support to school authorities in whatever steps they took to restrain student political activities. But outbreaks at Fukien Christian and Cheeloo universities in the fall of 1929 testified to the government's failure to enforce its edict, even among adherents of the ruling party.[86]

In addition to the missionary school tempest, other flareups occurred while the Kuomintang vacillated between encouragement and suppression of the youth movement. After almost a decade of hyperactivity, positive and consistent leadership would be necessary before the academic world returned to "normal." Some disturbances were, as before, ignited by trivial issues such as government prescription of school uniforms. Others, such as the sack of Foreign Minister Wang Cheng-t'ing's residence in December 1928, resulted from disappointment in Nanking's failure to deal forcefully with major national and international issues.[87] Though they differed in cause, these events had the same effect: an overall deterioration of student rapport with the new government.

In Shanghai, a political whirlwind filled the KMT policy vacuum. When leaflets and pamphlets attributed to the Communists and to the Chauvinists' Youth Corps were discovered at Ta-hsia University in February 1929, Minister of Education Chiang Monlin announced that this was typical of widespread "reactionary activities" in educational institutions.[88] A fortnight later representatives of the Shanghai Student Union delivered speeches described as "virulent" by an American diplomat, at a National Anti-Japanese Boycott Association meeting.[89] On March 8, more than two hundred students and workers demonstrated in celebration of International Women's Day. Students were imprisoned for possessing Communist printed matter, and three universities where radical literature had allegedly been discovered were dissolved.[90]

On March 5, with student unrest and leftism in the intellectual world approaching its greatest intensity since Party Purification, the government told its Ministry of Education that "school discipline must be as strict as army discipline."[91] The Kuomintang's Third National Congress, which opened in Nanking on the eighteenth, resolved to put an end to the "empty and sprawling student organizations" of the past, and advocated the creation of self-governing associations limited to the promotion of physical training, science, the arts, and publications.[92] (Such bodies had existed since the May Fourth period but had been eclipsed by politically oriented school groups, which had formed student unions on the city, county, provincial, and national levels.)

However, the influence of the Organization Clique in the Central Executive Committee was still to be reckoned with. Pending the promulgation of a new law, party branches were ordered to "gradually establish" student unions; members would be subject to Kuomintang leadership in extramural affairs, while officials under party control would take charge within the schools.[93] More than resolutions by national congresses would be needed to purge KMT policy of crippling contradictions.

In Shanghai the problem was particularly acute. On March 28, as the KMT congress drew to a close, the Shanghai Student Union met in defiance of warnings from the police and Party Headquarters and resolved to intensify its activities.[94] A Shanghai Student Organizations Reform Committee, hastily convened by the local KMT, thereupon ordered the Union to cease and desist, declaring that it was undemocratic, unrepresentative, and "reactionary," and insinuating that it was supported by subversive elements. After a majority of the city's schools had established party-approved organizations, a new union would be founded in place of the old.[95]

When these plans were unveiled, representatives of various Shanghai schools, including those closed down as Communist, held a clandestine meeting. The next day, twenty or thirty men, presumably the hard core of the student radicals, attacked the committee's headquarters, ransacked its files, injured a committeeman, and then proceeded to shout anti-government slogans in front of KMT Headquarters. On May 9 a large force of soldiers and police prevented a student mass meeting called to commemorate National Humiliation Day, but five hundred diehards gathered to shout anti-government, anti-KMT slogans and distribute subversive leaflets. Official sources reported that Communist students had been active behind the scenes.[96]

The Policy of Tai Chi-t'ao

The Shanghai crisis apparently convinced Kuomintang leaders that further inaction would be suicidal. Evidence of Communist machinations gave weight to arguments that students must not be permitted to meddle in politics. The most influential spokesman for this point of view was Chiang Kaishek's trusted colleague Tai Chi-t'ao. The KMT had been moving toward Tai's position since the settlement of the Tsinan Incident. The previous October Tai had been appointed to the CTM following Ch'en Kuo-fu's retirement. Continued intraparty turmoil during the subsequent year was indicated by frequent reorganizations of organs concerned with mass movements. Tai was named Minister of Training in April 1929; the fate of mass movements now depended on his decisions.[97]

The new minister lost no time in prohibiting the Eleventh NSA Congress, scheduled for September. The group was charged with illegally attempting to meet without Ministry supervision and control. Delegates were accused of not being representatives of student associations, and the standing committee was said to be dictatorially controlled by Peiping committeeman Chang Chia-fan. The young politicians ignored the ban and convened in the national capital on October 9, but the days of Kuomintang indecisiveness were over. Tai closed the assembly and disbanded the NSA.[98] This bold act destroyed a powerful force in Chinese politics during the post–May Fourth decade.

In January 1930, the Ministry of Training announced two basic laws that dissolved all non-academic organizations except the student self-governing associations.* The essentials of the new legislation were explained by the Ministry of Propaganda as follows: (1) The student movement would turn from the path of destruction to "follow the great road of construction and progress." (2) Student organizations would be confined to the schools but would receive orders directly from local Party Headquarters. Their structures would be "interwoven with that of the party." (3) These groups would create an environment of self-government based on the Three People's Principles. (4) They would emphasize "moral, academic, physical, and group education." (5) They would not interfere with educational administration.[99] Students were ordered to avoid active participation in national politics, were advised to rely on faculty guidance whenever political questions arose, and were cautioned to draw no conclusions without thorough investigation and discussion.[100]

The new laws represented a victory for Ts'ai Yüan-p'ei, Tai Chi-t'ao, and Chiang Kai-shek, and a crushing defeat for the Ch'en brothers and the Reorganizationists, as well as for CY, the NSA, the Shanghai Student Union, and all other youthful activists who sought lawful outlets for political expression.

Although students greeted the new regulations coldly, there

---

* For the texts of these two laws ("Principles of Organization for Student Groups" and "Outline of Organization for Student Self-governing Associations") see KMT-CEC, Hsüan-ch'uan-pu (Ministry of Propaganda) ed., *Ko-ming ch'ing-nien*, pp. 125–28. It is interesting to contrast the structure of the school self-governing associations shown in Figure 2 (p. 36) with Ch'en Kuo-fu's plan for a national organization shown in Figure 1 (p. 26).

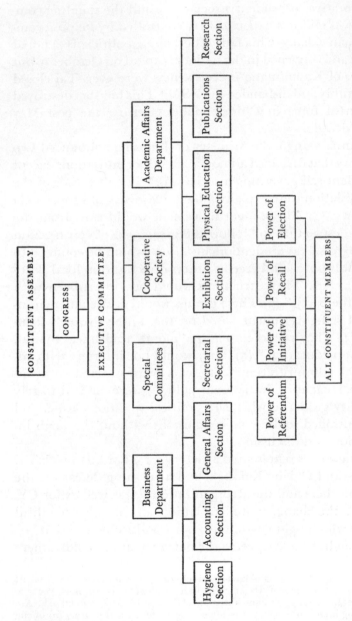

Figure 2. Organizational Plan for Student Self-governing Associations on and above the Technical School Level. *Source:* KMT-CEC Hsüan-ch'uan-pu (Ministry of Propaganda), ed., *Ko-ming ch'ing-nien* (Revolutionary Youth). Shanghai, 1929.

were no riots. Opposition was kept to a minimum by judicious interpretation and highly selective enforcement. Some organizations received permission to postpone reorganization until the fall semester, but all interschool bodies were ordered to disband at once. Kuomintang students were permitted to participate in extramural political activities that were taboo to others. With regard to Christian youth organizations, which were presumably outlawed by the legislation, authorities spoke like Legalists and acted like Taoists: they promised to enforce the law but did nothing.[101]

Harassed KMT leaders in Shanghai, on the other hand, suggested that the new laws did not go far enough, and asked that students be required to secure political guarantors to prevent subversive infiltration of the educational system.[102] But the CEC in Nanking felt this would be unnecessarily harsh: if schools failed to train young people properly, a guarantor system would be useless.[103] Yet when the Shanghai Student Union proved recalcitrant, the Ministry of Training was equal to the challenge. It decreed that youth groups in all schools be dissolved forthwith and speedily reorganized into self-governing associations. The Ministry reprimanded the Sixth Shanghai Student Congress for violating this order, and instructed the KMT's Shanghai executive committee to rectify the "mistake."[104]

KMT efforts to rally student support continued in spite of restrictive measures. In April 1931 the Ministry of Education announced that students would be mobilized during vacations for discussions, speeches, and other sorts of propaganda denouncing the unequal treaties.[105] A Kiangsu party organ proclaimed the importance of summertime propaganda activities and declared that college and middle school youths would be sent out to proselytize peasants, workers, merchants, elementary school pupils, and women to the KMT cause.[106] Thus, even after the decision to destroy student unions, the Kuomintang was reluctant to confine the younger generation to a life of study.

Internal discord continued to disrupt the KMT. The Nanking Student Regulatory Commission advocated abolition of

all youth organizations, while Ch'en Li-fu urged students to
carry on in the spirit of the Northern Expedition and the anti-
Japanese movement.[107] The party sought inspired agitators,
but was hostile toward young radicals. It drafted plans for
holiday activities, but failed to carry them out effectively.
Since KMT policy statements neglected to encourage student
participation in political life, young Chinese read them with
no enthusiasm, some antagonism, and much confusion.

A YMCA survey taken early in 1930 describes the Kuomintang's weak position in the schools, which resulted from vacil-
lation and contradictions in party policies. The director of this
study summarizes his findings: "On paper, the nationalist
party has a very big program. In practice the program is being
attempted in only a very few schools with any efficiency and
continuity." In a minority of institutions where the KMT was
reported to be influential, it had "acted with great harshness
and rigor," taking advantage of "its legal position as the official
agency promoting mass education and improvement of the
people's morale."[108] Three years after the beginning of Party
Purification, KMT influence in the schools remained essen-
tially coercive.

The Rise of Leftism

Throughout 1929 and 1930 the Nanking government suffered
a decline in the intangible but highly important area of public
opinion. The KMT projected an increasingly militaristic
image.[109] The party's left wing, excluded from positions of
power, had established itself as a rival claimant for popular
support.[110] No sooner had revolts by Chang Fa-k'uei and T'ang
Sheng-chih been suppressed in the south than Wang Ching-
wei joined with two warlords, Feng Yü-hsiang and Yen Hsi-
shan, to establish a military and political center for dissident
elements in the north. *The Survey of International Affairs*
for 1930 said that the Nanking rulers had begun the new decade "at the lowest point of their fortunes since their first establishment in 1927."[111] So tenuous was the government's
position that its very survival was considered the most important event of the year.[112]

Nanking's woes did not disappear with the defeat of the Yen-Feng-Wang coalition in the fall of 1930. Bandits continued to terrorize the countryside, a steep decline in the price of silver undermined fiscal stability, and political and intellectual leaders grew restless under party dictatorship. In the cities, public opinion castigated the government for the widespread disorder.[113] In the mountain fastnesses of Kiangsi and Hunan, Chu Teh and Mao Tse-tung organized a Red Army, which three government campaigns between December 1930 and October 1931 failed to dislodge.

The academic realm remained in political chaos. Unable to resolve factional schisms in his organization, Minister of Education Chiang Monlin resigned in November 1930. His successor was Chiang Kai-shek. Intra-clique conflict plagued education at every level; in many schools rival faculty and administrative groups passionately courted student support. During the fall semester of 1930, at least fifteen colleges and universities were shaken by strikes and other forms of student unrest.[114]

By 1930, the younger generation was largely disenchanted with the Kuomintang revolution. Civil war, continued poverty and misery, and corruption in government had dampened the buoyant spirits of those who had anticipated sweeping social and political changes. Now in a less sanguine mood, more and more students sought long-range solutions to China's problems.[115] Rejecting abstract, theoretical discussions, they demanded facts and exhibited a growing respect for the physical sciences and especially for the social sciences. University departments of economics, government, and sociology enjoyed record-breaking enrollments.[116]

The dominant mood among youth was by no means militant. Respondents to a questionnaire chose "pessimistic," "drifting," and "romantic" as the adjectives most descriptive of the students' view of life.[117] Even members of CY were infected by bohemianism.[118] Yet radicalism was far from dead. Quests for fundamental solutions that led some students to the laboratory drove others, less patient, to Marxism. In Shanghai intellectual circles, leftism enjoyed a renaissance. Dewey, Russell, and other foreign idols of the May Fourth period were eclipsed by Communists and social critics like Lenin, Gorky, and Upton Sinclair. At the same time, an indigenous proletarian fiction, which emphasized collectivism, realism, and revolt, and which delighted in exposing the weaknesses of the bourgeoisie, gained in popularity.[119] Leagues of social scientists, leftist writers, and leftist artists formed rapidly.

"Under the calm surface of discussion," wrote a Christian educator, "surges the rebellious current of desire for quick action." There was a restless search for shortcuts.[120] Communism offered one shortcut. Its unequivocally radical view of the social order and its comprehensive solutions to seemingly unsolvable problems attracted the best minds of the younger generation.[121] By contrast, the lofty but ambiguous tenets of Sun Yat-sen, conservatively interpreted by a party participating in unsavory alliances and internecine strife, could no longer appeal to the kind of young idealists who had rallied to the Kuomintang at the time of the Northern Expedition. Those who now joined the KMT frequently became cynical, vainglorious politicians. Consequently, public service was held in low esteem by college graduates.

Of nineteen YMCA correspondents who answered the question "What is the common attitude of students with regard to the aim of study?" thirteen checked "knowledge." None chose "government office."[122] At National Central University, the pride of party educators, students treated Monday morning Sun Yat-sen memorial assemblies with overt disrespect; they came late, chatted, laughed, moved about at will, and left before the meetings were over.[123] At other leading government universities—Tsinghua in Peiping and Sun Yat-sen in Canton —activists expressed their interest in party affairs by running KMT-appointed chancellors out of school.[124]

Wang Ching-wei, a popular spokesman of the non-Communist left until he joined the government in 1932, tried to appeal to young Chinese with the words of Sun Yat-sen: "The revolution is not yet completed." But even Wang was ambivalent about the students. His Reorganizationist Clique had no established youth group, and he, like many other KMT leaders, deplored the pernicious influence of school politics on education. Although he considered general political reform a prerequisite for educational stability, he was dismayed at the younger generation's transformation since the Northern Expedition. In 1929 he wrote:

The youth movement that developed after May Fourth reached its height in 1925–26 and has now become bankrupt.... Contradictions in the revolution, vacillations in government policy, the rifts in our party branches, and the reactionary current scene ... are enough to make young people vexed, depressed, disheartened, troubled, reckless, and opportunistic.[125]

Many of Wang's followers called for a renascent youth movement to play an active role in the continuing revolution. Student leaders were grateful for this support in their struggle to avoid political oblivion.

The disillusioned intelligentsia, which devoured leftist literature and hungered for social reform, was a ready target for Communist blandishments. Many contemporary writers noted a growing sympathy for Communism in the educational world.[126] Still, the commitment was more intellectual and emotional than political; few actually joined the CCP or CY.

Guided by the putschist "Li Li-san line," the Communists not only lost a golden opportunity to replace the educated cadres they had lost as a result of the Kuomintang purge, but dissipated much of their remaining strength in futile gestures of protest, especially in Shanghai.[127] In 1929 and 1930, when political realities demanded caution, party directives instructed cadres to demonstrate and distribute leaflets in the streets. Arrests, imprisonments, and executions followed, and the party was exhausted when conditions became more favorable for overt demonstrations after September 18, 1931.

Young Communists were active in some student disturbances late in 1930. In Shanghai, CCP followers organized resistance to a KMT-sponsored "Constitutional Law" at Shanghai Middle School, and established a Revolutionary Students' Association. There were other incidents involving Communists at Hu Shih's China Academy, at Chinan University, and at T'ung-wen Middle School.[128]

Shanghai police raids in October 1929 revealed that the activities of the Anti-Imperialist Youth League, a Communist front group, were widespread. Organizers had approached prospective members in fourteen schools, established branches in eight, and distributed five thousand copies of the pamphlet *Words to Young Students*. Branches of the League or organizations similar to it operated in Peiping, Canton, Hupei, Fukien, and Manchuria; members had been sent to Nanking, Wusih, Changchow, and Süchow to promote anti-imperialist agitation. The CCP ordered the League to devote particular attention to the YMCA conference on October 11 in Hangchow, and planned a gathering of all "anti-imperialistic youth" for Canton on December 11, 1929, the second anniversary of the disastrous Canton Commune.[129]

A government counterattack was swift and effective. The Ministry of Education closed schools, ousted leftist teachers, appointed new chancellors, and took other measures to restore order to the academic world.[130] KMT infiltrators disrupted and demoralized Communist organizations. In a surprise raid on a Shanghai restaurant, police arrested more than ten students and delegates of left-wing groups who were meeting under the auspices of the Anti-Imperialist Youth League. CY's Kiangsu Provincial Committee blamed the disaster on a secret agent who had represented himself as one of its own committeemen.[131]

While Shanghai Communists succumbed to KMT pressure, Peiping's importance as a leftist stronghold increased. The recollections of a former CY cadre in a city normal school indicate that Peiping Communists and their hard-core supporters numbered between five hundred and six hundred.[132]

A third major nexus of Communist youth work was the militarist-dominated province of Szechwan.[133] Until 1929, Szechwanese subversive activities were centralized in Chungking's Hsi-nan Public School. In the spring of 1930, after local authorities had imprisoned or killed many leading agitators from this school, the faculty and a hundred-odd students fled to Chengtu, where they re-established the school as Hsi-nan University. The university became such a storm center of mass movements in its new location that officials ordered it closed, along with two other colleges. Some two hundred students who resisted the order were seized and imprisoned; eighty of them and eight professors were later tried as Communist leaders. A month later, thirty-six students and eleven workers were arrested at a "reactionary" gathering; several were sentenced to death. The next semester, military authorities barred non-Szechwanese students currently studying in Szechwan from transferring to schools in their native provinces, and required special permits for students seeking to leave their quarters. A reign of terror ensued during which soldiers and police summarily killed students in the streets of Chengtu and other Szechwan cities.[134]

An internal shake-up in the Communist Party ended this era of hyperactivity. With the Red Army's failure to hold Changsha after its successful attack of July 1930, the fate of the Li Li-san line was sealed. Party directives now ordered student cadres to stress evangelization and consolidation rather than demonstration. Such peaceable means as lectures, debates, and plays were to be used to expand the party's influence.[135] Front organizations deriving from the new "united front from below" strategy were to win over "the revolutionary student masses."[136] Concrete student demands for improvements in educational conditions or for the abolition of military education could be used to promote support of the Kiangsi Soviet and the Red Army, though never as ends in themselves. Bourgeois reformism was still taboo.[137]

Under these directives, young Communists set out to walk the narrow road between right-wing deviationism and left-wing adventurism. In Peiping, for instance, demonstrations were still staged when possible, but efforts were primarily directed at weaning followers away from competitors such as the Youth Party and the KMT's Reorganizationist and Western Hills factions. In a Peiping normal school, a branch of the Anti-Imperialist Youth League formed additional front organizations (study groups, poetry societies, etc.), while a lending library distributed "progressive" literature. A League member became editor of the school newspaper, and the League at various times controlled the school magazine and the student association.[138]

However, during these years League cadres led a hectic and

hazardous life, attending long meetings, dodging detectives, and making furtive midnight excursions to distribute leaflets and paint slogans on walls.[139] The united-front-from-below approach failed to recoup for the CCP the mass support that had been lost during the period of not so splendid isolation following the April 1927 disaster. On the eve of the Mukden Incident, the CCP's fortunes were still at a low ebb in the schools of China.

The Kuomintang's Failure

Fortunately for the Communists, their provocative activities contributed indirectly to the further breakdown of KMT-student rapport, which had been deteriorating since April 1927. The KMT's positive "training" program was overshadowed by its intimidating warnings, which only antagonized a younger generation in search of encouragement and leadership. Chiang Kai-shek blamed school disorder on libertine attitudes toward discipline. He ordered educators to be strict, and he reminded students that demonstrations considered revolutionary during the warlord era were now counterrevolutionary. Offenders would be treated as "reactionaries."[140] To those who recalled the anti-Communist purge of 1927, his meaning was unmistakable.

A series of arrests in the summer and early fall of 1930 followed Chiang's remarks, but student activity actually increased in November and December. In December the Nationalist Government's Executive Yüan warned that reactionary students would be dealt with severely and that schools filled with incorrigible elements would be closed.[141] Chiang, in his new capacity as Minister of Education, reiterated the warning, told students they must surrender their personal freedom in return for their nation's freedom, and declared that opposition to government-appointed principals and teachers would be treated as insurrection.[142]

The Kuomintang was no longer a benevolent big brother, but an authoritarian father. After three years of indecision, the new regime had unequivocally asserted its determination to punish all student political activity not expressly sanctioned by party authorities. This clarification of the party's position was always in the background of its subsequent dealings with the rebellious younger generation.

Compared with the academic anarchy of the mid-1920's, the student world enjoyed a period of relative tranquillity following the downfall of the Wuhan government in the summer of 1927. Except for the patriotic surge at the time of the Tsinan Incident, no nationwide movement occurred until September 1931. The problem of these years was finding a satisfactory outlet for student nationalism.

From the Kuomintang's point of view, the problem was unsolvable. How could the KMT exploit the talents and revolutionary potential of China's students without destroying itself in the process? It was clear that China needed a future generation of well-educated leaders, that intensive student politics were incompatible with academic excellence, and that popular movements were susceptible to Communist manipulation. It was equally clear that the Kuomintang could not survive without mass support, that students were the group best equipped to rally the masses, and that Communists or other hostile groups would exploit youthful idealism and enthusiasm if the KMT did not. Had the Kuomintang been monolithic, composed exclusively of Confucian gentry or Bolshevized revolutionaries, military zealots or industrial capitalists, Westernized educators or professional politicians, or a happy combination of two or three of these, it might have enforced a consistent policy. But the conjunction of all these elements in a single party, beset by enemies and loosely bound by diverse ties of power, idealism, self-interest, and personal relationships, was too much. The result was inertia and confusion.

Every suggested solution had its pitfalls. Some Kuomintang policy makers attempted to bar students from politics by fiats, which could not be enforced. Other KMT leaders planned to mobilize idealistic students in a party-controlled movement, which the Kuomintang was too disjointed to organize. Moreover, it was not simply a question of formulating an effective student policy; China's young intellectuals wanted sweeping social and political reforms. Hungry for change, they could not stomach a potpourri of warlord politics, treaty-port economics, hybridized Western education, rural conservatism, neo-Confucian morality, and ossified Sun-Yat-senism.

The Communists, immeasurably weaker than the Kuomintang and forced to execute unrealistic Moscow-dictated policies, were in no position to take advantage of their enemy's weakness. Moreover, until the Manchurian Incident, the KMT still possessed one all-important source of strength: its nationalism. For all its shortcomings, the party that had unified China was still regarded by most students as the country's only hope. Relman Morin, who had studied at leading Christian colleges in Canton and Peiping, observed:

> For both the Kuomintang and the Communists, the Chinese student was a vast source of energy, a dynamo for galvanizing the Chinese masses. Neither group, curiously enough, seemed to fully realize this at the time. The Communists were already concentrating on the peasants. The Kuomintang made Dr. Sun's writings required study, and ordered many schools to observe a moment of silence in his memory every Monday morning. But something more than his image was needed to win the full loyalty and support of the student class.
>
> Nevertheless, at that moment in China's history, 1930, it appeared to me that the balance of student opinion was tipped toward the Kuomintang, especially in the missionary-founded schools.[143]

The great Kuomintang debate of 1927-29 demonstrated the party's willingness to discuss and try various proposals for solving the student problem. The end of this dialogue coincided with Chiang Kai-shek's emergence as the party's leading spokesman on the student question. "Chiang was not a fascist," writes a student of the Chinese labor movement. "He was a military bureaucrat. His solution was not to win over the workers but to sit on them."[144] This observation applies equally to Chiang's youth policy. But sitting on the students, as he soon discovered, was sitting on a volcano.

On September 18, 1931, at 10:30 P.M., Chinese troops clashed with Japanese railway guards a short distance north of the South Manchuria Railway center of Mukden. Within eight hours, three regiments of the Japanese Kwantung Army's second division had occupied the city. Two days later, Changchun, north of Mukden, was looted and burned. Elsewhere in the northeast, ambitious officers with crack troops at their command waited for a pretext to occupy the rest of Manchuria.

Student Response

Seven hundred miles south of the Great Wall, in the commercial and intellectual hub, Shanghai, and in the national capital, Nanking, the alarming events were announced by grim newspaper headlines on the morning of September 20. Following a tradition going back to the Twenty-one Demands, student reaction was immediate. Within hours, outraged young patriots were convening emergency assemblies, organizing anti-Japanese associations, and sending telegrams to Chiang Kai-shek demanding national unity (which meant a truce between the Nanking government and the Kwangtung separatists) and punishment of Chang Hsüeh-liang, the Peiping-based commander of the northeast forces, who was widely blamed for failing to resist the invader. Propaganda corps were formed, leaflets were printed, and boycotts of Japanese goods gained support.[1]

At a September 20 assembly convened in Shanghai by students from Hu-chiang University (operated by American Baptists), more than a hundred delegates from thirty colleges founded a Shanghai Students' Resist Japan National Salvation Association (RJNSA). By September 22, newly formed salvation associations in at least ten Nanking middle schools were able to send delegates to a city-wide RJNSA meeting. Teachers played an active role in numerous institutions: those from Chung-ying Middle School in Nanking led pupils to Kuomintang Headquarters to demand government action.[2]

The youth of Peiping responded with equal alacrity. Mass meetings protested the enemy invasion. Tsinghua students urged an immediate declaration of war, while their colleagues at Yenching advocated a total boycott of Japanese goods, requested military training, and informed the national government that "every Yenching man and woman stands ready to go to the front if necessary."[3] By the first week of October, a Peiping Students' RJNSA had been formed.[4]

Students felt duty-bound to alert their less sophisticated countrymen to the gravity of the national crisis. Within four days of the Mukden Incident, scores of Yenching and Tsinghua volunteers were analyzing the causes of the Manchurian situation for the unlettered masses of Peiping and its environs.[5] In the Yangtze delta, even grammar school children enlisted in the crusade. A Christian missionary was surprised to see some fifty primary school pupils, all wearing red crepe armbands board his train at a small town between Soochow and Shanghai. They had cut classes to barnstorm the countryside delivering impassioned speeches and distributing pamphlets. Their message, printed in large red type, was headed "An appeal, in tears, to our fellow countrymen," and concluded with these words:

Fellow countrymen, what the Japanese want is nothing less than the complete disintegration and subjugation of our country.... To save ourselves we must unite and discontinue all economic relations with Japan, and at the same time organize ourselves into volunteer troops to uphold our government. Our slogan is, "Let us all unite to withstand the common foe—even unto death." Let us stop all economic relations with the Japanese and buy nothing from them.[6]

This outburst of militant nationalism should not have surprised those responsible for educational policy. Anti-Japanese teaching, common at the time of the Twenty-one Demands, was now a government-sponsored program that sharpened student sensitivity to "national shame" and planted anti-Japanese bias in textbooks.[7] Such indoctrination reinforced a mistrust of Japanese ambitions that had been widespread since the Sino-Japanese War of 1894–95. To students in 1931, the only moral answer to attack was counterattack. Their ire, first directed at Chang Hsüeh-liang, eventually turned against the central government.

Nanking's dilemma, which was largely of its own making, reflected the post-Tsinan quandary. Two courses were available to the government: it could encourage the youth movement while trying to retain leadership, or could suppress it and urge students to quit the political arena and return to their classrooms. KMT sponsorship of anti-Japanese agitation and simultaneous appeasement of the foe might open the way for a Communist or a Reorganizationist exploitation of youthful indignation. If this happened, authorities who sought to stem the tide of student nationalism would be engulfed. Nevertheless, a policy of suppression would cost the government the sympathy of the younger generation, and would endanger the Kuomintang's status as China's preeminent nationalist party.

Initially the government chose the first alternative: school authorities were directed to intensify anti-Japanese education and military training and to emphasize the physical education program. Teachers were ordered to lead student meetings.[8] In Kiangsu province, the heartland of government power, a proliferation of hastily organized faculty associations culminated in the formation of the Shanghai Educational Circles' National Salvation Association. The meeting was held in the local Department of Education.[9] Official sponsorship was implicit.

Students were instructed to boycott enemy goods, to toughen themselves for severe conditions, to disseminate anti-Japanese propaganda, and to form volunteer armies. They were to refrain from strikes, romanticism, and pleasure seeking, and were to obey government instructions and regulations in all activities.[10]

Strong, responsible student organizations were essential for a government-controlled program. Authorities belatedly discovered that the ineffectual self-governing associations were incapable of containing the flood of nationalism. Without waiting for government orders, students created new extralegal groups, bypassing the KMT-dominated self-governing associations. Only the politically inexperienced middle school students proved amenable to Kuomintang control. In Nanking, they sought guidance from KMT City Headquarters. In Shanghai, the chairman of an organizational meeting for the middle school students' RJNSA requested that delegates honor the principles of party government, guard against machinations of the "reactionary clique," and keep anti-Japanese activities from interfering with studies.[11]

University students—many of them veterans of the agitation of May Thirtieth, the Northern Expedition, and the Tsinan Incident—were less restrained. One of the first acts of the newly organized Shanghai University Students' RJNSA was the declaration of a week-long strike, in open violation of government orders.[12]

Meanwhile, hungry, ragged refugees were streaming into Peiping and Tientsin from Manchuria; among them were thousands of students and professors still smarting from the indignities inflicted on them by the Japanese, and ready to listen to anyone who promised military action.[13] Young refugees were instrumental in the revival of Peiping student activities. Their reports of enemy brutality fanned the indignation of local colleagues; even pampered daughters of the rich at Nankai Girls' Middle School in Tientsin were inspired to play an active role in national affairs after hearing the newcomers' impassioned words.[14] The first RJNSA in Peiping was formed by refugee students; others followed, and before long some eighty universities and middle schools were represented in a Peiping Students' RJNSA.[15]

By the fall of 1931 Peiping Communists were bolder and

better organized than their Shanghai comrades.[16] They found embittered Manchurian refugees easy marks. Leftists went into action in the old city soon after the Mukden Incident, calling a meeting of urban masses for September 28. However, the local KMT countered by convoking a simultaneous assembly. The KMT attracted a crowd estimated at more than ten thousand.[17] "Not even the shadow of a single worker or peasant" was seen at the left-wing gathering, lamented a young radical.[18] Their own meeting a failure, leftists sought revenge by disrupting the KMT affair with anti-government slogans and a demonstration.[19]

The League of Nations' resolution of September 30, which noted Japan's promise to withdraw troops, brought a temporary lull in the Peiping anti-Japanese movement, but after further Japanese attacks, "progressive" students arranged for a second mass meeting. Their slogans demanded the restoration of mass organizations, proclaimed a struggle for civil liberties, and called for a union of workers, peasants, students, and soldiers. However, official pressure forced cancellation of the meeting. At Peita, the Kuomintang-controlled student association invited Hu Shih, T'ao Hsi-sheng, and other professors to address an assembly after the Mukden Incident, but a leftist motion to replace academic oratory with a discussion of policy toward Japan threw the meeting into chaos.[20]

Shanghai, where every student was nominally represented by a university or middle school RJNSA, was at first spared the violence of Peiping factionalism. However, the existence of the Shanghai organizations provided only a veneer of unity; for the first fortnight after September 18, most anti-Japanese activities were conducted by school and ad hoc groups. Student behavior continued to be unpredictable and very difficult to control, as the Kuomintang soon discovered. Young nationalists grew increasingly impatient with Nanking's failure to declare war. On September 25, following deliberations with two KMT representatives, the steering committee of the Shanghai University RJNSA decided to send fifty representatives to petition Nanking. Shanghai party headquarters agreed to provide them with letters to government and party notables.

Should the appeal for changes in foreign policy fall on deaf
ears, the emissaries planned to telegraph Shanghai students
who would then petition Nanking en masse. The representatives presented their petition to the government on September 27, but complaining that the occasion had been ignored
by the press, they remained in the capital to contact sympathetic academic groups. Meanwhile, a contingent of seven
hundred Futan University petitioners under faculty leadership arrived from Shanghai; still larger numbers of Shanghai
youth formed a Second Petition Corps to follow their colleagues to the capital.

On the rainy morning of September 28, Shanghai and Futan
delegations and more than four thousand Nanking students
paraded to Kuomintang headquarters. This uncoordinated
and poorly planned venture included a score of schools, each
with its own petition. The petitions varied in some particulars,
but were unanimous in their demand for resistance to Japan.
Further unity was evidenced by banners reading "Down with
Japanese Imperialism," "Down with the Non-Resistance Policy," "Down with [Foreign Minister] Wang Cheng-t'ing," and
"March Toward Tokyo."

At Party Headquarters, gray-bearded Control Yüan Chairman Yü Yu-jen received and addressed the petitioners. Students responded with pro-government and pro-Kuomintang
slogans. Finally Chiang Kai-shek appeared and invited them
inside, where he counseled calmness, preparedness, and loyalty.[21] But official exhortation could not divert the National
Central University contingent from its special target—Wang
Cheng-t'ing. According to student leader Yü Chi-chung, ani-
mosity toward the Foreign Minister stemmed from reports
by a professor whose brother was Minister to Japan. The professor alleged that Wang had ignored a warning that Japan
was about to strike and was vacationing at West Lake when
Manchuria was attacked. This story rapidly spread through
the university.[22] In the impassioned atmosphere of the day,
the epithets "villain" and "traitor" were heard around the
campus, and plans were devised for punishing the Foreign
Minister.

Central University students and a few professors (most notably Ho Hao-jo) sought out Chancellor Chu Chia-hua at Party Headquarters. With him in tow, they left their fellow marchers and proceeded to the Foreign Ministry in a torrential rain that poured water into their collars and out their cuffs. When Chu tried to reason with them, they pushed him aside and rushed into the Ministry to find their victim. After a preliminary search proved fruitless, most of the mob left to continue hunting at the Executive Yüan. A crowd of several hundred students remained at the Ministry to search further for Wang. Their efforts were soon rewarded; crouched in the corner of a room guarded by police with drawn knives was the Foreign Minister. Two girls stepped up to the tall Shantungese guards. "You look like good northern men," said one. "You love your country, don't you?" asked the other. The combination of feminine charm and the appeal to their patriotism was too much for the police; they stepped aside.

When Wang saw the mob rush in, he lunged toward the window, but students dragged him back and threw him to the floor. The girls stood aside and shouted encouragement as the boys beat the 49-year-old former YMCA leader and bombarded him with fists, feet, sticks, water glasses, and inkpots. Two crimson streams flowed from a head wound opened by a direct hit with a bottle of red ink.[23]

Professor Ho tried to intervene. "Enough, enough, you don't want to kill him!" he shouted. But rescue came only when Foreign Ministry servants entered through the window and carried away the unconscious Wang. So brutally had he been beaten that his survival was reported to be unlikely.[24] By the time police arrived, the assailants had escaped.

Back on the campus and in high spirits, the student-faculty Resist Japan Society sent a statement assuming full responsibility for the action to the Nanking Garrison Command and to Ch'en Li-fu at Central Party Headquarters. An aroused Chiang Kai-shek then convened the entire student body to give them a tongue-lashing and a pledge: "I will live and die with Nanking." The audience, deeply moved, received these words with thunderous applause.[25]

Petitioning the government became a popular pastime in the wake of the Nanking riot. Nearly three thousand Shanghai students in the Second Petition Corps arrived with almost no money and no clean clothing, vowing not to leave until the government yielded.[26] Reports that Japanese warships were steaming up the Yangtze prompted the Central University student body to march en masse to appeal to the government; once more Chiang had to appear in person to reassure them.[27] In the cities of Kaifeng and Taiyüan, and even in remote Kweichow Province, students clamored for government action.[28] In Japan twenty-three hundred Chinese students left school and boarded ships for home.[29]

The government, which had acted with restraint, became increasingly suspicious of the petitioners' motives. It ordered the arrest of four professors and students in the Futan delegation, which was so well disciplined that it was suspected of being controlled by professional politicians.[30] A delegate's protest that petitioning was in fact a sign of confidence in the government was ignored.[31] Nanking Garrison Headquarters seized the chairman of Central University's Resist Japan Society on suspicion of Communism, authorities in Peiping tore anti-Japanese placards from city walls, and an alarmed Ministry of Education ordered schools to attempt to relieve tension and to stop the spread of rumors.[32]

At the time of the Mukden Incident, a government program of military education was still mostly on paper. Although an estimated nineteen thousand students received some kind of army training during the previous school year, the authorized two to six hours a week of instruction were seldom given. A politically motivated requirement that only KMT members could be school military instructors sometimes proved to be self-defeating. At Yenching University, an annual appropriation of $2,000 for military training was reallocated to a scholarship fund because no qualified teacher could be found.[33]

After September 18, Nanking issued an "Outline of Education for the Volunteer Army," but this was primarily concerned with promoting student patriotism and morale and had nothing to do with military topics. While some argued that three months of rigid training would produce a student army strong enough to fight Japan, Chiang Kai-shek restricted his program to elementary drills on the grounds that students should continue studies to prepare for future service to the nation.[34]

Too impatient to wait for government leadership, students in north and central China organized their own volunteer armies. The Tsinghua University faculty cooperated by suspending classes for three weeks so that full time might be devoted to military training; local police provided rifles. Enthusiasts at neighboring Yenching and at other institutions agitated for permission to follow Tsinghua's example.[35] Peiping had its "Corps of Youth Determined to Die," Nanking its "Three People's [Principles] Iron and Blood Corps."[36] Local armies were formed in the schools of Taiyüan, while the Shansi students' RJNSA made plans for a province-wide unit.[37] The government met the demand by ordering the Bureau of Military Training to provide seven hundred instructors to train fifty thousand volunteers at Nanking, Shanghai, Hankow, Hangchow, Peiping, and Tientsin. A central office was established to direct the volunteer army movement in the schools.[38]

Though Chiang Kai-shek would rather have seen students remain at their desks, he preferred orderly ranks of soldiers to unruly mobs of demonstrators. He told petitioners that barracks for five thousand volunteers were being constructed in Nanking and that immediate military training would be available for all comers.[39] But enlistments were in the hundreds rather than in the thousands; the largest number for any city was Nanking's three hundred. Though representatives of Chinese students in Japan sought Chiang's encouragement to return from enemy universities to become soldiers, joining the army was still a drastic and unacceptable step for the vast majority of educated youth. Most of them inherited the traditional Chinese disdain of the soldier, and some rejected military service for fear of being used in China's civil wars rather than against Japan.[40]

Nanking encountered further difficulties in enforcing its

campus training program. At Yenching, a majority of those eligible for newly instituted military courses failed to register, reportedly because of widespread apprehension that these would duplicate other training activities.[41] However, there was massive popular support for a volunteer army program under auspices of the student Anti-Japanese Association.[42]

Many student leaders felt that the government-controlled regimen of elementary drillwork was too restricted; they clamored for arms. These demands were frequently coupled with even more embarrassing ones. The Nanking Student RJNSA asked for reinstitution of mass movements and of Sino-Soviet diplomatic relations; a Shanghai emissary boldly announced to a middle school audience that arming the students was only a first step to arming the masses.[43] Such pronouncements confirmed Chiang Kai-shek's suspicion of traditionally unmanageable Shanghai students; he reportedly gave preferential treatment in military training to those in the interior.[44] Not until January 1932, after Chiang had retired from the government and the Canton clique was in power, did the Department of the Army provide for training with real guns.

However, in the capital, the military training program and the ascension of moderate student leadership created an impressive degree of unity and discipline. On October 20, twenty thousand students from 42 Nanking schools paraded and held a mass meeting under RJNSA direction. Many marchers wore military uniforms; some carried guns and army mess gear. Strict order was enforced. The meeting opened with the Kuomintang party song, three bows to the national and party flags, and three minutes of silence for countrymen in occupied Manchuria. Later, the paraders formed ranks again and proceeded to central government offices to hear addresses by H. H. Kung, Ting Wei-fen, and Ch'eng T'ien-fang. This was the time of greatest student-government harmony in Nanking.[45]

Elsewhere, in spite of difficulties, the military training program produced substantial, if less dramatic, results. It symbolized government willingness to enlist school youth in preparation for war (presumably against Japan), and it absorbed so much patriotic energy that no major unauthorized demonstrations occurred in Nanking between October 1 and November 20.[46]

By mid-October, demonstrations and petitions were eclipsed by a nationwide boycott of Japanese goods.[47] In no other activity did students have such widespread support. Officials, merchants, workers, and consumers joined this attack on the enemy's pocket nerve. W. W. Lockwood wrote:

During my twenty-seven years in China I have seen nothing which approximates the present intense although suppressed emotion. . . . Students are carrying on an educational campaign in cities and rural districts with cartoons, pamphlets, and lectures; Chambers of commerce in the cities are concerning themselves with drawing the lines so as to prevent the purchase, sale, and transportation of Japanese goods. Chinese compradores of Japanese firms are resigning their positions. . . . Committees devoted to the salvation of China, representing merchants and students and all classes, are meeting daily to promote the economic boycott. . . . Shop windows and vacant walls are covered with slogans [which] declare aggressive action against Japan and command people to boycott the Japanese. We noticed several signs on one shop near this building which read (in Chinese): No Japanese are admitted here.[48]

However, the zeal of youth soon outstripped that of government authorities, and conflict arose when the students tried to impose their will on commercial interests. A typical case occurred in Wusih, an entrepôt on the Shanghai-Nanking railroad. At first, badgered by students, city businessmen agreed not to sell Japanese goods. When they broke their word, students confiscated all Japanese merchandise in the city. The boycott was abruptly terminated by the provincial government under pressure from the Chamber of Commerce.[49]

In Canton, a student-instigated boycott erupted into violence on Double Ten Day. An estimated fifty to one hundred persons were killed or wounded and another hundred arrested. When an association of students, workers, journalists, and other groups met in protest, the city was placed under martial law. A student walkout rapidly developed into a general strike; the chancellor of Sun Yat-sen University and the Provincial Commissioner of Education resigned.[50]

However, authorities elsewhere provided tacit encouragement. In Shanghai, a mob of several thousand students and workers attacked Japanese mills, stores, and homes; those arrested received only token punishment.[51] The boycott was still effective in June 1933.[52]

On October 6, 1931, approximately two years after Tai Chi-t'ao had forced the NSA to disband, the Nanking Students' RJNSA invited delegates to the capital to organize a country-wide anti-Japanese association.[53] By early November, when the congress opened, there were delegates from a dozen or more places, including Hunan, Honan, Fukien, Anhwei, Kiangsu, and Chekiang provinces and the cities of Nanking, Shanghai, Wuhan, Tsingtao, and Ningsia, with one expected from Peiping. Notably absent were representatives from Canton, headquarters of the rebellious faction of the KMT.

Pro-government elements controlled the assembly, limiting resolutions to vague proposals for a "revolutionary" foreign policy and an anti-Japanese economic boycott. However, a powerful eleven-man Shanghai delegation, perhaps sympathetic to the Canton mavericks, disrupted the proceedings with demands that the meeting be held in Shanghai and that each delegation be proportionate to the number of schools in a locale. Failing to secure a majority, the Shanghai students walked out and the congress collapsed.[54] Other factions that presented plans to revive a national student union failed even more abysmally. The numerous groups could not agree on a single chief of staff. The unity of the Northern Expedition period was irretrievably lost as long as student politics were confounded by the political, geographical, and personal issues that split the adult world.

As the abortive national congress ended and quiet was settling over Nanking and Shanghai, new forces gathered in the north. Four hundred students of Tientsin's Pei-yang College of Engineering, who had won a free ride to Nanking by lying on the railroad tracks, petitioned the government on November 9; 479 more petitioners arrived the next day. The chancellor of Mukden's Feng Yung University led a Northeast People's Youth Corps of his students and other Manchurian refugees (whom he later estimated to number nine thousand) to Nanking, Shanghai, and other cities on a barnstorming campaign to arouse the public against Japan.[55]

Inspired by General Ma Chan-shan's heroic resistance to the invasion of Heilungkiang, Shanghai students prepared for new patriotic displays in the middle of November. Their first step, a fund-raising campaign to aid the embattled general, was meticulously organized by the propaganda bureau of the university students' RJNSA.[56] On November 19, as Tsitsihar, the capital of Heilungkiang province, fell to the enemy, an estimated ten to fifteen thousand students streamed from more than thirty Shanghai universities, colleges, and middle schools, and swept through the city collecting funds and spreading propaganda. Incensed by this action, patrols of Japanese marines roamed the streets of the Foreign Settlement the following day, pounced upon isolated groups of students, beat them, and delivered them to local police.[57] Nevertheless, on the morning of November 21, a crowd estimated at one hundred thousand, including ten thousand students, rallied on the West Gate Athletic Field to climax the local anti-Japanese campaign.[58]

The Petitioning Persists

The nationalist crusade was spurred on by new Japanese advances in the northeast, continued failure of the League to act, and Nanking's refusal to declare war. As thousands of Shanghai students canvassed the city collecting funds for General Ma, a group of activists planned a second pilgrimage to Nanking.[59] Under the direction of Chou Hsiao-po, a handsome, flamboyant Futan student, some six thousand zealots gathered at the railway station.[60] Arrangements for transportation had been made in advance; discipline was impressive. As a huge crowd looked on, the neatly dressed students marched onto waiting trains chanting, "We won't come back until we have gained our goal!" After the last train had pulled out, some two thousand students left behind for lack of space abandoned good behavior to commandeer a train, and bullied the stationmaster into allowing them to leave for Nanking the following morning.[61]

Shanghai student leaders, preoccupied with their mission of

national salvation, spent little time splitting doctrinal hairs. The slogans that they composed on the train had something for each side. In addition to the routine anti-Japanese, pro-war themes, for KMT stalwarts there was "Long Live the Republic of China!" and for leftists, "Oppressed Peoples, Unite!" and "Masses Rise in Arms!"[62]

In Nanking, the new arrivals spurned offers of food and lodging at Central Party Headquarters and at the Central Military Academy and insisted upon staying at National Central University, where they could keep in touch with the city's foremost young politicians. Student-official relations thereupon deteriorated. When members of the Chinan University contingent awoke the next morning and found a number of their banners destroyed, they blamed KMT agents. Even more galling was a letter from the Nanking police charging the entire group with harboring Communist elements. To prove their innocence, hastily assembled representatives voted to investigate each other's units. The quest unearthed only a handful of Communist pamphlets.[63]

Despite their difficulties with the Shanghai college students, the authorities were highly successful in dealing with petitioners, who were now arriving at the Nanking and Pukow stations in an unending procession. Many accepted official hospitality. After a group had been fed and lodged under close surveillance, its leaders would be summoned to the Kuomintang's Ministry of Propaganda for an intimate talk about government plans to resist Japan, and secret party resolutions would be produced as evidence of sincerity.[64] High-level party and government officials would speak to the assembled students, who would afterwards be shepherded to the government offices to present their petition; Chiang Kai-shek would usually appear to say a few words. If they behaved very well, they might be treated to a pilgrimage to Sun Yat-sen's tomb before being escorted to a train waiting to take them home.[65]

After disposing of sixteen hundred Hangchow supplicants, the government faced an additional five thousand students from Wusih, Soochow, and Changchow. The routine approach was effectively used on the Wusih delegation. Shortly after arrival, recalls a participant, they were assembled for a speech by Chiang Kai-shek. He told them he was speaking to them first because they were the "purest" and that those from Shanghai, being under Communist influence, would not be granted an audience. Chiang compared himself to Yüeh Fei, the Sung dynasty hero who resisted Chin invasion. He likened the students to Yüeh Fei's commander-in-chief, the Emperor, but warned of a modern Ch'in K'uai (the crafty prime minister who had Yüeh Fei recalled and executed) trying to beguile them. If the "Emperor" would return to school and study, "Yüeh Fei" would fight the enemy. The following day, the Wusih students were taken on a sight-seeing excursion, then escorted to a home-bound train. Their trip had been a success: they had been well fed, they had seen the capital, and Chairman Chiang had spoken to them in person.[66]

While the Wusih contingent was sight-seeing, the eight thousand Shanghai college students that Chiang had vowed to ignore gathered before government offices to present him their war petition. They were greeted instead by Yü Yu-jen, who declared that their unruly conduct was a betrayal of the high hopes the nation had placed in them. The crowd responded with catcalls and demands to see Chiang Kai-shek.

At that moment, the Chairman was addressing Shanghai middle school pupils. Chiang was the fifth major official they had heard since their arrival the previous afternoon. Still unaware that their friends were waiting in front of the government buildings, they devoured a free lunch and returned for another harangue by Chang Tao-fan. These orations left them with little inclination to do anything but return to Shanghai without delay, which they did.[67]

Meanwhile, the college students were still waiting. By nightfall, although some had become ill and others had been driven away by snow and bitter cold, the vast majority remained, clamoring for Chiang (who was now at Party Headquarters talking to a newly arrived Tsinghua group).[68] Nanking students brought sorely needed refreshments, and the government offered its offices as temporary dormitories. In the morning, the besiegers gathered once again to continue their vigil.

Chang Chih-chung (Education Director of the Central Military Academy and the workhorse of government speakers) came out and replied to their petition, but they refused to leave until they had seen the Chairman.

At approximately 1 P.M., news spread that he was coming. Ranks were quickly straightened: in the front stood a group of chosen representatives; behind them assembled the throng, flushed, coughing, and shivering with cold and excitement. As Chiang appeared, hatless and flanked by a dozen bodyguards, the students snapped to attention.

Chiang's first words, "Are you aware of the anti-government moves in Canton?" revealed his suspicion that he was facing the lackeys of his southern rivals. Chou Hsiao-po replied without hesitation: "Chairman Chiang, we haven't seen a newspaper since we left Shanghai three days ago. How could we have any news of what is going on in Canton?" Having kept the students waiting more than 24 hours, Chiang then told them that their endurance of cold and hunger exemplified the indomitable spirit of the Chinese people, and that the nation's enemies should take note! If they had confidence in the government and were willing to cooperate with Chiang against the foe, their efforts would be crowned with success. However, if they became the tools of a small clique, they and the nation would lose. Students must work with the government to resist foreign insults and to save China in a fight to the end!

Chou Hsiao-po assured Chiang that the petition was entirely patriotic and voluntary, and not controlled by outsiders. He said that the school representatives had just voted to condemn the Canton recalcitrants and label them public enemies, and he reaffirmed his fellow students' faith in the government and in the Chairman's ability to recapture Manchuria. But he said that as representatives of Shanghai youth, they would welcome a written promise to take back to their constituents.

Chiang responded that they could trust him to do his duty; this evoked deafening applause. After he had withdrawn to prepare a statement, Chang Chih-chung invited the petitioners to retire to the Officers' Academy for refreshments, but they insisted on waiting while Chiang composed his declaration. Only after the Director of Education had displayed and read aloud Chiang's handwritten message did the crowd disperse. These were the Chairman's words:

I am deeply pleased to see you, motivated by patriotic ardor, coming to the capital to petition. I resolved long ago to devote my life to the Party and the Nation. I accept your petition. In regard to the questions of military affairs and diplomatic relations, I have sent Director of Education Chang to explain everything to you. You students can fulfill your duties as citizens by calmly studying and supporting the government.[69]

With this piece of paper as a trophy, the bedraggled petitioners returned to Shanghai to face student political rivals. The very day they had left for Nanking, a radical Shanghai Universities' Volunteer Youth Army had held a demonstration in the workers' quarters of Chapei, shouting "Long live the liberation of the Chinese Nation!" and "Masses of the nation arise in arms!" Participants doubtless included Communist students who saw more hope in stirring up the masses than in petitioning a hopelessly reactionary government.[70] On the other hand, the Kuomintang-controlled University Students' RJNSA had met while the petition corps was absent and had sent a telegram to the government repudiating the petition. The association had also decided to review membership qualifications for the group, for the presumable purpose of eliminating the rival faction.[71]

Meanwhile, students in the Wang Ching-wei camp had called their own national conference at the Ta-tung Hotel, with representatives from Canton, Kwangtung, Kwangsi, Amoy, and Shanghai, dubbing themselves the "National Student Association." The conference had passed a resolution asking the government to control "illegal" student unions throughout the country. Urgent telegrams were sent to student leaders in other parts of China, inviting them to join the conference.[72] While the organizers suspended proceedings to await answers, Shanghai's student politics grew more chaotic than ever. The students, victims of the city's sophisticated, pluralistic political environment, had divided into warring camps and had become incapable of effective action.

Pacifism Rejected

In the weeks immediately following the Manchurian invasion, Western-trained intellectuals urged the younger generation not to abandon hope. Tsiang Ting-fu, chairman of the Tsinghua history department, told a Yenching audience on October 15 that Japan refused to withdraw only because China lacked a government strong enough to protect Japanese interests, and that the nation's sole hope was a ten-year development plan. Yenching history professor William Hung, who cautioned against underestimating the enemy, called for "more practical work and less talk."[73] Three days later, speaking from the same platform, the YMCA leader T. Z. Koo optimistically predicted a Russo-Japanese war within twenty years and announced that Chinese nonmilitary resistance in Manchuria, if successful, would aid the Geneva disarmament conference scheduled for February 1932.[74]

But China's youth had already decided that the era of the Kellogg Peace Pact had ended, though it would take their government five years (and the United States a full decade) to reach the same decision. As the League studied and discussed the crisis, many Chinese grew cynical about the efficacy of words against tanks and planes, and looked elsewhere for assistance. Even those unsympathetic to the Bolshevik regime raised their voices for a renewed Sino-Soviet alliance.[75] However, the fervently patriotic younger generation viewed the problem as moral, not military: China must fight back, with or without allies. Their government's continued failure to resist aggression provoked a radical change in student attitude. As a foreign observer commented: "The students felt the government policy to be only a supine submission, a sign of decadence; and that the rest of the world would so interpret it, having respect only for those who courageously stand up for their rights and are willing to fight in their defense even in the face of inevitable defeat."[76]

Thus in late November, the Nanking government was compelled to brace itself for a new invasion by students. Enraged by the Japanese provocation in Tientsin and by the attack on Chinchow along the Mukden-Tientsin railroad, and encouraged by the example of earlier crusaders, they began to converge on the capital from every direction. Between November 29 and December 2, more than four thousand had arrived or were en route.[77] Rather than attempt to dissuade them from coming, the Ministry of Education simply instructed them to board trains in a disciplined manner and to avoid disorder and violence.[78] Nearly every group was granted the honor of half an hour or more of exhortation from Chairman Chiang. However, burgeoning forces of radical nationalism soon would compel the authorities to reconsider their permissive policy.

These forces were strongest in Peiping, where impatient students were pushing their Union toward the left. The new mood in the old city was expressed in a Double Ten editorial in the Yenching student newspaper, which advocated awakening the masses and placing less faith in "national leaders."[79] In keeping with these ideas, the Union intensified propaganda among workers, peasants, and fellow students. However, the organization met opposition both from Peiping KMT Headquarters and from its own conservative faction: the KMT ordered the police to stop the Union's meetings and the press to ignore Union activities. Some Union conservatives refused to cooperate in a protest strike and petition to Chang Hsüeh-liang. Others broke away to form a pro-KMT "New Student Union."[80]

The splinter organization was too preoccupied with its own problems to rejoice at the discomfiture of the left. The right wing was caught between fear of antagonizing the government and the realization that only inflammatory nationalistic agitation could arouse mass support. During the final week of November, the new group timidly telegraphed a corps of Tsinghua youth in the capital to deliver a petition for war on its behalf. By the beginning of December, however, the tide of popular nationalism had swept away caution and forced it to organize a mass petition to Nanking.[81]

The nucleus of leftist strength was at Peita. Here, where the

regular student association remained under the control of Kuomintang supporters, radicals created an "extraordinary" association and requested a school assembly. The old guard retali-
ated with signs on dormitory bulletin boards: "Guard Against
Communist Disruption."[82] A stormy gathering on November
30, punctuated by cries of "Down with the Communist Party!"
voted for strongly worded anti-government slogans and decided to demonstrate in Nanking.[83]

The term "demonstrate" had profound implications for the
young revolutionaries: the petition was a legal device, useful
only when a government was truly representative of the people
and worthless when it worked hand in glove with the imperialists; a demonstration, on the other hand, was a revolutionary
weapon to incite the masses to rise against their rulers. The
change from one to the other was a shift from fighting only
the "external enemy" (Japanese imperialism) to attacking the
"internal enemy" (the treacherous government).[84] Their resolution proclaimed: "When the government is unable to repre-
sent the interests of the people; unable to expel the Japanese
army with military force; unable to protect the independence
of the Chinese nation, we cannot but withdraw our trust from
it and expose it."[85]

The Peita Demonstration Corps, more than two hundred
strong, constituted the most potent pro-Communist student
group in China at the time. More than all others, it altered the
direction of the anti-Japanese drive, forced a drastic revision
of government policy, and brought the whole movement to a
violent finale. Nonetheless, this disciplined, fanatical group attracted comparatively few followers. Upon arrival at the railroad station for the crusade to Nanking, the Corps found all
available second- and third-class coaches occupied by sixteen
hundred rivals from the New Peiping Student Union, which
had now decided to lead a Peiping Petition Corps to the
capital. A Petition Corps for a Declaration of War Against
Japan was also ready to depart. The Peita demonstrators had
to be content to make the long, cold trip in antiquated baggage
cars.[86]

The Demonstration Corps compensated for numerical

weakness with sophisticated organizational techniques. They boarded the train equipped with materials for posters and banners and $97 from solicited contributions. Not a moment was wasted en route. Already organized into five sections (secretarial, communications, propaganda, investigation, and general affairs), it further divided into four squads, each with five ten-man groups. Slogans demanding the restoration of mass movements, arms for the people, and "the liberation of the Chinese nation" were adopted. Finally, an overall strategy was mapped out. They would refrain from petitioning with other groups, but would welcome all those who wished to join them in demonstrating. (This technique reflected CCP united-front-from-below strategy.) For the remainder of the journey, all hands were busy writing propaganda, making banners, holding meetings—and dealing with espionage. Like the *Simplon Orient* the train had its spy, one Kuan Shu, a senior majoring in English, closely connected with Peita's right-wing union; he was one of those who had fought to break up the November 30 meeting. Kuan was discovered and put off the train when it stopped at Tsinan. He was seized again several days later when he appeared in Nanking.[87]

When the Peiping students arrived at Pukow, across the river from Nanking, the government perfunctorily announced that the Peiping Petition Corps would present its suit at eight the next morning, followed by the Petition Corps for a Declaration of War at ten. No mention was made of the Peita Demonstration Corps.[88]

From the moment they stepped off the train, the Peita students clashed with the authorities. They refused a KMT offer of transportation across the river; instead, they established headquarters in the gymnasium of National Central University (on the Pukow side). However, even dedicated revolutionaries do not enjoy sleeping in unheated gymnasiums in December; when a KMT envoy offered better accommodations at the Central Officers Academy, a Peita student was sent to investigate.[89] The emissary was ushered into a room where he saw a group of students (later revealed to be members of the New Student Union's Petition Corps) seated around a table with

Fang Chüeh-hui of the KMT CEC. Taking the new arrival aside, Fang expressed concern over rumors about the Peita students and warned that no disturbances by "reactionary elements" would be tolerated. The representative refused to discuss anything but lodging. When this was arranged, the main body of students trekked through rain and mud to the Officers Academy, but returned to Central University when the actual accommodations fell short of what had been promised.

Irritated by this rebuff, Kuomintang Headquarters threatened to cut off food supplies unless the Peita radicals agreed to petition rather than demonstrate. The students retorted that they would buy their own food. Antagonism developed into open conflict: spies infiltrated student meetings, and the Nanking Garrison Command confiscated four thousand copies of the Corps' "Report to the People" and arrested the printer.[90]

Stating that the government was spreading false rumors about them, the Corps delegated two members to hold a press conference.* When most of the "reporters" appeared to be spies, a note of protest was sent to the head of the Garrison Command. In reply, he scolded them for not following normal petitioning procedures, censured their provocative behavior and seditious slogans, and cited a telegram from the Peita Students' Association which disclaimed any responsibility for the action of the Corps and ordered it back to Peiping. The group was then directed to return there immediately.[91]

The Peita leaders replied contemptuously that they would demonstrate the next morning. Would the Garrison Command kindly send gendarmes to "supervise"? The students who delivered the letter were jailed. Several hours later they were joined by 180 comrades arrested while demonstrating and shouting, "Down with the government that sells out the nation!" and "Oppressed masses organize and arise!"[92]

Central University students were emerging from morning classes when the remnants of the Peita demonstrators straggled onto campus crying of their heroic struggle and lamenting the

---

* One of the two was Ch'ien Chia-chü, now a prominent mainland economist, who was excoriated during the anti-rightist drive of 1957.

fate of their imprisoned comrades. They found a receptive audience. Earlier that morning, Chancellor Chu had refused demands for a student assembly and for suspension of schoolwork to allow more time for anti-Japanese activities. The return of the bruised and angry Peita demonstrators provoked an emergency meeting, which spawned angry resolutions: "To the aid of the Peita students!" "Against government suppression of the mass movements!" "Call a general strike!" "To the streets!" Students rushed to the chancellor's office for the university flag. School secretary Kuo Hsin-sung tried to stop them and was pushed aside. Within minutes, several hundred were marching under the banners of Peita and of the Central University Demonstration Corps. They paraded to the Garrison Command to demand the release of the imprisoned Peita students. When a frontal assault on Garrison Headquarters failed, students waited in vain for a satisfactory answer and reluctantly dispersed at about 10 P.M. By the end of the day, Chancellor Chu Chia-hua had tendered his resignation, and authorities had placed Nanking under martial law.[93] That night, the imprisoned Peita revolutionists were roped together, herded aboard a special train, and sent north to Peiping under armed escort.[94]

Crisis in the Capital

During the first week in December, the government had to contend not only with subversive activities by several hundred Peita and Central University left-wingers, but also with nearly three thousand Peiping and 580 Tsinan students. Groups in Wuhan, Taiyüan, and elsewhere were also preparing to join the movement. By the end of the week, Peiping's universities were completely disorganized, several presidents had resigned, and classrooms were empty. In Nanking, by now under martial law, hundreds of police and guards patrolled the streets, government officials went into hiding, and a fire brigade was alerted to stand by in case of further trouble.[95]

Central authorities realized that the uninterrupted rush on the capital could no longer be tolerated. As police jailed Peita agitators, and as Central University comrades marched to their assistance, the government issued a new order: students must immediately cease coming to Nanking.[96]

The edict was ignored. Students assembled in railroad stations, holding up trains by lying on the tracks. Only force could have made the order effective, but the Kuomintang was reluctant to repeat the English mistake of May 30, 1925. Moreover, the presence of an aroused public pressing the government for a declaration of war might have been regarded as a useful diplomatic bargaining point in negotiations with Japan; and as an American diplomat observed, students could be more easily controlled at close range than in railroad stations hundreds of miles away.[97] Hence, barely two days after ordering the students to stop coming, the government tacitly nullified its injunction by requesting them to observe regulations while riding the trains.[98]

On December 7, Chiang Kai-shek informed high government officials at the weekly Sun Yat-sen memorial meeting that although he had personally answered more than ten student petitions, he was reiterating his position on their major demands: China would continue to seek peace through the League of Nations but if driven to the wall would wage total war against Japan; the government was doing its utmost to peacefully promote national unity. Finally, in response to demands that mass movements be permitted, he pointed out that the government had followed a permissive policy since the Manchurian Incident, even when the masses had been misguided by propaganda, but he implied that such leniency might not continue indefinitely.[99] Leaflets dropped from airplanes on student demonstrations voiced a note of vexation, reminding students that government patience was not inexhaustible:

Patriotic students: The government has repeatedly announced that (1) it definitely will not negotiate directly with Japan, (2) it definitely will not create a neutral area at Chinchow but will, on the contrary, oppose that measure, and (3) there is no proposal to create joint control of Tientsin. Do not believe Japanese counterpropaganda.[100]

The increasing momentum of the left-wing movement provided Nanking with the opportunity to take the offensive instead of making apologies. Pamphlets denouncing the Pei-ping student leaders as Communists were circulated in the schools of the capital; Chiang called one group of petitioners "unconscious tools of the nation's enemies." In an attempt to oust the radicals from their home base, Central University was closed for an early winter vacation.[101]

Government efforts to quarantine Nanking failed to contain the youthful radicals. While 180 Peita demonstrators were reluctantly beginning the long trip northward, representatives from student groups and other anti-Japanese associations met in Shanghai to discuss further activities. Their deliberations were interrupted by a strange youth who burst in and ran up to the platform. In a voice hoarse from shouting slogans he announced that he was from the Peita Demonstration Corps and described the callous treatment he and his fellow patriots had received at the hands of the government.[102] The assembly grew incensed and voted to support the Peita students with a demonstration the next day and with a demand for an explanation from the government. At this point, KMT observer Shao Li-tzu intervened.* He explained that China was too weak to fight Japan, and that therefore she was using diplomacy, not force, to defend herself. He said that the Peita Corps' agitation in Nanking was worse than useless; it was dangerous: the group had distributed reactionary leaflets, waved red flags, shouted Communist slogans, and assaulted policemen. The Peita student denied Shao's charges of Communism in an eloquent rebuttal. The former Youth Bureau chief had no defense against the impassioned young man, and delegates remained adamant in their determination to support the Peita students.[103] Within 24 hours, three thousand copies of the Peita Corps' manifesto had been circulated, and Shanghai students were enraged. Some five thousand went on strike, fifteen thousand demonstrated; liaison agents scurried back and forth between Shanghai and Nanking, and the RJNSA warned that thirty thousand would descend upon the capital unless the government made amends for its brutality. Authori-

* A founder of the CCP, Shao had switched to the KMT and had served as director of its Youth Bureau; he was then a member of the party's Standing Committee.

ties responded with underworld tactics. On the morning of December 9, Hsü Hsiu-ch'en of the Peita Demonstration Corps and a comrade from National Central University were assaulted by a gang of men after delivering incendiary speeches before a meeting of Shanghai university students. Hsü was whisked away in a black sedan.[104] That afternoon, an estimated eight to nine thousand students protested before the city government offices, asserting that a KMT strong-arm man named Wang Fu-sheng and an official from Shanghai party headquarters had been among the attackers. They demanded that Mayor Chang Ch'ün release Hsü and punish the men responsible for the incident. Other young rioters wrecked the railway station at Chenju, several miles from Shanghai on the Nanking line. The same evening, seven hundred Futan extremists gutted Shanghai Kuomintang Headquarters.

The students won their demands. The mayor resigned, Hsü was released, and Wang was hauled before a "People's Court" presided over by a law student. After a brutal beating, Wang confessed that he had kidnapped Hsü by order of KMT superiors. The Shanghai RJNSA, apparently satisfied by this local victory, forgot its threat to send 30,000 students to the capital.[105] But Nanking was far from placid after the Peita demonstration. Propaganda teams of Central University leftists agitated in the streets, and government officials continued to be burdened with endless speaking assignments before hostile student groups.[106]

While party leaders waged a war of words, student reinforcements gathered in Peiping. On December 4, more than two thousand from 21 schools flocked to the Ch'ien-men West Station demanding transportation to the capital. Railroad authorities, under instructions from Nanking, refused. A three-day battle of attrition ensued; students jammed both Ch'ien-men stations, lay on the tracks and stopped all rail traffic, while Marshal Chang Hsüeh-liang's envoys begged them to disperse. The mayor, the directors of the Bureau of Public Safety and the Department of Education, and the Assistant Chief of Police successively pleaded in vain. A telegram from Chiang Kai-shek on the evening of December 6 extricated Chang from his dilemma. The wire instructed him to "deal with the situation in an appropriate manner." With considerable relief, he directed railroad officials to give the obstinate agitators free transportation to the capital.

The train was scheduled to depart the next morning. As the appointed time drew near, hundreds of students who had left the station to demonstrate in front of Chang Hsüeh-liang's headquarters or to catch a few hours of sleep returned to get on board. Police stopped them at the gates, and scuffles broke out. Disorder was compounded by the arrival of a train bearing the 180 Peita demonstrators and four hundred Fujen University students, who gleefully threw themselves into the melee. The train finally left for Nanking at eleven A.M. with two thousand shouting, singing passengers.[107]

Further obstacles were encountered en route to the capital. Local authorities at Tientsin and Tsinan refused to allow the train to pass, but they were reluctant to detain several thousand troublesome agitators, and they finally stepped aside. "When I come to think of it today," reflected a former member of Communist Youth some 26 years later, "this was [the result of] the contradiction during that era between the local warlords and the Kuomintang central government; the party and CY cleverly exploited this contradiction."[108]

Nanking's political climate was returning to normal as the whirlwind swept in from the north. The southern student front had been disrupted by charges of Communism in the movement; leftists and rightists were too busy arguing to play a significant role in the conflict that followed. While the Peiping-Tsinan students were arriving, several thousand local petitioners made their last plea; leaders accepted the official reply and voted to return to classes.[109]

In other cities too, many students saw no point in continued agitation, which they felt could only embarrass the government and weaken the country. Some were openly critical of their less restrained comrades. For example, a Hangchow Christian College undergraduate was appalled that some students from his city had refused to travel in third-class coaches, and that hotheads in Shanghai had wrecked railroad offices.

He concluded that moral self-cultivation was the first step toward national salvation.[110] The northern newcomers disagreed. Though the Peiping and Tsinan groups included many factions, a preponderance of revolutionaries made these groups much more radical than their predecessors. Upon arrival in the capital, the "demonstration" faction conferred with members of the Peita Demonstration Corps who had stayed in the capital as advisers.[111] The story of the Peita group whetted appetites for action, but police surveillance and intimidation compelled them to await reinforcements from Shanghai.[112] Meanwhile, hoping to rally all possible forces under left-wing auspices, Peita and Central University radicals sponsored a meeting of Peiping, Tsinan, Nanking, and Shanghai representatives. The delegates established a central office as an initial step toward a national students' congress and a national RJNSA.

Petitioners acted while demonstrators talked. A group led by Tsinan students marched to the Government Building for a lengthy address from Chiang.[113] The following day left-wing organizers, realizing that further delay would cost them support, led some fifteen hundred demonstrators to the same place and listened to a talk by Ts'ai Yüan-p'ei; but they failed to agree on what to do next, and the demonstration collapsed. Though six hundred Tsinan radicals stormed the Ministry of Foreign Affairs and wrote slogans on walls, doors, and windows, student disunity forestalled greater violence.[114]

Disheartened by factional bickering, many Peiping students left for home. The youth of Nanking was likewise divided and discouraged. At this critical juncture, fresh support began to arrive. On December 14 and 15 more than twenty-five hundred recruits from points in the lower Yangtze Valley had reached the capital or were en route. Rioting Taiyüan youths wrecked offices of the Department of Education and the *Minkuo jih-pao* newspaper. In Hangchow and Tientsin only military blockades prevented students from leaving their schools for the crusade.[115]

The government was desperate. Young agitators had already forced the resignations of the Mayor of Shanghai, the chancellor of Sun Yat-sen University, the commissioners of education in Kwangtung, Chekiang, and Shansi, and Foreign Minister Wang Cheng-t'ing. Wang's appointed successor, Shih Chao-chi (Alfred Sze), had refused to assume office, and the next Foreign Minister, Ku Wei-chün (Wellington Koo) had unsuccessfully offered to resign. At Central Party Headquarters, endless conferences were held to examine possible solutions to the problems; Vice-Minister of Propaganda Ch'en Pu-lei was at his desk twelve hours a day.[116] The Ministry of Education was immobilized; on December 11, pending a reorganization of this office, a Special Educational Committee of the Central Political Council, headed by Ts'ai Yüan-p'ei, was established to handle the situation.[117] On December 17, in a characteristic maneuver, Chiang Kai-shek retired, mainly because of internal KMT politics, but partly because of student pressure. The party's new Provisional Standing Committee thereupon created the Secret Committee on Mass Movements to spare the Chairman of the Government the embarrassing responsibility of replying directly to mass petitioners. It was hoped that a committee of educators under Minister of Education Li Shu-hua could "guide and lead the students."[118]

The Peiping Demonstration Corps took advantage of the government's confusion to hold its most violent demonstration to date. On December 15, several hundred students gathered at Central University and paraded to the Foreign Ministry. According to the official newspaper, the *Chung-yang jih-pao,* they carried red flags and wore pieces of red cloth over their left shoulders and on their chests, and were escorted by a squad of "inspectors" carrying large wooden clubs.[119] Following orders of the student general command, a number of them ransacked the Foreign Ministry and clubbed officials who attempted to flee, while about two hundred others proceeded to Central Party Headquarters.[120]

Meanwhile, a crucial meeting of the KMT's CEC was in session; the committee had just accepted the resignation of Chairman Chiang Kai-shek when the students burst into the outer courtyard. Ch'en Ming-shu, newly appointed Acting Chairman, and Ts'ai Yüan-p'ei, head of the Special Educational Committee, met them. Suddenly shots rang out, whether from students or police is not clear; the mob grabbed Ts'ai and Ch'en and carried them off as hostages. Aided by party workers, police finally rescued them, bruised and disheveled, and arrested some of the demonstrators, but Minister of Education Li Shu-hua resigned in despair. The next day, the *Chung-yang jih-pao* printed a photograph of a flag allegedly captured from the students. It read, "Long Live the Chinese Communist Party!"[121]

The Authorities Act

After the December 15 brawl, delegates from the demonstration corps of six cities met at Central University and voted a repeat performance for December 18. Nanking student leaders, wary of radical Peiping agitators and afraid of bloodshed, planned instead an earlier petitioning by all local schools, including middle and primary schools. Nanking students would also be free to participate, but only as individuals. Some youths were so embarrassed by the outbreak of violence that they offered apologies to Kuomintang officials.[122]

The demonstration erupted a day ahead of schedule. On the afternoon of December 17, Peiping leftists, several hundred sympathizers from Shanghai, and a handful from Central University assailed KMT Headquarters but a strong contingent of troops compelled them to retreat. About half of the group then stormed the Examination Yüan, where they were repulsed by forty or fifty guards. Gathering strength, a mob of two thousand converged on the offices of the *Chung-yang jih-pao*.[123] Several hundred extremists, enraged by the newspaper's hostility and especially resentful of its efforts to label them Communist, climbed over sandbag barricades, broke in, and ransacked the building. The pillage was interrupted by government troops. In the ensuing melee, several students jumped or fell into the icy Chin-huai River behind the newspaper office, and at least one drowned (a middle school pupil named Yang Tung-heng).[124] By 7 P.M., when the fighting was over, 62 students had been arrested and many members of both sides had suffered injuries.[125]

This display of violence and vandalism drew strong criticism. An abbreviated edition of the next day's *Chung-yang jih-pao* carried photographs of "reactionary" leaflets to prove that Communists had been responsible for the riot. More than one hundred fifty disillusioned Tsinan youths attempting to return home were obstructed by Peiping leftists and had to fight their way to the train. A 528-name Central University manifesto accused a small minority of expropriating the name of the student body and of illegally using the school flag.[126] The extremists had overplayed their hand.

There was no demonstration on December 18. Before dawn, police encircled the Central University campus, where battle-weary students were sleeping, and rounded up the out-of-town guests. By mid-morning, the Tsinan and Shanghai contingents were on their way home, but the defiant Peita Demonstration Corps was kept waiting on the frozen drill grounds until nearly noon. As they marched to the station under heavy police escort, they shouted revolutionary slogans.[127] Nanking officials doubtless breathed more easily once their train was on its way to Peiping. Elsewhere local authorities were directed to stop trains if necessary to keep agitators away from the capital. Convinced that students were becoming tools of the Communists, the government called a halt to demonstrations and directed the military to deal severely with further uprisings.[128]

But authorities were sensitive to public opinion and aware of a national tendency to sympathize with young patriots; they took pains to explain their suppressive measures. The Chief of the Nanking Garrison Command said that nothing short of mass expulsion from the capital could have forestalled further violence; moreover, the police were preventing a minority from coercing the majority of students, who wanted to return to their studies.[129] Generally Communists were blamed for compelling the government to use force.[130] However, it appears that one high official, to escape censure for the December 18 roundup, circulated a rumor that the government had resorted to such severe action only because of pressure from a "certain" foreign ministry (reportedly the American).[131]

With this notable exception, the official explanation is accurate. In the earlier stages, when nearly all petitioners were pro-government, Nanking had been lenient, patiently discussing, arguing, placating, and explaining the reasons for its foreign policy. Moderates, either satisfied or exhausted, had then retired from the arena, leaving it to hard-core leftists, who were responsible for the violence of December 15 and 17. By the morning of December 18, with public opinion turning against the extremists, the authorities had been able to strike with effectiveness and relative impunity.*

By chance, design, or intuition, timely government action dealt a death blow to the student movement. The vision of a national union vanished. In spite of isolated outbursts, there were to be no more mass invasions of the capital.[132] Communist students and their allies—exhausted, alienated from the "student masses," and hounded by police—had gone underground. About 16,600 students who had gone to the capital during December were dispersed all over the country.[133] Only a few of the less fortunate remained in Nanking—in prison. The capital was quiet once again.

Communist ineptness contributed to KMT success. The Mukden Incident had caught party leaders off balance. Lacking detailed directives, some Shanghai cadres had participated in petitioning the "reactionary government" in order to expose the KMT's "traitorous visage," hoping to take this opportunity to spread propaganda that the CCP favored resisting Japan.[134] Such clumsy attempts to use a patriotic movement for purposes of insurrection were doomed to fail; nonetheless, the party line hardened as Communist leaders moved to eradicate "Kuomintang illusions."[135] Followers were warned to avoid alliances with Reorganizationists, Chauvinists, and Trotskyites. Instead of seeking to form the broadest possible united front, the CCP fomented class warfare in the schools. Young Communists were ordered to abolish anti-Japanese organizations controlled by the KMT and the "compradore

---

* On the other hand, the history of the May Fourth, May Thirtieth, and December Ninth movements suggests that police action at the outset of a movement stimulated student activity.

class" and to create in their stead national salvation societies of students, workers, peasants, and soldiers. CCP directives claimed that even KMT volunteer armies could be transformed into armed or semi-armed organizations of impoverished students.[136]

These belated Communist declarations could not possibly compensate for the lack of earlier guidance; they could lead only to suicidal heroics. The sack of the *Chung-yang jih-pao* offices was a Pyrrhic victory that made suppression all but inevitable. The commitment of overwhelming KMT strength sealed the fate of a bankrupt CCP policy.

Students Subdued

Not until January 1932 were students sufficiently recovered from the December debacle to resume efforts to incite public opinion against the government and Japan; results were meager. Individually and in small groups young politicians shuttled between Peiping, Shanghai, and Nanking attempting to reestablish lines of communication. In Peiping, a new Union for the Resist Japan National Salvation Movement, founded by Peita and half a dozen other schools, sent representatives to contact the students of Shanghai and to visit Wang Ching-wei. Others went to the capital to petition the government. Canton's students, deeply involved in local politics as usual, sent a 136-man delegation to Nanking to urge authorities to send troops north and permit the Kwangtung-Kwangsi military to contribute its own expedition.[137] Students at the missionary-run Nanking and Lingnan universities appealed in person to Chiang Kai-shek, Wang Ching-wei, and Hu Han-min to mend the Nanking-Canton rift that was crippling the nation.[138]

The only significant demonstrations between December 18 and the end of January were staged in Shanghai, and left-wing students seized the initiative. On January 5, agitators unsuccessfully demanded that Chinese merchants in the Foreign Settlement join a general strike to protest Japanese occupation of Chinchow. On January 10, the University Students' RJNSA organized a memorial service and parade for student martyr Yang Tung-heng, and warned Wang Ching-wei, Chiang Kai-shek, and Hu Han-min against "cheating the people of the nation." A week later, fighting began at a leftist rally when Reorganizationists and Third Party adherents distributed anti-Communist pamphlets.[139]

Activities of the more moderate middle school union struck a similar note of futility. When 53 representatives of thirty schools once again traveled to petition Nanking, no one in the government would answer them.[140]

The handful of Wang Ching-wei partisans who had met in Shanghai at the beginning of November to convene a national students' RJNSA congress were still deliberating in January; only a Peiping delegation had responded to their appeal for additional representatives. After resolving to hold conferences in Peiping and Canton preparatory to a national meeting, the body faded into oblivion.[141]

A few groups, realizing that the hour for petitions, demonstrations, and manifestoes had passed, prepared to join guerrillas in Manchuria or arranged with Nineteenth Route Army officers for training in the use of arms.[142] These were the only indications of purposeful action in Shanghai's schools.

By mid-January, the Shanghai student movement was disintegrating. The university RJNSA had split into two warring factions. Small groups of student politicians bickered constantly, while critics deplored the lack of leadership. A student from the College of Law claimed that the force of the anti-Japanese movement had dissipated because a few leaders had rigidly adhered to discredited techniques, failing to build a strong organization or to devise and execute rational plans.[143] The CCP was still directing student cells to promulgate an ambitious program of school strikes, student-proletariat alliances, a militant boycott movement, continual propagandizing, the creation of revolutionary volunteer armies, and the coordination of the students' struggle with that of the Red Army.[144] In September this strategy might have been effective. By January it was only an ironic commentary on a Communist Party that had lost contact with the "student masses."

Four months after Mukden, the Japanese ruled the Northeast, Chiang Kai-shek was in retirement, national politics were more confused than ever, and the students were silent.

The Challenge in Shanghai

The Japanese attacked Shanghai on January 28, 1932. The Nineteenth Route Army's heroic defense afforded local students a unique opportunity to prove the sincerity of their declarations of readiness to die for their country. Most of them failed to convert their words into deeds. Several days before the attack, rumors that a large Japanese fleet had entered the Whangpoo River and was preparing to besiege the city put thousands of terrified students to flight. After the attack, many youths who had bade farewell to their loved ones and started off with great bravado turned back before they reached the field of combat.[145]

But the student role was nonetheless impressive. At least eight hundred students, and perhaps many more, the majority of them from Shanghai, participated in support activities for the Nineteenth Route Army. Several hundred volunteers were reportedly turned down because they lacked training and because the commander was opposed to sacrificing educated youth.[146] It is impossible to estimate how many more would have gone if Nanking had wholeheartedly supported the Nineteenth and encouraged anti-Japanese activities.

The largest student unit to enlist was the 500-man Shanghai Schools' Volunteer Army, which marched to the front as the Youth Propaganda Brigade. There were also noteworthy instances of individual patriotism. Three Nanking students proudly sewed the Nineteenth Route Army insignia on their school military uniforms and reconnoitered the topography of a vital stretch of coastline. (It made little difference that they correctly predicted the Japanese landing place, because the Nineteenth was too small to offer resistance.)[147]

The Futan University Volunteer Army wrote an exciting chapter in the annals of the Battle of Shanghai.[148] When winter vacation interrupted their regular military training program, a group of Futan volunteers prevailed on Commander Weng Chao-yüan of the Nineteenth to provide special training during recess. They were on the verge of abandoning these plans for lack of recruits when the news reached them that Weng's battalion had been ordered to withdraw from the city in compliance with a Japanese ultimatum. Frustrated and indignant, and encouraged by Commander Weng, the Futanese spread propaganda and rallied support for the Nineteenth. That night, soon after the agitators had retired, Japanese troops attacked the Chapei district.

The Futan patriots immediately remobilized under Commander Weng. Joined by students from the College of Law and China Middle School, they formed sections for intelligence, transportation, morale boosting, public relations, and propaganda. Those in the intelligence section, disguised as truck drivers and messengers, gathered useful information. Two students from the transportation section were reported missing in action while hauling ammunition to the front.

As fighting intensified and danger increased, students were ordered to the rear to disseminate propaganda along the Shanghai-Nanking railroad. Propaganda was their forte; brevity of expression was not. They called themselves "The Propaganda Corps of the Shanghai University Students Volunteer Army Training Group Attached to the Nineteenth Route Army." Starting out on February 12, the group spent six weeks traveling from town to town, shouting slogans, distributing leaflets, haranguing streetcorner crowds, presenting plays, glorifying the heroic story of the Nineteenth, and rousing the people against Japan. Their plays bore such names as *Iron and Blood*, *Repay Your Country with Ardor*, and *Wake from Your Drunken Dreams!* In Soochow, they invaded teahouses to preach their gospel; in Wusih, they presented four plays in eight days before audiences of several thousand.

News that the Nineteenth Route Army had retreated to its second line of defense reached them in Changchow. Only the Japanese bombs that cut the railroad, and an absence of orders from their commander, prevented the students from returning to the front. Instead, they intensified propaganda, calling an emergency meeting to tell the people of Changchow to mobilize immediately and prepare to fight to the last man or leave a scorched earth in the event of Japanese invasion.

At Chinkiang, students worked under the constant surveillance of police and spies sent by suspicious local authorities.

Across the Yangtze in Yangchow, they performed *The New Hope,* a pantomime urging all classes to unite against Japanese imperialism, and *The War for Survival,* which vividly depicted Japanese rapacity. Numerous converts who wanted to join their corps were urged to organize local groups instead. Thus, the seeds of propaganda produced first aid corps and funds for front-line soldiers. These results were gratifying. "The masses are not stupid," observed a student chronicler, "nor can we lay at [their] doorstep the crime of being a 'sheet of scattered grains of sand.' This is actually the fault of the government, which doesn't provide leadership, and of the intelligentsia as a whole, which is unwilling to take command."[149]

Recalled to Wei-t'ing for military training, the corps entertained soldiers with comedies, music, and didactic drama. When the volunteer armies were ordered to disband after the April armistice, the students proclaimed that they would continue to serve their country so long as one Japanese soldier remained on Chinese soil. Therefore, three volunteer divisions, including one composed of Shanghai students, were attached to the Nineteenth Route Army. These reluctantly disbanded when the Nineteenth received orders to move to Fukien, but their spirited activities revealed what the students could do when given a cause to serve. A foreigner on the scene paid them tribute:

Something new was born in the life of the nation when that army of ill equipped fighters, with their cloth shoes and soft caps stood against one of the best equipped armies in the world. . . . China can hold her head with pride among the nations that proudly point to their valiant sons who died bravely in defense of their soil. The students share in that glory.[150]

It was the Nanking government's misfortune that it could offer them no comparable opportunity to march against the nation's enemy under the Kuomintang banner.

Evaluation: A Fiasco

Almost every student movement in recent Chinese history has had a discernible political impact. The May Fourth Movement of 1919 compelled the government to adopt a stronger foreign policy; from 1925 to 1927, students paved the way for the Northern Expedition; the December Ninth Movement of 1935–36 was the forerunner of a united front against Japan; and postwar student riots hastened Chiang's downfall and Mao's victory. Compared with these, the student movement of September 1931–January 1932 was a fiasco. It failed to force the government to fight Japan; Nanking continued its policy of accommodation in the following years despite student demands for war. Businessmen refused to surrender Japanese goods to committees of young vigilantes; workers did not strike in their support. The press, lukewarm in September, had become openly hostile to them by December. No major literary or intellectual movements followed in the wake of student political activities.

The crusade of 1931 had at least one distinction: More students were moved greater distances with a larger cumulative total of passenger miles than in any other student movement in Chinese history—perhaps more than any other in world history. The characteristic device was the petition, which brought great crowds before government and party offices to hear high officials defend the policies the listeners detested. A smaller number of demonstrators assaulted any person or institution that symbolized appeasement of Japan.

In spite of the apparent unity of thousands drawn to a single magnetic center, the movement was uncoordinated and incohesive. At no time did students achieve nationwide organization; local units created to fill the vacuum left by a negative government policy were soon shattered by political and ideological controversies. Only one common element, nationalism, held them together and gave them momentum. That the movement survived as long as it did is a tribute to the patriotism of China's youth and not to any political party.

In January 1932, a Trotskyite publication, analyzing the chaotic situation in student politics, said that strong Kuomintang influence was limited to faculties and administrations. It reported that the Reorganizationist faction had a small organized following among the students of Shanghai, where Chauvinists also enjoyed some popularity, and that the Third

Party had been quite powerful in Peiping until the execution of its leader, Teng Yen-ta, by the Nanking government. Communists were organizationally weak but had numerous sympathizers, especially in North China, with considerable drawing power in Shanghai and Nanking.[151]

With no single party in a dominant position, competition and conflict among student factions bred confusion and thwarted formation of a permanent nationwide organization. The Kuomintang, though handicapped by an unpopular foreign policy and an ambiguous attitude toward student political action, handled the situation tactfully and managed to emerge relatively unscathed. Its permissiveness toward mass petitioning not only deprived critics of a clear target, but provided government and party leaders with an opportunity to speak directly to thousands of students. When the authorities finally resorted to coercion, their victims were primarily self-proclaimed foes—the Communists and fellow travelers.

In the early weeks of the movement, immediately after the Mukden Incident, the Communists were unprepared and ineffective. Their city apparatus still suffered the effects of KMT Party Purification. The CCP was further weakened by its own militancy and exclusiveness. Its truculent, uncompromising attitude frightened away potential allies when the timely use of broad patriotic slogans could have won student support.

By the middle of December moderates, weary of political activity, lost control of the movement by default to leftists. Had the latter been able to present themselves as persecuted martyrs without the violence and destructiveness of the riots of December 15 and 17, these rebels might at least have achieved a propaganda victory. As it was, the Communists lost as much sympathy by their reckless tactics (compounded by the Red Army's continued insurrection during a period of foreign aggression) as the KMT did by its policy of appeasement.

Though national and international crises compelled the central faction of the Kuomintang to retire temporarily, acceding to its Cantonese rivals, the government had won a victory over student critics. Face-to-face encounters with seasoned KMT politicians had neutralized potential mass support for the radical opposition. Many petitioners returned from Nan-king convinced that China needed time to prepare for war. The campus military training program, for all of its inade-quacies, was at least a token sign of Nanking's preparation for a showdown with the enemy.

However, a gulf of suspicion still separated youth from gov-ernment. Students could never fully respect a regime that failed to resist enemy attack. Though few became Commu-nists, many welcomed the Chinese Soviet's declaration of war on Japan in April 1932. Former China correspondent Relman Morin has recently written:

Great numbers of students and intellectuals who had been loyal to Chiang Kai-shek began to withdraw support from him and the government. This is not to say that they switched immediately to the Communists. . . . My friends told me they were simply con-fused, disheartened, badly disappointed in the Generalissimo and his associates. The wedge had been driven.[152]

During the subsequent five years of peace, the government did what it could to heal the breach. Realizing that legislative attempts to abolish the student movement had failed, it acted to stabilize academic conditions and to silence radical critics. These measures ranged from regularizing school budgetary allocations to staging gestapo-like raids on dormitories shelter-ing suspected subversives. The younger generation was ef-fectively squelched; it took four more years of Japanese aggres-sion and government appeasement to bring students into the streets again. By that time, the CCP, careful not to repeat its mistakes of 1931, was able to take the offensive, and the KMT, having forgotten its earlier lessons, was left defenseless.

Chaotic conditions prevailed throughout China from late 1931 to the middle of 1933. The Kwantung Army, after occupying southern Manchuria, continued into Jehol, meeting only token resistance. Japanese marines attacked Shanghai on January 28, 1932, plunging a major part of the city into five weeks of bloody war. On January 30 the Chinese government, fearful of a subsequent assault on Nanking, established a temporary capital in Loyang. For the next ten months, liaison officers commuted the five hundred miles between Nanking and Loyang, and some government bureaus actually operated in railroad coaches.

Internal problems wreaked even greater havoc than did Japanese imperialism. The rice-rich Yangtze Valley struggled to recover from the 1931 floods, the worst in half a century; the following year, an abundant harvest dropped grain prices below the profit margin. The chronically impoverished northwest was crippled by devastating drought and famine. Shansi roads were choked with peasants abandoning farms to avoid exorbitant taxes.

These were difficult years for students with limited means. The Yangtze floods that destroyed twelve million homes also impoverished countless students and forced many to leave school. Because of the deluge, students all over China had to economize rigorously or quit their studies. Japanese attacks in Manchuria and Shanghai further disrupted the academic scene. More than ten thousand northeastern refugees flocked into Peiping and Tientsin to resume schooling, and the Battle of Shanghai totally or partially demolished ten colleges, forcing students with sufficient resources to seek instruction elsewhere. An estimated twenty thousand students were affected by all these calamities.[1] Repercussions of Japanese aggression ruined the financial stability of the families of many urban middle class students. Unemployment for intellectuals, clerks, and officials followed in the wake of the occupation of Manchuria; small businessmen faced cutthroat competition from smuggled enemy goods.[2] By 1935, even though the general situation had improved, thousands were still dropping out of school for lack of funds.[3]

China's woes seemed interminable. The Communists remained entrenched in Kiangsi despite the government's first four "extermination campaigns," which took place between 1930 and 1933. Continued wrangling between the KMT's central faction and the Kwangtung clique had paralyzed the ruling party. Fiscal anarchy ensued when powerful financial interests refused to cooperate with Chiang Kai-shek's successors, following his retirement in December 1931. Salaries of officials and teachers fell months in arrears, and national offices lacked such necessities as coal and tea. The Kuomintang, after four years at the helm, found that its prestige had hit an all time low.

From the middle of 1933 until the beginning of the war, the national picture brightened considerably. The Tangku Truce of May 1933 brought China two years of relative immunity from enemy attack. In October 1934, the government's fifth extermination campaign forced the Red Army to flee Kiangsi and begin the Long March, during which its troops were decimated. While German advisers helped Chiang prepare for war against Japan, "reconstruction" became a national byword. Finances were modernized under T. V. Soong and H. H. Kung; telephone and telegraph systems, roads, and railroads were built; and the government began to manifest a serious interest in rural reconstruction and mass education. In the cities, a monetary deflation made possible an improved standard of living for salaried employees, officials, and teachers.

Stabilization of Educational Administration

Chu Chia-hua, the fourth Minister of Education in as many years, held the position from December 1931 to April 1933. During this period, China's colleges and universities suffered a variety of afflictions as a result of national conditions. Educational appropriations slowed to a trickle because of the financial crisis, and unpaid teachers went on strike at many institutions. Schools were inadequately equipped, teachers' qualifications were not standardized, and chancellors were preoccupied with politics. Fundamental issues of organization remained unresolved; in 1932, disgruntled teachers complained that Peiping's academic institutions had been subjected to as many as five major reorganizations during the preceding six or seven years.[4]

Throughout 1932, while authorities were stamping out the last vestiges of the anti-Japanese movement, a succession of "student tides" (*hsüeh-ch'ao,* local school disorders provoked by dissatisfaction with educational conditions and personalities) swept through government schools. During this year, not a month passed without major incidents, which affected, in all, more than a dozen universities and countless middle schools in twenty provinces.

Student tides were very different from student movements (*hsüeh-sheng yün-tung*), which were nationwide reactions to major domestic and foreign problems. However, both phenomena can best be understood when viewed in the context of political, economic, and educational chaos. Ever sensitive to their environment, students reacted violently to foreign aggression, domestic injustices, and instability in the school system. Campus unrest was also symptomatic of personal economic problems; hard pressed to pay tuition and fees, fearful of unemployment after graduation, students joined dissatisfied teachers in strikes, or staged walkouts of their own.

Student tides were concentrated in three areas: the northwest, where political injustice and economic disaster were especially acute; Peiping, the center of radical activities; and Shanghai, where government efforts to reorganize education met strong opposition. In almost every instance, Communists played a prominent role. With the decline of the patriotic movement, the party had decided to concentrate on problems involving students' self-interest. Occasionally young CCP cadres were able to manufacture issues; more often they capitalized on existing discontent about tuition, unpopular administrators and professors, government manipulation of school affairs, political intimidation, and other grievances and misunderstandings.

Once aroused, students organized, struck, sought publicity, demonstrated, and sometimes assaulted opponents. The Communist plan was to intensify conflict, to pit students against authorities and against each other, and to expand altercations into a broader "revolutionary struggle." Such tactics invited violent suppression, which in turn roused popular indignation. Nonetheless, the Communists often failed to achieve their objectives. For example, agitators skillfully expanded isolated disturbances at Peiping University and National Normal College to create a city-wide strike, but order was restored before the revolutionary potential of the situation had been exploited. Party spokesmen blamed this failure on right-wing deviation among cadres.[5] In Paoting's Second Normal School, however, Communist students and a number of unwitting accomplices were martyred in a pitched battle with army troops. The soldiers had been ordered to remove students from the campus, where they had barricaded themselves for a lengthy siege. From the Communist point of view, this was a great success.

The Ministry of Education resorted to extreme methods; it closed down centers of radicalism, ordered obstreperous youngsters to be expelled, and said lawbreakers should be remanded to the police. Government attempts to reorganize or dissolve Workers' University and other Shanghai schools, combined with faculty agitation for back pay, led to disturbances in which students and teachers were arrested, and prompted an exodus of disgruntled professors to Peiping.[6]

Student disorder continued into 1933, but subsided by the fall semester of that year as national educational administration was stabilized, and radical agitators were imprisoned, expelled, or driven underground. Communists waged a rearguard action against the new order, especially in Peiping, where a series of left-wing fly-by-night journals battled liberal educators on the subject of "educational fascism."[7]

Government suppression did not preclude efforts to deal with the underlying causes of unrest. In 1932, a midsummer conference of leading academicians urged that expenditures for education be made an independent budgetary item. The adoption of this suggestion eliminated the major immediate source of faculty and student discontent. Ch'en Li-fu and others, insisting that a slavish imitation of American liberal education had produced anarchy, made some headway in instituting a utilitarian curriculum at the expense of the humanities and social sciences.

Without doubt, there was some truth to charges that Ch'en's goals were political rather than educational. The Communist critic Ho K'o-ch'üan had reason to fear that proposed reforms would reduce the supply of left-wing activists, who had chiefly been recruited from departments of liberal arts.[8] Whatever Ch'en's motives, the Ministry of Education agreed that China needed chemists, physicians, and engineers more than lawyers and litterateurs. In October 1932, it announced that henceforth not only universities but also senior middle schools were to emphasize scientific and technical subjects, relegating liberal education to the junior middle schools.[9] From mid-1932 to the summer of 1933, steps were taken to amalgamate or reorganize colleges of liberal arts, schools of law and business, and departments of literature and social welfare in Peiping and other cities.[10] The following year, the Ministry of Education established restrictive entrance quotas for such institutions as liberal arts colleges, teachers colleges, and law schools.[11]

Other measures had the dual effect of raising standards of scholarship and controlling student behavior. Increased academic burdens allowed little time for extracurricular student activities; diligence and orthodoxy were encouraged by monetary incentives; scholarships and cash awards were based on essays discussing party principles as well as on academic excellence. In 1932 the government instituted comprehensive examinations necessitating study along prescribed lines. Middle school students had to pass these in order to graduate and compete in college entrance tests. Compulsory primary-school examinations were instituted at the same time but were quickly abandoned in face of mounting criticism.[12]

Such policies and the improvement of political, economic, and especially educational conditions restored order to the campuses and laid the foundations for a golden era under Minister of Education Wang Shih-chieh. The length of Wang's term of office, which lasted from 1933 to 1938, symbolized the new order of stability.

The transition from chaos to construction is clearly illustrated by developments at two leading government universities, National Central in the capital and Peita in Peiping. In both schools, Western-trained chancellors subdued unruly student politicians and made efforts to modernize and strengthen the curricula. At National Central, a perennial battleground for Kuomintang cliques and a vortex of radical activity during the 1931 demonstrations, disagreements between KMT student factions had left the school without a chancellor after Chu Chia-hua's resignation in December 1931. Executive Yüan Chairman Wang Ching-wei named a new chancellor without consulting the students, and the appointee (Vice-Minister of Education Tuan Hsi-p'eng) was beaten senseless by a mob when he arrived to assume his post. However, Lo Chia-lun, who took over in August 1932, was an immediate success. Six months after Lo's inauguration, a university official took note of the unaccustomed good behavior of Central's students; their hostility was subdued, and was directed toward Japan, not against the school administration.[13]

While Lo was pacifying young KMT politicos, Chiang Mon-lin, the chancellor of Peita since 1930, fought against Communists and fellow travelers who had made his university a center of left-wing action. The Peita demonstrators, who were shipped back to Peiping after the December 1931 debacle in the capital, had been hounded by police agents and their student union had been disbanded. In response to CCP directives, they now deemphasized anti-Japanese slogans and focused their attack on the Peita administration, especially Chancellor Chiang, and the Dean of the Arts College, Hu Shih. At the beginning of the 1932 fall semester, a strike was called to protest Chiang's refusal to abolish tuition. The expulsion of nine student leaders prompted a mass meeting at which the chancellor was charged with using high-handed policies to destroy the "spirit of Peita"; his resignation was demanded. To restore order, Chiang reinstated the expelled students and then withdrew to the Western Hills. When agitators renewed their demands, he simply took a trip to Nanking. Lacking a target, the barrage subsided.[14]

Since direct action had failed to dislodge Chiang, leftists resorted to the printed word. They charged that he was using the tuition requirement to rid Peita of impoverished students, the bulwark of "progressive ranks," and accused him of importing reactionary professors and students to oppose the free tuition movement.[15] Though leftist charges against him grew bolder, the chancellor stood his ground, and the revolt died for lack of support. By 1933, Peita had lost its reputation as the Mecca of the student movement and had regained its academic aura.

Foreign missionary institutions as well as government schools enjoyed an era of tranquility and progress. The anti-Christian movement, a powerful force during the 1920's and still noticeable on the eve of the Mukden Incident, was now virtually lifeless. Realizing that Christian theology was no longer an important issue among the younger generation, farsighted missionary educators at Nanking, Cheeloo, and Yenching universities intensified their efforts to direct students into rural reconstruction activities.[16] Thus youthful idealism was diverted from both political and religious struggles, and directed toward China's critical socioeconomic problems.

By the end of 1934, strict discipline controlled the nation's schools, and a remarkable improvement in university administration, planning, and finances was evident.[17] Hailing the new order, an exultant *Ta-kung pao* editorial of May 3, 1935, declared that student political disorders were a thing of the past.[18]

Kuomintang Youth Policy

The Kuomintang had been visibly shaken by its inability to
control the anti-Japanese movement after the Mukden Incident. A foreign policy of appeasement, even though couched
in terms of "preparation to resist," had inevitably lost support for the party, which had built its reputation upon anti-
imperialism. It was imperative that the KMT break the bond
between nationalism and Communism and win back the
younger generation. Chiang Monlin and Lo Chia-lun felt
that improvement of the academic environment would encourage students to concentrate on their studies. Other KMT
elements, disagreeing with the liberal educators, argued that
the developments of late 1931 had proved the impossibility of
isolating students from national issues. Instead, they favored
positive political measures to guarantee that future patriotic
outbursts would benefit the Kuomintang rather than the Communists.

Suggested solutions were as numerous as the factions of the
KMT. One possibility was to supplement existing legislation,
such as the regulations of January 1930, which outlawed multi-
school unions. Hence an ordinance passed by the CEC on August 1, 1932, reiterated this prohibition and subjected all other
youth groups to "party guidance and government supervision." Associations would not be chartered until they had obtained permission from local KMT headquarters and government officials, had stated their adherence to the Three People's
Principles, and had obeyed party and government directives.
Individuals having records of anti-revolutionary activities or
accused of illegal acts were ineligible for membership.[19] This
law would have confined student political activity to small
groups within the school, strictly controlled by the KMT. As
will be seen, it did not prevent opposition groups from oper-
ating underground, nor was it allowed to stand in the way
when Kuomintang students sought to form unions.

To complement legal control, the party used subversive
methods to infiltrate and manipulate student organizations
and other groups. Members of these organizations who were

already in the KMT were ordered to form "working committees" disguised when necessary under names such as Academic Research Group or Recreation Club. These cells were
responsible for planning and directing activities for party
members, publicizing KMT ideology and policies, and ferret-
ing out counterrevolutionaries. Where no party members were
available to establish cells, KMT Headquarters would devise
means of infiltration or would entice officers of the organization into the party. Thus, the ruling party resorted to the
same clandestine tactics employed by the "Red bandits" in
contending for control of the masses.[20]

In the spring of 1934, the Committee for the Direction of
Mass Movements, finding that student organizations remained
inchoate and directionless, issued an outline to serve as a guide.
Groups were directed to foster a national literature, to promote the use of Chinese products, to regulate extracurricular
activities, to carry out the New Life Movement (which will be
described subsequently), to study local sociological phenomena, to operate schools for mass literacy, and to organize secret
networks to spy on the activities of traitors in North China
and the coastal provinces. This ambitious program was never
energetically pursued, although at least one major group, the
Shanghai Middle School Union, adopted many of its precepts.[21] Had strong, popular student organizations not been
discouraged by other KMT policies and attitudes, such directives might have been more effective.

The Kuomintang's most promising approach was the rural
reconstruction program put into effect in sections of Hupei,
Hunan, Anhwei, Fukien, and Kiangsi. In the Hupei project
(which at least one observer considered the most successful),[22]
a group of one hundred twenty normal-school students and a
handful of recent college graduates descended upon ten coun-
ties that had been greatly influenced by the Communists. The
young people shared the simple food and lodging of the peasants. In ten months they opened a hundred schools with a total
enrollment of fifty thousand, they assisted economic development, and they helped farmers to defend themselves against
the "Red bandits." Meanwhile, several dozen lecturer-propa-

gandists traveled from village to village speaking about economic and political problems. Thus an outlet was provided
for idealistic students, intellectual unemployment was alleviated, and peasants and government were benefited by social
progress.[23] Such programs, if vigorously promoted as early as
1927, might well have been more effective in consolidating
KMT rule than were the numerous and costly campaigns
against warlords and Communists. However, the rural reconstruction effort, instituted as a defensive reaction to Mao's
soviet regime, and with only four years to operate before the
war with Japan, had only a limited effect.

The New Life Movement, launched by Chiang Kai-shek on
February 19, 1934, was an attempt to revitalize China by ce-
menting together her four hundred million "scattered grains
of sand" with a Confucian puritanism. Chiang, whose guiding
hand in this program was ever apparent, believed that the nation's traditional values could be resuscitated by the button-
your-shirt-don't-spit-in-public approach, beginning with the
minutiae of social habits. He thought that school problems
would be ameliorated by improving student attire. On one
occasion he declared, "If we don't start with these little things
no educational method will have any vitality, no educational
method will have any use."[24] Interpreting the movement for
the younger generation, P'an Kung-chan, commissioner of
both the bureaus of social affairs and of education in the
Shanghai municipal government, urged students to practice
self-cultivation, to develop a sense of shame, and to adopt
habits of strict good behavior in accordance with the ancient
virtue of propriety (*li*). He said:

They should be respectful of teachers and elders, friendly to fellow
students. When attending class, they should sit properly and listen
to the lecture. When improving themselves, they should study
assiduously. On the training field, they should march in strict
order. Coming in and going out, they should observe the proper
etiquette of precedence. In their homes, they should be filial and
respectful to their parents and kind to their siblings. In public,
they should treat people in a trustworthy manner and practice
mutual help.[25]

The New Life Movement struck a responsive note in Chinese puritanism.* In its early days the Movement attracted some support from Kuomintang-indoctrinated middle school and boy scout groups. As late as November 1934, in a manifestation of the New Life spirit, seven hundred Shanghai undergraduates formed an alliance to stop fellow students from attending dance halls. However, the narrowly defined New Life program failed because it did not satisfy the students' hunger for social reform and resistance to foreign aggression, and because its Confucian philosophy was quite unacceptable to the heirs of the iconoclastic May Fourth tradition.

The Fu-hsing She (Regeneration Society), popularly known as the Blueshirts, shared the New Life Movement's preoccupation with military discipline, but was more dynamic, since it was modeled on twentieth-century Communist and fascist methods rather than on Confucian precepts.[26] This quasi-secret body was formed by a clique of Whampoa zealots who felt that the KMT's civilian organization was too soft, bureaucratic, and corrupt to carry on the spirit of Sun Yat-sen. They regarded themselves not only as the embodiment of China's revolution, but indeed as its only hope. The middle and lower echelons of the Blueshirts were composed of lower-ranking Whampoa alumni and recent graduates of the Officers' Academy. In response to student demands for military training, these junior officers swooped down on China's campuses, where they recruited student activists and organized fronts for underground warfare against Communists and fellow travelers. However, their appeal to the young intellectuals failed. College students considered these military teachers crude, unsophisticated, and at best semi-educated. For all their modern

---

* The Communists have used this puritanism more skillfully. Campaigns to reform public manners and morals, the objects of sardonic criticism in the 1930's, have appeared less comic in Communist hands. To Chiang, these efforts were part of a conservative program which sought to achieve national revitalization through individual discipline. For Mao, they have been part of a sweeping social revolution successfully implemented by totalitarian techniques. Mao would doubtless be reluctant to admit that the first campaign to exterminate flies was initiated by "imperialistic" American missionaries or that expectoration was a sin even under the "reactionary" Kuomintang.

ideas, the students still subscribed to the old Chinese adage, "You do not use good iron for nails; you do not use good men for soldiers." The group also acquired a reputation for being fascist, hence the pejorative term Blueshirts. And finally, it suffered a weakness common to all KMT factions—it was unable to offer a coherent, attractive ideology to compete with Communism.

Some students began to view military education as a farce. Those who had vehemently demanded training found that instead of the instruction in military science and the use of weapons they had anticipated, they drilled, saluted, and wasted time in seemingly useless ritual. By December 1934, many Peiping students were in open revolt against military training and considered their drillmasters power-hungry, though somewhat inept, conspirators.[27]

While the KMT was endeavoring to create a loyal and docile youth movement, it employed the sternest methods to destroy all other student political activities. In the dormitories of Peiping, and to a lesser extent in other academic centers, 1933, 1934, and 1935 were years marked by pre-dawn police raids, surprise searches, and secret arrests. The White Terror, as it was called by leftist critics, was a negative yet highly effective response to overt student radicalism. Secret police organizations, aided by professional KMT students, Blueshirts, and sympathetic faculty members and administrators, were able, as Helen Snow observed, to "behead the movement and demoralize it from within."[28] Newspapers reported frequent arrests of students and faculty members. All organizations and meetings were regarded with suspicion. Even a summer conference of the Student Christian Alliance in North China had difficulty getting permission to meet. An American organizer complained that "police demanded complete records of all who attended and a full copy of the program."[29] The Know and Do Club, a social service group established by the student department of the YMCA, was placed under surveillance after holding a commemorative service for Sung dynasty patriot Wen Tien-hsiang, and had to be disbanded and reorganized under a different name.[30] Members of a Resist Japan Association at Peita, participants in a Modern Lecture Society at Tsinghua, and delegates to an anti-war conference from the College of Fine Arts were among those jailed during these years.[31]

The White Terror was especially prevalent in Peiping after Chiang Kai-shek's nephew, Chiang Hsiao-hsien, arrived with his Third Gendarmes Corps to rid the city of subversives. Despite his relentless efforts, Communists often escaped, abandoning less crafty fellow travelers to Chiang's net.[32] According to one account, from April to September 1932, 471 students were arrested, 22 were killed and 95 wounded in fights with the police, and 113 were expelled.[33] Between June 1932 and the end of January 1933, a hundred Peiping students and professors were reportedly imprisoned for political crimes.[34] A college teacher estimated that three hundred students, professors, and intellectuals were arrested in North China in 1934.[35] Two hundred thirty Peiping and Tientsin intellectuals were taken into custody between November 1934 and March 1935, according to a special survey.[36] These statistics, though unofficial, suggest the broad dimensions of the White Terror.

The successful intimidation of non-KMT groups and the New Life Movement's failure to enlist college student participation resulted in a dearth of campus political organizations.[37] Moreover, standardized government examinations and curricula (the latter, including scouting and athletics, totaled sixty or more hours a week for most middle school students), and universal military training in secondary schools and colleges indicated growing regimentation. This was especially evident in the middle schools.[38] Beginning in 1934, every junior middle school pupil was required to join the Boy Scouts (*t'ung-tzu chün*, literally "boys' army").[39] Disciplined squads of these uniformed youngsters became a symbol of the new order. A former American missionary in Hwaining (now Anking) recalls:

The rise of the war spirit was very marked. . . . At certain hours of the day—early morning, noon, and late afternoon—the streets were filled with lads in uniform. . . . Elementary-school children were constructing tanks and airplanes and other war paraphernalia. They were going without their lunches to contribute to the purchase of planes to "save the country."[40]

Andrew T. Roy, an American teacher in Nanking, viewed with misgivings the "wartime psychology in the schools." His impressions foreshadowed the reaction of a later generation of Westerners to Communist China's "blue ants" society:

Formerly the students had self-government and many extracurricular activities; they were independent, noisy, and not well disciplined. Now every student is in uniform, everything is immaculate, the students clean their own classrooms, give implicit obedience, are courteous, walk to the left of all flower beds, the girls have stopped curling their hair or using cosmetics, and one would think a Fascist utopia had been let down from heaven upon the spot. It's all very neat and wonderful but gives me a slightly shaky feeling inside.[41]

The KMT's successful regimentation of lower-Yangtze-Valley middle schools was outbalanced by its failure in other sections of the country, especially in the universities. The philosophic premises of the New Life Movement were antithetical to those of the Western education sought by university chancellors and high officials of the Ministry of Education. The militarist Blueshirts competed with the party's civilian authorities in the CC Clique. In addition, the organizational efforts of political activists thwarted the pedagogical aims of liberal educators.

Although the KMT's many faceted approach to the students had constructive as well as destructive aspects, destruction had the greater impact. The White Terror, immediately successful in ridding campuses of many insurrectionists and at frightening others into silence, was suicidal in the long run. The party had gained an unsavory reputation as a result of its oppressive techniques, and was able to enlist mainly the opportunistic, the indigent, and the frightened. An atmosphere of fear clouded government-student relations and provided excellent propaganda material for Communists. Moreover, the students were only temporarily subdued. As early as January 1933, a writer in *Ch'ing-hua chou-k'an* (The Tsinghua Weekly) observed that Kuomintang oppression was producing more student radicalism than it destroyed.[42] When the anti-Japanese movement erupted once again in 1935, it was immediately expropriated by the left.

Students and Communism

While the Kuomintang sought an effective policy, the CCP, its urban apparatus crumbling under government assaults, fought for survival in the schools. However, as in previous times of crisis, the party placed little confidence in "petty bourgeois" intellectuals. Furthermore, student cadres were burdened with orders to deemphasize anti-imperialist agitation and to concentrate on an insurrectionary program.[43] Such extremism could not fail to frighten off the majority of anti-Japanese youth, who though disillusioned were still not ready for revolution.

From late 1930 to mid-1935, the official Communist line was based on the United Front from Below, which involved opposition to all other political leaders—Trotskyites and third parties as well as the KMT—while appealing to followers to unite under its own aegis. In the schools, this exclusive policy emphasized the distinction between "capitalist counterrevolutionary" and impoverished "proletarian" students. Another technique of the party line was to soft-pedal political slogans so as to transfer agitation from the anti-Japanese issue to the "vital demands" of the students. Thus, young cadres instigated campaigns to oust "reactionary" chancellors, to abolish or lower tuition, to strengthen school facilities, to improve the cuisine, to oppose inspection of student mail and dormitories, and to protest expulsions. In these ways the party sought to weaken and discredit KMT educational policies.[44]

Intensification of the White Terror in the cities and the isolation of the Kiangsi Soviet virtually cost the Communists their contact with the student masses. What saved the party was not its tactical maneuvers or the United Front from Below but its anti-Japanese propaganda, which was zealously spread by cadres though granted a low priority in the new party line. The CCP's "declaration of war" against Japan, and its verbal support of the Fukien rebels perpetuated its popular image as a dedicated spokesman for a war of resistance. Party resolutions might stress internal revolution, but skillful propagandists cried, "Resist Japan!" Had the Communists been devils incarnate, this slogan would still have made them appear to be bearers of sacred writ.

Although the CCP had practically no organized strength in the cities, the party acquired valuable assets in the minds of China's young intelligentsia. There were Marxist disciples in the KMT and among unaffiliated elements, but only the Communists stood to benefit politically from the immense popularity of Marxism. To the young man seeking a comprehensive analysis of a confusing and hostile environment, the explanation that reactionary "feudal" or "bourgeois" classes were allied with warlords and imperialists seemed plausible enough. The social reformer was eager to work among the peasants and workers, the alienated rebel was attracted by the radicalism of the Leninist solution, the moralist discovered in the austere simplicity of the Communist Party a refreshing contrast to the materialism of the Kuomintang elite. The same poverty-ridden rural milieu that provided legions for the Red Army supplied leftists for city schools. Disproportionate numbers of student radicals came from the lowest income groups that could afford a post-grammar-school education—landlords and "wealthy" peasants.[45]

"As the result of foreign insults combined with misgovernment at home, left wing ideals have captured the imagination of most of our younger men," wrote Liang Shih-ch'iu, a prominent author and Peita professor who was by no means a radical, in the *Ta-kung pao* of February 24, 1935. He continued:

Of recent years the Government has steadily introduced measures of increasing severity against left wingers. But the Government can only control actions, not thought; and the more actions are controlled, the more do thoughts incline towards the left.... The Government ... fails to see that the drift towards the left wing in the younger men caused by [its] restrictive measures largely increases the danger.[46]

The findings of a YMCA survey supported Liang's theory that police terror merely increased the students' desire for socialist and communist ideas.[47]

Sympathy for Communism was usually expressed as admiration for the USSR. While the Chinese soviets were isolated from the world by government blockades, and news from the West revealed devastating economic depression, reports from the Soviet Union indicated that Stalin's Five-Year Plans were transforming a backward nation into a modern industrial power. Students contrasted the vigorous program of their northern neighbor with China's interminable and fruitless talk, which failed to solve critical problems.[48] The plans excited strong interest even in missionary middle schools, and when the Soviet ambassador spoke on the subject at Yenching University, receptive students submitted more than a hundred questions.[49] The failure of the Western powers to provide something more effective at halting Japanese aggression than moral platitudes forced China to look to the USSR for assistance. Chinese students were delighted by the resumption of Sino-Russian diplomatic relations in 1932.[50]

Although membership in the CCP and CY was still too dangerous to attract many students, those who did join were serious and dedicated. Classmates generally held CCP members in high esteem, though they assumed that KMT followers were rank opportunists. James Y. C. Yen, who in his Tinghsien rural reform projects was trying to offer an alternative to Communism, observed that "the more earnest and intelligent" of China's middle school graduates were joining the Communist Party because it seemed to offer the country the only way out of its difficulties.[51]

Even though the CCP and particularly the CY lost vast numbers of registered members during these years of persecution, Communism attracted a superior segment of the younger generation and accumulated a reservoir of good will. After 1936, it was able to tap this hidden store through an anti-Japanese united-front policy.

The Decline of the Anti-Japanese Movement

By the end of 1931, the ascendancy of left-wing students in the anti-Japanese movement had frightened away supporters and invited government suppression. Nonetheless, sporadic activi-

ties continued through the spring of 1932, especially in Peiping, the radicals' stronghold. There student leaders conferred
with their Shanghai and Tientsin colleagues and formed a
series of organizations in an unsuccessful effort to regain the
momentum of the previous year. These included an alliance
of Manchurian refugees, academic reform associations for free
tuition and independent educational funds, and national salvation unions. However, vigilant authorities rendered these
groups impotent and dispersed several hundred students
and others who attended mass meetings on the anniversary of
May Thirtieth. Elsewhere, boycotts, once encouraged by the
KMT, were now suppressed. By the end of the spring semester,
the anti-Japanese student movement had been crushed.[52]

In North China, government oppression coupled with frequently unopposed Japanese advances shattered morale.
When enemy troops attacked Shanhaikuan in January 1933,
and then marched toward Peiping and Tientsin, students who
had once demanded resistance at any price formed the vanguard of a panicky flight from the two cities.

This display of fecklessness furnished government officials
and liberal educators with a welcome opportunity for revenge
on the self-styled patriots, even though some professors had
also taken to their heels. Vice-Minister of Education Tuan
Hsi-p'eng, still scarred from his beating at the hands of a student mob six months earlier, castigated spineless students for
using the enemy's invasion as an excuse to evade their studies.[53] Chancellor Mei Yi-ch'i begged Tsinghua's nine hundred
undergraduates to act as models for society by remaining in
the city for examinations; only three hundred responded to
his appeal. Even those who did not leave town were absorbed
in "erotic adventures, skating, dancing, and other forms of
dissolute life."[54] The respected scholar Fu Ssu-nien led the
chorus of criticism:

These last few days, the strange events in Peiping have really laid
bare the evil nature of the Chinese. . . . Strangest of all is the fear
on the part of the university students, who have been running
helter-skelter demanding that examinations be eliminated, or that
school authorities should at least guarantee their safety. . . . When

one thinks back to the petitions, demonstrations, military training, anti-Japanese work, etc., of over a year ago, this is really the lowest kind of comedy. Looking back on the past from the vantage point of the present, they seem to have acted according to the following formula: When they themselves bore no responsibility, they petitioned; when no harm could come to their own persons, they demonstrated; when they knew full well there was no need to go into battle, [they wanted] military training; when separated from the Japanese by the greatest distance, [they shouted] "resist Japan." One fine day, trouble broke out, and they were faced with the possibility of difficulties or danger, so they took the path of least resistance and ran. . . . This is China's so-called "superior element!"[55]

The student exodus was a result as much of despair as of cowardice. The government appeared to be firmly committed to a policy of appeasement (or in KMT terminology "pacifying within before resisting without," in practice, they amounted to the same thing). Few retained faith in petitions, demonstrations, mass meetings, or propaganda. Sixteen diehards who had stayed in Peiping to organize an anti-Japanese association discovered the futility of their efforts when they were arrested on January 11.[56] No political activity could escape the watchful and hostile eyes of the authorities.

The foreign-based YMCA was the only non-official organization that might openly engage in patriotic work without inviting government suppression. One YMCA worker wrote:

Owing to the Japanese invasion and the chaos in the country, there is a feeling among the population in general and especially among the students that life is not worthwhile. The Association has attempted to organize activities which will give an outlet to patriotism and help people to feel they are doing something which really counts.[57]

The YMCA carried out a program of popular lectures, dramas, and discussion groups. Its leaders hoped to put patriotic energies to constructive use through service work for China's fighting men and a "National Goods Movement," an attempt to redefine the anti-Japanese boycott in positive terms.[58]

The Peiping branch of the YMCA had just concluded a drive to collect winter clothing for Manchurian volunteers when the Japanese attacked Shanhaikuan on January 1. Mem-

bers of a Government University Bible Class established a
Youth Service Fellowship; the group made bandages, studied
first aid and nursing, and went to the front to build roads and
do relief work. In May, as enemy planes showered Peiping
with intimidating leaflets, and as bombers buzzed the city to
further frighten residents, students and YMCA workers discussed "the Christian attitude toward the situation," and proposed sending a delegation of Christian students to Japan.
Even after the proximity of battle had forced the closing of
government schools, students continued to enroll in service
projects.[59]

As a foreign-led organization with pacifist tendencies, drawing its membership principally from missionary schools, the
YMCA could play only a transitory role in the patriotic drive.
Nevertheless it is worth noting that the revival of the student
movement in the fall of 1935 began at Yenching and Tsinghua
universities, both YMCA centers.

The eventful 1932–33 school year in North China ended
abruptly in late May. As Japanese troops advanced within
shooting distance of the gates of Peiping and enemy planes
flew so low that the bombs under their wings could be plainly
seen, chancellors of several government universities encouraged students to return to the safety of their homes. Once
again there was a mass exodus from the old city and morale
deteriorated further.[60] When the government negotiated an
uneasy truce through the humiliating Tangku agreement of
May 31, young China looked on in stunned silence.

In the lower Yangtze Valley, there was less KMT terrorism
than in Peiping, and the party took a more positive attitude
toward student political activities, hoping to manipulate
rather than coerce. The government had several advantages:
the area was only indirectly threatened by the Japanese, hence
students were more willing to accept long-term solutions; the
economic situation was more promising than it was in the
north; and most important, Kuomintang hegemony was unchallenged in Shanghai and Nanking, where the KMT was
in a position to carry out more precise and effective policies
than it could enforce at points hundreds of miles away.

When the Japanese attacked Shanhaikuan, a group of left-wing KMT student leaders in Shanghai organized a union to "support the government in its resistance to Japan."[61] Kuomintang Headquarters in Nanking sent an emissary to stifle this new group lest it develop along anti-government lines as others had done in the past. However, when the union's leaders responded with assertions of their loyalty to the KMT and their determination to proceed with their plans, the party's envoy reluctantly gave in. The organization was formally inaugurated on April 16, 1933. A month later a middle school union was started;[62] KMT authorities were more successful here than in the university union.* The middle school group built its program around activities favorable to the ruling party: raising money for "national salvation airplanes," organizing lectures on "saving the nation by learning," conducting volunteer schools during summer vacations, promoting the New Life Movement, and denouncing the USSR for selling its interests in the Chinese Eastern Railroad to Japan's puppet state of Manchukuo.[63]

The university union was less willing to follow the KMT's prescribed course, preferring a program of direct action reminiscent of the student movements of 1931 and earlier. During summer vacation, Shanghai students under union auspices spread propaganda over the radio and in person in five provinces. The group was unwilling to renounce the outlawed anti-Japanese boycott. At one stage, the KMT sent a special agent to mobilize its cadres in the union and teach them how to deal with "reactionary elements." A degree of success is suggested by the union's reorganization of its "Committee for Inspecting [Japanese] Goods" as a "Committee to Promote the New Life Movement."[64]

The Shanghai unions represented a KMT victory insofar as they provided open, officially sanctioned outlets for the patriotic energy of activists. Shanghai students remained friendlier to the government than did their Peiping counterparts. When

---

* As a rule, middle school students were more easily indoctrinated by both KMT and CCP than those of college age. It depended largely on who reached them first.

the latter demonstrated on December 9, 1935, Shanghai's university union defeated motions for a sympathy strike and parade. Radical elements defied the union and held a demonstration, but Kuomintang efforts prevented the Shanghai movement from approaching the proportions of Peiping's.

Responses to a Bleak Environment

Events between the successful defense of Shanghai in February 1932 and the Tangku Truce of May 1933 produced a dramatic transformation in the outlook of China's students. Their mood changed,

from an elation amounting almost to intoxication, through a more rational period of hopeful, determined resistance expressed in concrete projects in support of the volunteers; girded by a new confidence inspired by international vindication and sympathy; intrigued by a possible way out via Russian cooperation, finally to complete disillusionment, hopeless depression of spirit, and a feeling of shame before the world.[65]

The students had lost faith in international justice; China's inability to defend herself provoked feelings of national inferiority, deep despair, and searching introspection. They wondered whether the nation's weakness was due solely to military backwardness, whether China was inherently inadequate, or whether she had been betrayed by reactionary rulers. In such perilous times, students tended to measure all ideas against the standard of China's survival. In a debate at Yenching University, opponents as well as defenders of a scientifically oriented curriculum argued their positions on the grounds that national strength was the primary goal of education.[66] One YMCA worker reported, "It is almost futile to deal with matters which cannot in some way be shown to be relevant to national issues."[67] Another observed that the "supreme test of Christianity" to many students was whether it could "help to make the Chinese race a strong and respected equal with all other races in practical world affairs."[68] Thus, both religion and science were evaluated in terms of utility for national survival.

After the Tangku Truce, the pace of Japanese aggression

relaxed, and many students turned from foreign affairs (which were manifestly beyond hope) to social and individual reconstruction. Feeling isolated and impotent as individuals, they sought a unifying discipline.[69] Some of them (primarily middle school pupils) enlisted in the New Life Movement, large numbers turned to Marxist beliefs, but the most attractive program for socially conscious youth was the rural reconstruction movement. This developed under government, Christian, and private auspices. James Y. C. Yen, Liang Sou-ming, and T'ao Hsing-chih commanded large followings among educated youngsters.[70] At the University of Nanking, students received training under foreign reconstructionists John H. Reisner, John L. Buck, and Frank Price, while sociologists Stewart Burgess and Sidney Gamble taught at Yenching.[71] Government-sponsored projects in the recaptured soviet areas of Central China also attracted many students to the villages. However, the immensity of China's problems soon caused, in the words of Kiang Wen-han, "an increased feeling of disillusionment about such isolated rural experiments' [being] a fundamental solution."[72]

While radical members of this impatient generation were seeking a panacea for foreign and domestic maladies, some of their classmates turned their sights from such thankless tasks to career goals. A foreign commentator likened these opportunists to the old mandarin class, saying: "They cherish no idealism, their one ambition is to get well located."[73] Other students surrendered to nihilism, occupying themselves with erotic literature and love affairs. Growing despair was reflected in the frequency of youthful suicides.[74]

After the Tangku Truce, increasing numbers of Chinese students expressed a mood of futility and cynicism by flocking to study in Japan. An estimated eight hundred sailed in September and October 1934, and three thousand left in 1935.[75] This should not be taken as evidence of affection for the "dwarf slaves." A favorable foreign exchange rate and a desire to learn more about the foe were strong motivations. Nevertheless, considering the thousands who had angrily returned from Japan after the Mukden Incident, this trend indicates a new orientation: no longer did China's young men believe they could save their country by political action, and a showdown with the enemy appeared remote; in the meantime, study, even in Japan, seemed to many the least of several evils.

These widely divergent responses to an oppressive environment are symptomatic of a malaise that KMT reforms failed to cure. There appeared to be no solution to social injustice, intellectual unemployment, and Japanese invasion. The students of the middle 1930's were seeking a way out of the darkness, but none was apparent. The government forbade collective activity; individual efforts seemed pointless. The result was much anguish and little action.

Thus, from mid-1932 to mid-1935, the forces of stability and instability in the schools were delicately balanced. Although Japanese imperialism, along with the deeply rooted tradition of Chinese nationalism and chronic economic and emotional problems, continued to plague the students, the increasingly settled conditions in the economy and education, a temporary lull in Japanese aggression, and the absence of the radical leaders who had been purged by the White Terror discouraged political adventures. However, any significant change in the balance could have released the latent fury of student nationalism. The balance began to change in June 1935.

The Japanese military, which had suspended aggression in North China since 1934, made new demands in the spring of 1935. On June 10, enemy threats forced the Chinese government to sign the Good Will Mandate, which outlawed anti-Japanese words, deeds, and organizations. The Ho-Umezu Agreement of July 6 set the stage for the removal from Hopei province of all military and political persons and groups unfriendly to Japan; these included the dreaded Third Gendarmes. Throughout the summer and early autumn, the Japanese manufactured "incidents" that served as excuses for further pressure; the Nanking government tried to stall, but was forced to make concession after concession. In October, the situation in China's northern provinces was summed up neatly in a newspaper headline:[1]

CHINESE IN NORTH CHINA UNEASY
NO RECOGNIZED RULER OF THIS PART OF THE COUNTRY EXISTS

The same words would have described Peking on the eve of May Fourth.

The aggressor quickly took steps to fill the power vacuum. On October 28, Premier Hirota formally announced his famous Three Principles, which advocated a Japan-Manchukuo-China axis to oppose Communism and develop North China. Japanese leaders subsequently proposed the establishment of a North China Autonomous Region.

On November 1 there was an attempt to assassinate Wang Ching-wei, the appeasement-minded chairman of the Executive Yüan. The next day, the Peiping Political Council ordered its agencies in North China to suppress any group whose activities were prejudicial to friendly relations between Japan and China.[2] Still unappeased, the Japanese had their soldiers arrest prominent "enemies" in Peiping and Tientsin.[3]

The foremost instrument of Japanese expansionism was Major General Doihara Kenji, a reckless adventurer and chief of the Kwantung Army's Special Service Section. Doihara, called "the Lawrence of China," threatened invasion unless a North China Autonomous Council was established for the provinces of Hopei, Shantung, Shansi, Chahar, and Suiyuan. In Tientsin, a Japanese-inspired "People's Association for the Promotion of Self-Government in North China" supported his demands.[4] The only effective Chinese force in the area was the Twenty-ninth Army commanded by General Sung Che-yüan, who was restive under the yoke of Nanking and rumored to be willing to head an "autonomous" regime.

On Peiping campuses, bitterness and despair prevailed as the shadow of Japanese militarism covered North China in the spring of 1935. Four years earlier, Manchurian students had been uprooted by the Japanese. Now the youth of Peiping saw their lives, their careers, and their beloved city jeopardized. Student cadets wept openly when ROTC units disbanded under enemy pressure.[5] The former December Ninth leader Chiang Nan-hsiang (currently president of Tsinghua University) recalls, in a eulogy of his fellow-student Yang Hsüeh-ch'eng:

By the summer of 1935, a change had come over him, and he was often in the reading rooms avidly reading the contents of the daily newspapers. . . . National events were his main concern. The humiliating Ho-Umezu Agreement . . . had been signed, and the Kuomintang government had acceded to the demands of the Japanese Military Command and withdrawn from Tientsin and Peiping. . . . The city of Peiping, situated near the outer perimeter of our national defense line, was already in turmoil. It was the events of these stormy times that carried the diligent scholar Yang Hsüeh-ch'eng into the turbulent political stream. He could not passively continue his "tranquil" studies in this turmoil of events. There were thousands of other patriotic young students in this ancient cultural city, with its glorious revolutionary tradition, who were similarly awakened and stirred into action.[6]

Only the imminence of final examinations forestalled a violent nationalistic outburst. Before departing for summer vacation, a Tsinghua student wrote on his dormitory wall:

> For ten years
> An impoverished student,
> I entered Tsinghua,
> Failing to foresee
> That our beautiful land
> Would be ours no more.
> How sad, how hateful![7]

During the fall semester students became increasingly irate when they saw the remaining obstacles to Japanese control crumble. Anxiety mounted as precious books and works of art were removed from vulnerable libraries and museums to safer places in the south. Rumors spread that even the colleges would be evacuated. However, four years of police suppression and "saving the nation through study" had obliterated all traces of the militant spirit of 1931. Untold numbers of activists had been killed, imprisoned, or forced into hiding. The result was a complete lack of leadership.

"What can we do?" asked one desperate youth in a letter to the leftist periodical *Life of the Masses*.[8] But in November 1935, this magazine, which would soon become a staunch supporter of the renascent student movement, could offer nothing more than a series of denunciations against "feudal remnants," "warlord officials," and "merchant capitalists," some Marxist platitudes about the "world economic crisis," and a reminder that the globe was divided into two "irreconcilable camps." To the students of Peiping, such jargon was as useless as Nanking's favorite aphorism, "First unify within, then resist the enemy without."

Not surprisingly, the first signs of concerted protest appeared at Yenching and Tsinghua universities rather than at Peita, the traditional center of student politics. Five miles northwest of Peiping, Yenching and Tsinghua had kept alive a spirit of freedom that had been crushed within the city walls since the suppression of the 1931 movement. Yenching, an American missionary school partially protected by extraterritoriality, had a strong liberal tradition. Peita students who wanted to read the Marxist classics with impunity borrowed them from the Yenching library. Tsinghua, though a government university, had originally been established with American Boxer Indemnity funds as a preparatory school for Chinese students planning to continue study in the United States. When the Japanese attacked the Great Wall in 1933, students at these two schools took steps to aid Chinese troops. During the middle 1930's, Yenching's outstanding sociology department was a center of rural reform and social surveys, and its school of journalism championed freedom of the press. In March 1935, when most Chinese universities were too subdued to require official pressure, Tsinghua and Yenching were raided by police, and about a dozen students in Tsinghua's Modern Lecture Society were imprisoned.[9]

Late in October, the incipient protest began to take form. A visiting friend from Tsinghua suggested that the Yenching student body place itself on record against government suppression of civil liberties and academic freedom.[10] At a Yenching assembly the following day, a student named Kao Ming-k'ai, serious, liberal, and a forceful writer, asked a crowd of six hundred to send a sharply worded petition to the Sixth Plenum of the Kuomintang's current CEC, which was about to convene in Nanking. The idea won unanimous approval.[11] In the short interval before the November 1 opening of the party conclave, Yenching envoys secured the signatures of representatives from Tsinghua, National Peiping Normal University (which also had been raided the previous March), two Hopei provincial colleges, and half a dozen Peiping and Tientsin middle schools. Copies of the statement were sent to four hundred schools, libraries, and cultural institutions.[12]

The Kuomintang plenum received this impassioned appeal:

After the establishment of the government at Nanking, according to newspaper reports, the number of youths slaughtered totaled no less than three hundred thousand, and the number of those who have disappeared and been imprisoned cannot even be estimated. Killing was not enough, they were buried alive; imprisonment was not enough, they were even subjected to torture; hell itself has been brought to humanity!

... [We] petition that the spirit of the Provisional Laws be respected and that the rights of free speech, press, assembly, and association be put into effect and the illegal arrest of students be stopped. We present this petition believing that in this period of national crisis each citizen must individually shoulder responsibility and act to save his country.[13]

In Nanking, the petition was overshadowed by the attempted assassination of Wang Ching-wei, and in North China the students were not visibly moved. It required more than a cry for civil liberties to rouse them from their apathy. As a Yenching student leader later wrote:

Some thought the proclamation was useless; some thought the government would pay no attention to us; some thought we were trying to beat the drum for the Yenching Student Association. Moreover, these were all borne out by the facts, though this did become the prelude to December Ninth.[14]

The quest for a more effective form of action brought Chang Chao-lin, the Manchurian-refugee president of the Yenching student body, to the home of young American writers Edgar and Helen Snow.* Mrs. Snow recalls:

Chang Chao-lin was very unhappy. He said he had come to find if there was any information on what was happening in Manchuria among the resistance fighters. He said he did not believe a word of anything in the Chinese press and that the refugees from Manchuria were despondent and did not expect the central government to ever resist the Japanese invasion, either there or in North China. Chang was angry about the suppression of anti-Japanese sentiments in the press. . . . It was a time of desperation for the Tungpei exiles and he was ready for anything.[15]

Although the Snows could do little but offer Chang sympathy and share his indignation, Helen Snow suggested to the school newspaper editor that the students form a mock funeral procession, bearing the "corpse of North China" through the

---

* Edgar Snow was at that time teaching journalism at Yenching. He had written *Far Eastern Front* and would later became famous for *Red Star Over China*. Helen F. Snow, who generally used the pen name Nym Wales, was taking courses at Yenching. She covered the student movements for the *China Weekly Review* and later wrote several books, including *Inside Red China* and *Notes on the Chinese Student Movement*, the latter being the most thorough English-language documentary source on the subject.

streets of Peiping. The young journalist reacted coldly; he was not receptive to irony. "This was no time for satire," Helen Snow observed. "They wanted nothing less than the 'correct line' of the world revolution."[16] The funeral proposal was rejected, but the Snow household became a rendezvous for Yenching student leaders. The Snows knew the power of the press, and urged any kind of protest that would make news.

Meanwhile, Yenching and Tsinghua activists were building on the foundation laid by the November 1 petition. Their task, to rouse and organize the students of Peiping, was not easy; years of intimidation had worked only too well. If there was any remnant of the Communist apparatus in Peiping, it was unknown to them, although they would have been quite happy to accept help from anyone favoring resistance to Japan.[17]

The week after the petition, an interschool organizational meeting was convened in a Yenching student dining hall. The students' fears that the presence of some two dozen strangers would attract the attention of the district government office proved groundless; but merely getting organized posed great problems. This was the first interschool meeting in Peiping since the Tangku Truce. Of the ten schools represented, only Yenching, the I-wen Middle School, and the First Girls' Middle School had student associations. It would be difficult for such an amorphous gathering to take action. Nothing short of a city-wide student union could hope to be effective, but there was no obvious way that one could be convened. It was decided that schools without student associations or national salvation associations might be represented by delegates from other student groups; meanwhile Yenching and the two middle schools would form a nucleus.[18]

While underground work was proceeding at the other nine schools, Yenching leaders undertook a publicity campaign among their own classmates. The university's weekly, *Yen-ta chou-k'an,* was pressed into service; the issue of November 8 was devoted to the Japanese question. In large red letters, wall-newspapers proclaimed, "Youth: Unite to Struggle for the Liberation of the Nation!" Both a forum on the problems of youth and a current events discussion group attracted large numbers.[19]

But throughout November the Yenching student body remained divided on the question of collective action. A petition to Ho Ying-ch'in (Minister of War and head of the Peiping office of the Executive Yüan) was suggested, but its opponents argued that Yenching should not act without the participation of other schools, which were lagging behind organizationally.[20] Another proposal called for a proclamation condemning autonomy for North China and demanding armed resistance to Japan. Even though this plan did not involve mass action, it seemed preferable, for its contents were stronger and it would provide an opportunity to coordinate work in the various schools. It passed with an amendment by Shen Ch'ang-huan (today the Chinese Nationalist Foreign Minister), which provided that Yenching would organize a delegation of representatives from Peiping schools to present these views in petition form to Ho Ying-ch'in. This was the modest origin of the December Ninth demonstration.[21]

The Peiping Student Union, defunct since early 1932, was reborn on November 18 at the First Girls' Middle School. The new organization was not impressive. Though students from 22 schools attended, there were formal delegates from only nine universities and middle schools and only three of these represented their entire student bodies.[22] The delegation from Tsinghua, where radical and conservative elements had already clashed openly, spoke only for the left. The Union's initial proclamation, unlike the November 1 petition, was concerned with the critical situation in North China rather than with Nanking's dictatorial rule; but its denunciation of the government was nonetheless severe. KMT rulers were accused of sacrificing Chinese territory and citizens for their own selfish interests. The Union declared its opposition to the separation of North China from the rest of the country and called upon the people of that region to launch "a great, holy, national revolutionary war."[23]

The day after the organization's inaugural assembly, Chiang Kai-shek summarized his foreign policy in the often quoted words, "We shall not forsake peace until there is no hope for peace. We shall not talk lightly of sacrifice until we are driven to the last extremity." However, five days later a number of chancellors and professors from Peiping and Tientsin universities proclaimed their support of the Union's stand against autonomy for North China, although they spoke of Nanking more respectfully than the students had. These proclamations were ignored. On November 25, Major General Doihara inaugurated the East Hopei Autonomous Council under a puppet chairman, Yin Ju-keng. The capital of this "autonomous federation" was Tungchow, only thirteen miles east of Peiping. In Tientsin, the Japanese promoted demonstrations demanding self-government for the North. On November 29, as Japanese warplanes droned ominously overhead, Sung Cheyüan wired Nanking that he could no longer withstand the pressure for autonomy. The students expected that it would be only a matter of days before North China would become another Manchukuo.

The December Demonstrations

The growing resentment in Peiping academic circles moved Chinese and Japanese authorities to action. The Kwantung Army commander in Peiping summoned Peita Chancellor Chiang Monlin to the Japanese barracks for interrogation. Chiang was accused of anti-Japanese activities and was asked to go under military escort to Dairen for a talk with Lieutenant General Itagaki Seishiro. He declined the invitation and was released.[24] Armed police disbanded student associations at Peita and Chung-kuo College and arrested half a dozen Manchurian refugees in a raid on Northeastern University. An incipient student self-governing association at Normal University was suppressed by school officials.[25]

Police interrogated the pupils of several institutions, notably the First Girls' Middle School, the birthplace of the new Peiping Union. Seven leaders at Yenching heard rumors that they had been marked for arrest. Since their flight would have disrupted the mechanism of student organization, they continued to work by day but hid at night to avoid capture in dormitory raids, which were customarily made before dawn.[26]

During the last week of November, Edgar Snow made a radical proposal to his Yenching student friends. As a journalist, Snow was in continual contact with military and diplomatic personnel. Time was running out, he said; if students were to have any impact on public opinion, they would have to move rapidly. He called for a massive student demonstration against autonomy, to take place no later than December 10.[27] In view of the deteriorating situation in North China, the students agreed. On December 3, General Ho Ying-ch'in arrived in Peiping; the students interpreted his visit as a prelude to Nanking's surrender of North China. On the same day, the Peiping Student Union voted to march en masse to Ho's headquarters on December 9, with a petition urging: (1) opposition to the so-called autonomy movement, (2) open conduct of foreign relations, (3) cessation of arbitrary arrests, (4) protection of territorial integrity, (5) termination of all civil war, and (6) freedom of speech, press, assembly, and organization.

The Union's plans reveal the intricate organization and meticulous division of labor that were the hallmarks of Chinese student movements. A central command bureau, a supervisory corps, a communications corps, and a first-aid corps were quickly established, though only a few insiders knew when the demonstration would occur. The delegates returned to their schools to rally classmates to the cause. At Tsinghua a meeting was called for the evening of December 3; a right-wing minority opposed the idea of a demonstration but agreed to cooperate because of their basic agreement on the principles involved.[28] Yenching student leaders chose as their delegate to the central command force Wang Ju-mei (who later rose to a high position in the Chinese Communist foreign service under the name Huang Hua). A student assembly to approve the plan of action was called for the night of December 6.[29]

On the eve of the demonstration, students were preparing leaflets, posters, and flags. Chang Chao-lin was making arrangements with Yenching authorities. Headquarters established a succession of command. If the leader was arrested, his lieutenant would take charge; if the lieutenant was then seized, another deputy would assume control. These plans were kept secret so morale would not suffer. The commander-in-chief of the Yenching squad later recalled:

[A student] told me that there were three girl students who would bring bandages, astringents, etc. While I thanked her, my heart jumped a beat. But this excitement quickly subsided. We absolutely had to avoid causing a conflict. We had to preserve our young lives. Certainly our influence would be still wider if there were deaths, but we absolutely would not make this kind of opportunistic plan.[30]

During the afternoon, representatives of the Peiping Student Union made final arrangements in an upstairs corner of the Yenching gymnasium. Delegates with detailed strategies for the next day rode the last bus into Peiping. That night, at a Yenching student assembly and in dormitories of more than a dozen other Peiping schools, the word spread: "Tomorrow we march!"[31]

With the first light of dawn, Tsinghua and Yenching students rose, put on their padded gowns, scarfs, fedoras, and fur hats, and ran out into the cold. The Yenching leaders, who had planned to commandeer university buses for the five-mile journey to the city, discovered that the vehicles had disappeared and that police were guarding the main gates. The marchers slipped out through side entrances and set out across the frozen fields toward Peiping.

Within the city walls, other students, carrying propaganda leaflets, flags, and placards, drifted into the streets in small groups. They began putting up posters, and distributing leaflets to pedestrians or inducing newsboys to slip them into morning papers. Thirty or forty enthusiasts at Chung-kuo College broke through the gate, which had been closed by school police, and marched westward toward the Chü-jen T'ang, Ho Ying-ch'in's headquarters, near the Hsin-hua Men (gate) in the West City. (See accompanying map.) They halted en route to rally pupils of the Associated Girls' Middle School; a dozen of the boldest girls ignored the warnings of their teachers and left a Sun Yat-sen memorial meeting to join the march. At a Northeastern University gathering, organizers announced that the day had arrived for action to keep North China from becoming another Manchuria. Some of the young refugees were moved to tears as the assembly voted to join the demonstration. Marching shoulder to shoulder, four abreast, they too headed for the Hsin-hua Men. Peiping University's College of Law had been surrounded by police, but dozens of students scaled the wall and rushed to join the demonstration. Similar scenes were taking place at other schools throughout the city.

Troops of the Twenty-ninth Army and police of the Fourth Precinct confronted the column as it approached the Hsi-ssu P'ai-lou (arch). The marchers tried to win over the police with such slogans as "Down with Japanese imperialism!" and "Chinese don't strike Chinese!" But the police stood firm, and the students had to charge the lines. A number of them were beaten with clubs, leather belts, and the blunt edges of swords, and the wounded were left to be carried off by the enemy. The battle-tested Northeasterners were soon among the crowd gathered in front of the Chü-jen T'ang.[32]

A committee of representatives stepped forward with the petition to Ho Ying ch'in; they were met by a functionary who announced that General Ho was spending the day at the T'ang-shan hot springs resort. He offered to accept the petition on Ho's behalf, and tried to assure the students of the government's sincerity. His words only irritated the crowd. Meanwhile, couriers arrived saying that the Yenching and Tsinghua contingents were demonstrating outside the Hsi-chih Men, which had been barred to prevent them from joining the rest of the students. The masses cried, "To the Hsi-chih Men," turned their backs on the official, and marched toward the northwest section of Peiping.

When soldiers with broadswords and armed police met the students at the Hsi-tan P'ai-lou, the intrepid students handed leaflets to their attackers and implored them to fight the Japanese. The leaders finally reorganized their lines, and, fearing another and more disastrous clash at the Hsi-chih Men,

Map of Peiping Showing Key Points
of the December Demonstrations

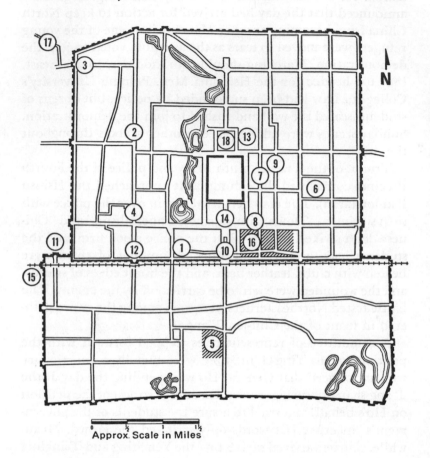

Approx. Scale in Miles

1	Chü-jen T'ang, Hsin-hua Men	10	Ch'ien Men
2	Hsi-ssu P'ai-lou	11	Hsi-pien Men
3	Hsi-chih Men	12	Shun-chih Men
4	Hsi-tan P'ai-lou	13	Peita
5	T'ien Ch'iao (shaded)	14	T'ien-an Men
6	Foreign Ministry	15	Railroad Gate
7	Nan-ch'ang Road	16	Legation Quarter (shaded)
8	Ch'ang-an Street	17	Road to Tsinghua and Yenching
9	Wang-fu-ching Street	18	Coal Hill

turned their remaining followers to spread the demonstration to the eastern part of the city. En route, reinforcements joined them from several schools, though only a few came from National Peking University, home of the May Fourth Movement. This small contingent marched under a cardboard box top inscribed with the proud name "Peita."

When the procession approached the Legation Quarter along Wang-fu-ching Street, fire hoses scattered the crowd with a stream of icy water. The students retreated, and police and soldiers set upon them, slashing, kicking, and arresting those who could not escape. The rest straggled back to their dormitories. Outside the walls, nearly a thousand disappointed Yenching and Tsinghua students turned and began the long, cold trek home.[33]

The same evening, representatives of the participating schools met at Peita and voted to begin a general strike in the morning. The following day, mass meetings in more than a dozen schools supported the Union's decision to strike, and approved its demands for the immediate release of the arrested students, for punishment of the police and soldiers who had injured demonstrators, and for a satisfactory reply from Peiping authorities, especially from General Ho, to the previous day's petition. By December 13, almost all students were on strike at Yenching, Tsinghua, Normal University, Peita, Chaoyang, Fujen, National Peiping University, and five middle schools.[34]

The strike was more than a weapon of protest; it gave the students time to organize and expand the movement. A multitude of committees, subcommittees, and work groups sprang from individual school associations, many of them recently formed. In the vanguard of this activity was Tsinghua University, where a National Salvation Committee led by active left-wing students, and basing its legitimacy on mass meetings, circumvented its parent body, the self-governing association. The prominence of such organizations after December 9 foreshadowed a drift to the left. As the movement developed, organizers whom Edgar Snow has called "the professionals" steadily came into power.[35] This was probably unavoidable, since the only groups trained and disciplined for political

action were Communists and Communist sympathizers at one
extreme and Kuomintang cadres at the other. In a movement
critical of government policy, the former had an obvious advantage.

Tsinghua's National Salvation Committee created special
units to meet new needs. (See Figure 3.) On December 11,
police and soldiers surrounded several schools, and arrested
nine Northeastern University students. To prevent similar
incidents from occurring on their campus, the Tsinghua Committee formed a Department of the Guards, whose 200-man
Sentry Division guarded the school gates 24 hours a day, and
protected the campus by patrolling it on bicycles. The Guards'
communication section disseminated news, sent messages, and
maintained liaison with other schools. Another department,
specializing in propaganda, dispatched units to proselytize
nearby villagers, published a monthly periodical, *Nu-hou pa*
(Roar in Anger), issued three intelligence reports daily, and
turned out twelve different kinds of propaganda materials.
Its Foreign Language Section translated the December 9
petition and other items into eight languages for overseas
distribution.[36]

On December 14, the chancellors of the Peiping universities
sought to end the strike, pointing out that most of the imprisoned students had been released the previous day, but the
Union refused to comply because its other demands had not
been granted. Any hope for a return to normal was smashed
by the simultaneous announcement that the often postponed
inauguration of the Hopei-Chahar Political Council would
take place in two days. The Student Union met on December
15 and voted to stage a protest demonstration the following
morning to coincide with this event. Detailed plans were
mapped out; schools would march in four divisions, led by
Northeastern, Chung-kuo College, Peita, and Tsinghua. A
troop of approximately one hundred students from Yenching
and Tsinghua, fearful of being locked out again, spent the
night in the city.

The spontaneity and courage of December 9 seem insig-
nificant beside the magnitude and drama of December 16.
Though small compared with the well-rehearsed extravagan-

zas of the Communist era, December sixteenth saw what was probably the largest student demonstration ever held in Peiping up to that time. According to figures published in one campus newspaper, 7,775 students from 28 schools took part.[37] Early in the morning, determined students broke through police lines to follow predetermined routes to the working-class T'ien Ch'iao district, where a mass meeting was scheduled. According to plans, they would then march to the Foreign Ministry Building, where the political council was to convene.

The students were organized and disciplined; so were the forces that met them. All over the city, police and soldiers confronted columns converging on the central line of march. Authorities exercised less restraint than they had the previous week, using clubs, swords, gun butts, and belts on the unarmed students, who had been ordered to offer no resistance. The main column, several thousand strong, marched down Nan-ch'ang Road into Ch'ang-an Road, and near the scene of the December ninth hosing, was again deluged with water. This time, Peita students wrested away the hose and turned it on the police. However, other students, unaware that their side was in possession of the hose, cut it and turned off the water.

With the way cleared, the procession continued through Peiping's south gate, the Ch'ien Men, to the T'ien Ch'iao neighborhood in the outer city. Here its numbers were increased by the Yenching-Tsinghua students, who had walked more than ten miles to reach their comrades. Having found the Hsi-chih Men closed once again, they had marched southward outside the city wall and had finally gained entrance by breaking down a Peking-Hankow Railroad gate. Five hundred more demonstrators arrived from the besieged Normal University campus; they had escaped when a passing column of Tsinghua students diverted the attention of police. Further reinforced by thousands of T'ien Ch'iao residents, the meeting resolved that the masses be armed to resist Japanese imperialism.

The students then lined up and set out for the Foreign Ministry Building to "ask the city government why the local authorities were selling out the nation," in the words of one re-

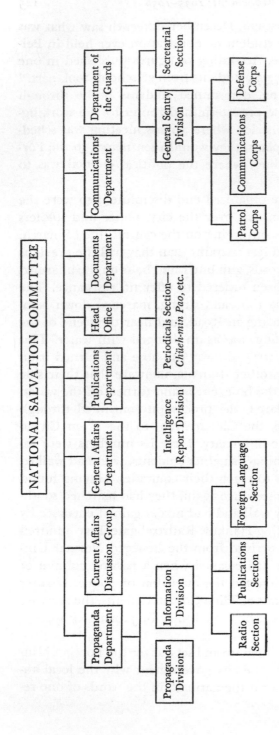

Figure 3. The National Salvation Committee of the Tsinghua University Student Self-governing Association. *Source: Chiu-wang yün-tung pao-kao-shu*, edited by Ch'ing-hua ta-hsüeh hsüeh-sheng tzu-chih-hui chiu-kuo wei-yüan-hui (The National Salvation Committee of the Tsinghua University Student Self-governing Association). Peiping, May 9, 1936.

porter.[38] The column, nearly three-quarters of a mile long, was led by the Tsinghua contingent, marching under three enormous banners denouncing the Hopei-Chahar Political Council, other "traitors," and Japanese imperialism.

But the approach to the inner city through the Ch'ien Men was barred. As students flocked into the square in front of this gate, rifle squads from the local police station fired blanks into the crowd, creating near-panic. When order was finally restored, leaders began negotiations with the police, hoping to gain peaceful admission to the city. The police feared a violent demonstration at the Foreign Ministry if the students were permitted to pass. A compromise was finally reached: several hundred marchers were allowed to enter the city through the Ch'ien Men; the others were guaranteed access through the Shun-chih Men in the western quarter of Peiping (across town from the political council's meeting place). However, the students discovered upon arrival that they had been deceived; the Shun-chih Men was bolted. On the other side, police dispersed a contingent led by Peita students as they shouted encouragement to their comrades across the wall. Suddenly, a diminutive girl ran out of the crowd outside and rolled under the gate. She was dragged away by police as she tried to open the lock. The young heroine, Lu Ts'ui, became the main subject of the dispute.* At 7 p.m., after involved negotiations, she was allowed to roll back to join the cheering throng. This was followed by a sit-in to force the police to open the gate, but the night was too cold for the students to persevere. By 8 p.m. the Yenching-Tsinghua group had begun the three-hour march home; at 9:30 the others left to spend the night at the Normal University dormitories in the outer city. As they began to disperse through the dark streets, the students were once again assaulted by soldiers. Too exhausted to resist or to run, many were injured. In all, 85 students were severely wounded and 297 were less seriously hurt during the demonstration.[39]

* This action began her political career, which culminated in her appointment as Secretary-General of the All-China Democratic Women's Federation after the Communist victory.

The political results of the demonstration were encouraging. Though the Hopei-Chahar Political Council was inaugurated on December 18, the Japanese were forced to drop their five-province autonomy scheme, and the new Council was not the puppet organ they had envisioned. Frustrated, they issued denunciations of the demonstrations, blaming them on Communist, Kuomintang, and American machinations. In addition, Sung Che-yüan's position was immeasurably strengthened by the students' action. Already largely freed from Nanking's control by the Kwantung Army, which had compelled other Chinese military units to leave the area, he was now provided with a bulwark of public opinion against further Japanese demands. Sung was quick to take advantage of the situation. The day after the December 9 demonstration, he informed Doihara that further negotiations would have to be postponed and that he could not assume responsibility for maintaining order in the city if autonomy were proclaimed.[40] However, Sung displayed no public gratitude toward Peiping's students; in an open letter he accused them of having been misled by Communist agitators.[41]

Nanking authorities also had reason to be thankful. Ho Ying-ch'in had come north armed with nothing but his own eloquence; student demonstrations had enabled him to secure from Sung a pledge of loyalty to the central government. For this reason, and because it was remote from Japanese military power, the Nanking regime spoke less harshly of the student patriots than did Sung. The Ministry of Education said that both the December 9 demonstration and the earlier anti-autonomy manifesto of Peiping's educators were "patriotic," though it remained silent concerning the November 1 diatribe. Peiping authorities were instructed to accord due protection both to students and to faculties. Only after the strike and the second demonstration did Nanking's friendly attitude cool.[42]

Not until eleven days after December 9 was there an official reaction from the embattled forces of Mao Tse-tung in northern Shensi. (This argues strongly against alleged Communist control at that time.) The Communist Youth Corps proclamation of December 20 lauded the new movement but warned students to seek support from workers, peasants, soldiers, and merchants if they wished to avoid the fate of the 1931 efforts.

In an open bid for leadership, CY promised to cooperate with all anti-Japanese groups and announced that it was forthwith renaming itself the "Resist Japan National Salvation Youth Corps." It would be open to "all patriotic youth, whether or not they believe in Communism . . . with the sole stipulation that they are willing to resist Japan and save the country."[43] Although the attempt to attract mass support away from other groups was a familiar tactic, the elimination of ideological prerequisites for membership in CY was unprecedented, and the offer to cooperate with other anti-Japanese organizations was an important step toward a broad united-front policy.

The Movement Spreads

Reports of the dramatic events in Peiping soon reached every part of the country. In spite of government censorship, most newspapers were able to publish at least an official version of the demonstrations. The students were their own best publicity agents. After the December 9 outburst, the Peiping Union's propaganda section sent members to other major cities and mailed thousands of circulars to colleagues throughout China. (At least one appeal for support was written in invisible ink.)[44] Yenching and Tsinghua dispatched joint delegations to cities in the Yangtze Valley. More than half of a twenty-man Tsinghua bicycle corps reached Nanking after pedaling more than six hundred miles in the cold of winter, only to be rounded up by government detectives and returned to Peiping.[45]

Proclamations, telegrams, strikes, demonstrations, and propaganda campaigns in support of the Peiping students came from Hangchow (December 10), Canton (December 12), Shanghai and Sian (December 14), and Tsinan (December 16). The December sixteenth demonstration completed the destruction of student apathy begun on December 9. From December 18 to 22, the youth of sixteen cities added their voices to the uproar; by the end of the month, approximately 65 demonstrations had occurred in 32 different areas. Throughout China students were rededicating themselves to the ideal of anti-imperialistic nationalism.[46]

School walkouts and the prospect of further demonstrations alarmed authorities. On December 19, Minister of Education Wang Shih-chieh ordered local officials everywhere to prohibit petitions, parades, and strikes. In Peiping, Twenty-ninth Army Commander Sung Che-yüan convened a special meeting of chancellors to seek a means of stopping student activities. Officials in Peiping and other storm centers scheduled early winter vacations in an attempt to scatter the troublemakers. In Shanghai, where the KMT had habitually fostered and attempted to control student political action, a newly established Student Union asked the government "to protect legitimate patriotic movements and speech," but this conciliatory language failed to mollify pro-KMT students, who requested a thorough investigation of the Union. Mayor Wu T'ieh-ch'eng announced that the city government and KMT Headquarters would lead the patriotic movement.[47] Wu's tact succeeded where Sung Che-yüan's uncompromising stand had failed. He complied with the request of two hundred Futan petitioners by asking Peiping officials to release the imprisoned demonstrators. To end a siege of the North Station he granted activists from Futan and other schools transportation to Nanking, leaving it to Shanghai and Nanking officials to turn back the contingent at Wusih. Before long the academic scene returned to normal.[48]

At the Süchow and Kaifeng railroad stations, thousands more gathered, likewise hoping to repeat the pattern of 1931, when petitioners had won free transportation to the capital; but officials halted train service until they dispersed.[49] Similar tactics turned back Nantung University students, who had waited three days for river transportation up the Yangtze.[50] Patriotic activities in Nanking, isolated from outside reinforcements and watched carefully by government authorities, were also short-lived. At National Central University, focal point of the 1931 movement, Chancellor Lo Chia-lun (a May Fourth veteran) once again displayed his deftness in handling student politics. On the condition that students return to their dormitories, he secured the withdrawal of the troops that had surrounded the campus to prevent demonstrations at the Japanese Embassy.[51]

Authorities in the Wuhan cities at the junction of the Han and Yangtze rivers tried unsuccessfully to maintain order by halting ferry service, but an early winter recess prevented a school strike. Similar methods stymied the Canton student movement following a demonstration on December 12.[52]

Only in Peiping, birthplace of the nationwide movement, were leaders able to prolong activities beyond the initial burst of mass enthusiasm; but there too many difficulties arose. It is questionable whether the movement would have survived without strong leftist leadership. The strike continued after December 16, but some schools lost contact with the Peiping Union, which still lacked central headquarters. A December 26 consolation meeting for arrested and wounded schoolmates revived spirits and provided a forum for impassioned oratory. Printed propaganda also helped; countless newspapers, periodicals, and bulletins from the Union and its member schools vividly described the demonstrations, exposed police brutality and government treachery, censured "national salvation through study," discussed tactics for the strike, and attacked allegedly pro-Japanese officials and scholars.[53] Elaborately organized student groups performed a multitude of tasks. Among those responsible to Yenching's headquarters were an intelligence department, a Peiping city-residence agent, Student Union representatives, and a delegation for soliciting the participation of other schools. There were also editorial and statistics groups; committees for communication, information, and political discussion; propaganda corps, nursing corps, and wireless corps; and a temporary library.[54]

Student activities attracted support from the older generation and brought about the formation of a left-wing National Salvation Movement, an invaluable asset to the Communists in developing a united front. This effort had forerunners in groups such as Mme. Sun Yat-sen's League for Armed Resistance Against Japan (1934), but reached nationwide proportions only after the December demonstrations. Shanghai, where political and cultural nonconformists sought refuge under foreign law, was the center of the Salvation Movement. Most prominent among Shanghai's active writers, teachers, politicians, and financiers were the "Seven Gentlemen," who earned the title and national renown when they were arrested in November 1936. Shortly after December 9, the noted educator T'ao Hsing-chih founded the National Crisis Education Society, which included four of the seven. Two of them, the journalist Tsou T'ao-fen and the banker Chang Nai-ch'i, established the Shanghai Cultural Circles' Education Society. National salvation associations of women, teachers, cultural workers, and film makers followed. A Workers' Anti-Japanese National Salvation Association was subjected to especially harsh persecution by Chinese and Japanese authorities.[55]

The majority of Peiping's college faculty members tacitly supported the students; a vocal minority openly encouraged them. A manifesto by the North China Cultural Workers' Association endorsed the November 1 declaration, and other groups mushroomed after the two demonstrations. More than 150 delegates attended the January 27 inauguration of the Peiping Cultural Circles' National Salvation Association Simultaneously, the Peiping Student Union drew up a comprehensive scheme of organization for all anti-Japanese groups in China.[56]

Journalists, chafing under press censorship, went into action after the Peiping demonstrations. Some Chinese reporters openly sympathized with the students on December 9, but their stories were omitted from Peiping's Chinese-language papers. The *Pei-p'ing ch'en-pao* (Peiping Morning Post) protested this censorship by conspicuously inserting an advertisement ("Pianos Rented and Repaired") in the center of a roughly effaced photograph of the demonstration.[57] The *Shih-chieh jih-pao* (Daily World) was more outspoken. In a "Lament," the editor deplored the suppression of freedom of the press and protested that "an event witnessed by thousands of eyes must be blocked out of the newspapers."[58] A crusade to abolish censorship began in the Yenching department of journalism and led to the formation of the Chinese Journalists' Association of Peiping and Tientsin.[59] However, it must not be assumed that press support was unanimous. The *Ta-*

kung pao lived up to its French name, *L'Impartial,* by criticizing both government policies and student methods of protest. An editorial published simultaneously in the *Chung-yang jih-pao* and eleven other pro-government newspapers expressed "respect and admiration" for the students' motivations, but appealed to them to cooperate with the government and to renounce strikes and disorder.[60]

Hu Shih's article, "A Word on the Student Movement," provoked the most thorough discussion of the function of school political activities since the great Kuomintang debate of 1927–29.[61] Then the issue had been "How can the students best help the KMT build a new China, by study or by political action?" Now it was "Does the government merit the younger generation's loyalty at all?" Hu urged students to use verbal protest rather than mass action, to act within the spirit of the law, and to remain vigilant against minority manipulation. He stated that at a time of unprecedented crisis, as always, the foremost responsibility of students was to develop their own knowledge and abilities. Following leaders blindly, believing without thinking, making arbitrary decisions, allowing oppression by a minority, hoodwinking the masses, working for selfish ends, and destroying the law must be considered inappropriate to the period of learning.

Point-by-point criticism of this article was offered by two radicals writing under the pen names Wei Li and Mo Ning.[62] Both said Hu was naïve to assume that words alone would move a government that betrayed the nation, oppressed the people, and closed its ears to public opinion. They denounced the charge of minority control as patently false. Furthermore, argued Wei, students were actually obtaining a more useful education in the salvation movement than they could in the classroom. These critics argued that study as usual during a time of national crisis would lead to national enslavement. Mo Ning concluded that Hu Shih was "a running dog of imperialism and the traitorous government, a criminal who swindles the masses."[63]

Most students did not endorse such extreme criticism of the Peita dean; but it is clear that many supporters of the December Ninth Movement were inclined to cast aside the liberal gradualism of Hu Shih in favor of more radical national salvation doctrines. Legalistic niceties and parliamentary democracy seemed trivial to Chinese youth in this period of national crisis. Considering that China had known nothing but crisis for nearly half a century, it is not surprising that the vanguard of the younger generation eventually rejected Hu for Lenin and Mao.

The Rural Crusade

On December 18, the fourth congress of the Peiping Student Union resolved to broaden the scope of the movement in order to "rally the oppressed masses" against imperialism.[64] Twelve days later, a meeting of more than a hundred college and middle school representatives decided to organize a pilgrimage to Nanking, where they would present demands to high officials, and to seek to rally support in the countryside en route.[65]

These tactics were not novel. Ever since the May Fourth period, Chinese students had felt a duty to spread their ideas of national salvation to the workers and peasants. In 1919 and 1920, Li Ta-chao's disciples formed lecture groups to speak on street corners and in villages. Early Kuomintang and Communist attempts to develop the labor movement mobilized student propagandists. Student agitators played an important role in the Northern Expedition, and after the Mukden Incident, young intellectuals in Shanghai and Hangchow organized drama groups and propaganda teams to spread anti-Japanese doctrine in cities and villages of the lower Yangtze Valley. Idealistic students of the 1930's became zealous rural reconstructionists under KMT, CCP, and Christian auspices. The campaign of January 1936 was the best organized of these crusades.

The newly founded Peiping-Tientsin Student Union organized four corps, three from Peiping and one from Tientsin. These were subdivided into platoons and squads, each containing a leader, four propagandists, two scouts, and specialists in communications, organization, investigation, and first aid.[66] About five hundred students made the pilgrimage, walking in long columns across the frozen countryside of northern Hopei during the first three weeks of January. Nanking, their ultimate destination, became increasingly remote as they immersed themselves in the crusade to awaken the rural masses. Patriotic songs, didactic plays, and impassioned speeches in a babel of dialects filled the air of winter-bound villages. Students distributed an impressive array of propaganda written in simple vernacular, which the few barely literate peasants or schoolchildren could read to the illiterate majority, for example:

Men, women, children! Listen to what we say: Have we seen those things flying overhead every day? Those things are called "airplanes." Sitting in them are the devils of the Eastern Sea, the Japanese devils. They speak a foreign tongue, live in the Eastern Sea, and fly their airplanes over here.

Do you know what they are coming to do? . . . They are coming to kill every single man and woman with their guns and knives, and to ravish our daughters and wives. . . .[67]

But the North China peasant's traditional suspiciousness and lethargy were not easily overcome. Indifference was compounded by linguistic and class barriers, observed Hubert Freyn (a Viennese student who accompanied the Yenching group), and speeches were presented in an atmosphere of "frigid curiosity."[68] At best, despite the villagers' unresponsiveness, "it was apparent that a great deal of the information the students were making known to them was news, and the method of presenting it was novel."[69]

Official hostility increased the students' difficulties; government agents harassed them continually along the route. One report stated that "large numbers of detectives were sent out in advance of the students to instigate the local authorities against them and to spread terrifying rumors."[70] Many a long day's march ended outside a locked city gate.

Only among the educated and the young did the students receive a warm welcome. Teachers and sometimes principals willingly housed them in local schools. While adults listened impassively to patriotic drama and oratory, children registered enthusiastic approval. In meetings with pupils and teachers, the Peiping delegations founded rudimentary anti-Japanese organizations. Freyn describes the relationship between the students and their hosts:

The social gap between the simple village school teachers and some of our *jeunesse dorée*—sons and daughters of millionaire merchants, high officials, wealthy landowners—was indeed wide, yet it made no difference. They were united by the bond of patriotism and the privileges of education; they belonged to the great fraternity of learning.[71]

On January 8, the four corps convened in Kuan, approximately thirty miles south of Peiping. The following morning they exchanged information on the attitudes they had encountered. The authorities and their deputies had been hostile, the few soldiers and factory workers had been friendly, organizations other than schools (guilds, village elders, etc.) had been impassive and indifferent. The attitude of the peasants had been "95 per cent curiosity and 5 per cent sympathy":

They had heard about Japan—somewhere, indistinctly—but about Manchuria, the nearest point of which [was] barely seventy-five miles distant, most of them knew nothing. The appearance of the column of singing and shouting students was a spectacle to be looked at—like a wedding or a funeral a break in the day's monotony. . . . One of the farmers had countered the patriotic appeal of a student with the words: "The present government seems all right. Our taxes are lower than before. Why bother us?"[72]

The failure of anti-Japanese propaganda accentuated an ideological dispute that had divided Peiping students since 1931. On one side were those whose sole goal was to rally the country to resist aggression; on the other were the Communists and fellow travelers, who saw the anti-Japanese movement as a vehicle for spreading Marxist political and economic doctrines. At Kuan, radicals proposed that subsequent propaganda emphasize the slogan "Down with Imperialism!" (not merely Japanese imperialism), that it urge an open revolt against the gentry, and that it denounce Chiang Kai-shek. Moderates, on the other hand, wanted slogans restricted to denunciations of Japanese imperialism, advocated a general support of economic betterment, and asked that any attacks be limited to the provincial authorities who aided the imperialists. Extended arguments produced a compromise which provided that "economic propaganda, but in a moderate tone, should henceforth form the main subject."[73]

Fear of Communist manipulation prompted a minority of corps members to return to Peiping after the Kuan meeting.[74] The remainder reorganized into three groups and branched out on the morning of January 10, arranging to meet again farther south in the Hopei provincial capital of Paoting. The crusaders had new slogans: "Refuse to pay unnecessary taxes!" "Organize to resist the invasion by Japan *and* the encroachments of your landlord!" and "Chase out the Dwarfs *and* the usurers!"[75] The emphasis upon economic propaganda was an immediate success. A Yenching girl wrote:

The peasants felt economic oppression more bitterly than Japanese invasion. . . . They know nothing about political affairs. They understand that they must pay taxes if they have land. But they don't know why. They were madly glad when the preachers explained the situation and told them to resist [taxes] and to overthrow the bad officers.[76]

The young propagandists had but a short time to test their new approach. Two days after leaving Kuan, the third corps was intercepted and put on a train to Peiping by detectives and police sent by the Hopei-Chahar Council. The first and second corps were rounded up on January 21 as they convened at the outskirts of Paoting, and were promptly shipped back to Peiping.[77]

As the last of the pilgrims disappeared, life on the dusty plains of Hopei returned to normal. Although their endeavors had rendered the area more susceptible to wartime guerrilla activities, the strongest impact had undoubtedly been not on the peasants but on the students, who gained firsthand knowledge of the life and thought of China's masses and became aware of the enormous problems of communication. This was a unique preparation for war and revolution.

The abrupt termination of the January crusade did not prevent students in Peiping and elsewhere from following this example and carrying the national salvation message to the people. Enthusiastic reports by representatives of the Peiping-Tientsin Student Union inspired activists in Tsinan,

Süchow, and other North China cities.[78] In villages near Peiping, Tsinghua students established day and night schools for workers and other interested persons. Yenching and Tsinghua squads made weekend trips to neighboring factories and villages. Later, soldiers of the Twenty-ninth Army became the principal targets of student propaganda.

Immediately after returning to Peiping, the Yenching-Tsinghua contingent organized a Chinese Youth Salvation Vanguard Corps "to comprehend and grasp the correct theory for carrying out the anti-imperialist, anti-feudal national liberation movement."[79] The group planned to read books on social philosophy and economics, to do daily gymnastic exercises, and to play a leading role in future student activities. It was understood that "advanced members" would be "selected for some other organization" (presumably the Communist Youth Corps).[80]

Five days later, after the first and second corps were surrounded by police near Paoting, and were waiting to be sent to Peiping, they decided to form a permanent organization to perpetuate their spirit of unity. They called themselves the National Liberation Vanguard. After its return to Peiping, the new group joined with the Yenching-Tsinghua organization and the Tsinghua Bicycle Corps to form the Chinese National Liberation Vanguard (CNLV),[81] which became the major Communist front organization in the student movement. The Vanguard was organized along Leninist lines, with democratic centralism, a cellular structure, and strict regulations to ensure secrecy and discipline. The group expanded from three hundred members at its inception on January 21, to six hundred in May and twelve hundred in September 1936. In the year and a half before the beginning of the war, it was the nucleus of left-wing student activity in North China. Afterwards, many of its members became cadres in the Communist border-area governments.[82]

Assault from the Right

As leftist elements became increasingly prominent in the student movement, the Nanking government took countermeasures. A fortnight after the December 9 demonstration,

Chiang Kai-shek ordered the Ministry of Education to convene a meeting of educators and student representatives in Nanking. The announced purpose was to exchange opinions on the current situation, but the evident aim was to mount a counterattack against student critics.

Both the Peiping and the Peiping-Tientsin Student Unions firmly resolved to boycott the conference. The former denounced the meeting as "an effort to divert attention from the real issues, to disperse our movement, and to prevent the Chinese masses from organizing themselves for the Anti-Japanese War of Resistance."[83] Chiang's proposal evoked heated discussions in every school. Students at Nankai University and other Tientsin institutions elected representatives to the conclave, but most Peiping students refused to participate. Many delegates secretly chosen by anxious chancellors dared not accept; others had to slip away quietly to Nanking to avoid retaliation from irate schoolmates.[84]

On January 13, while detectives were rounding up the third corps at Kaopeitien, two hundred nationwide delegates, including 130 students, were on their way to Nanking. At a special meeting in the Executive Yüan, high government officials listened patiently as some fifty students stated their views on the internal and international situations. The orators called for the punishment of traitors, for an openly conducted foreign policy, for preservation of "territorial and administrative integrity," and for special education to meet the current crisis. In reply, Chiang Kai-shek promised not to sign any treaty detrimental to China's interests, and implored listeners to have faith in the government. He declared that national salvation was the responsibility of every student, but that demonstrations and strikes were not.[85] In a final session, 164 university and middle-school chancellors supported the students' plea for education to meet the national crisis, but advocated "the suppression of such student activities as will tend to upset school order and discipline."[86] Thus, the conference offered an undefined program of emergency education as the only outlet for youthful nationalism.[87] However, student representation in Nanking excluded the alienated left-wing leaders, whose hostility lay at the root of the government's troubles in the schools. Until these radicals were ready to come to terms, conciliatory gestures were doomed to failure, and "suppression" became the key word. Instead of preparing for a truce in the academic world, the Nanking gathering mobilized pro-government forces for battle.

The return of the delegates to Peiping inaugurated a new period in the student movement, one of bitter warfare between the left—now rallied around veteran propagandists of the Vanguard—and the right, led by the conference representatives and their supporters among faculties, administrations, and students. Meetings were held by both sides. Angry leftists demanded that the Nanking conference delegates be expelled; in some cases, delegates' possessions were burned or thrown out dormitory windows. A Peita delegate saved himself by defying an aroused mob of his fellow students—he stood on his desk and vowed he would defend his freedom of conscience with blood.[88] Though open fights between left and right occurred in Chaoyang and Tsinghua universities (Peiping), Nankai (Tientsin), Futan (Shanghai), and Sun Yat-sen (Canton), the war was predominantly verbal rather than physical. In Shanghai and Canton, the KMT troubleshooter Liu Chien-ch'ün persuaded skeptical student audiences to be more tolerant of Nanking's policies, while pro-government elements in the north tried in vain to win support for a Peiping-Tientsin-Paoting Union in opposition to the Peiping-Tientsin Student Union.[89]

Once again taking a lesson from Communist methods, the Kuomintang also attempted to establish front organizations. Most notable were the Endeavor Societies, such as the one led by Yenching student Wang Chüeh. This organization attempted to compete with the Vanguard by offering activists a disciplined program of village surveys, rural reconstruction, and self-cultivation.[90] Such an appeal, which excluded the Japanese issue, could not succeed.

Tsinghua, though a left-wing bastion, earned Communist denunciation as "the most powerful stronghold of the reactionary elements."[91] To oppose the broadly based National Salvation Committee and the hard core of the CNLV, the right wing enlisted more than a hundred members for a School

Aid Corps, and published the *Tsinghua Critic* (*Ch'ing-hua p'ing-lun*), a vehement anti-Communist newspaper that denounced the National Salvation Committee and the Peiping Student Union as "Red," defended the Nanking conference delegates, and reprinted Hu Shih's arguments against school strikes.[92] The *Critic* adroitly called for a united front against Japan without abandoning its ultimate anti-Communist goals. "We want an orderly, disciplined [effort] united to resist the enemy," read an editorial. "After our enemy has been driven out, we will close our door and clear our old accounts."[93] At the same time, the publication served notice on the Nanking rulers: "We never support the present government blindly. We support the government that will resist the enemy. If the present government takes no steps to resist the enemy within the year, we also want to throw it out."[94]

Thus, for a fleeting moment, this anti-Communist student newspaper threatened to steal Mao Tse-tung's thunder by advocating an all-inclusive united front. The CCP, painfully groping its way toward a similar line, was not to reach this conclusion for nearly a year. (One student was even expelled from party ranks for advocating a policy of "unconditional unity.")[95] History might have been different had the KMT decided to champion the farsighted ideas disseminated by its sympathizers on the *Tsinghua Critic*. Instead, the KMT resorted to its old divisive tactics and created a "New Student Union" in Peiping (officially named the Peiping City Students National Salvation Union); but it was unable to compete effectively with its left-wing rival, which was henceforth known as the "Old Student Union." The right also suffered from a tendency to attract the wrong kind of support. Sung Che-yüan's warnings of Communist manipulation rang hollow after his broadsword brigade had attacked student ranks. Yang Li-k'uei, chairman of the Normal University physics department, further discredited the progovernment cause by refusing to produce facts to support his charge that the Peiping Student Union was receiving Communist funds. His reason—that he was withholding evidence only to protect students from arrest —was unconvincing.[96]

In arguing for immediate preparation for war and an end

to appeasement, the left had an enormous advantage over government spokesmen. Only an occasional KMT educator like Lo Chia-lun had the political vision to propose a curriculum geared to imminent war. The party as a whole assumed a defensive attitude, warned its members to beware of Communist national salvation propaganda, yet offered no popular alternative.[97]

For the moment, the left was too incapacitated by political and ideological differences to capitalize on the Kuomintang's difficulties. The problem was whether to pursue militant tactics in order to keep the movement alive or to make concessions that would win student moderates, faculty members, and school administrations. The united-front line dictated the latter approach. Typical of friendly criticism was an article in *Life of the Masses,* which counseled young radicals to seek advice from "progressive" professors and to cease treating those who cooperated with school authorities like "running dogs."[98]

Indeed, ideology reinforced by necessity was pushing the students toward a more moderate position. In its report of January 28, 1936, the Peiping Student Union retreated from the extremist slogans of November 18. Thus, the label "enemy" was transferred from the "anti-Communist autonomy movement" to "any North China puppet organization." Support of a "Chinese revolutionary war," with its overtones of civil insurrection, now became support of a "revolutionary war to oppose the encroachments of the Japanese imperialists." The proposal "make a mutual aid agreement between the people of China and the Union of Soviet Socialist Republics" was changed to "Unite all people in the world who treat us on an equal basis [a direct quote from Sun Yat-sen's will] and cooperate to oppose Japanese imperialism." Though the phraseology was Marxist, an orthodox Communist might have been appalled by the suggestion that the petty-bourgeois students, and not the proletariat, should lead China's revolution.[99]

The students' retreat from militancy became obvious during the first days of February, when most schools in Peiping and Tientsin resumed classes for the first time since December

9. On February 8, a proclamation by the Peiping Student Union officially ended the strike, admitting,"Our force is weak and our knowledge is insufficient."[100] The Union explained that the return to classes was simply a new tactic for continuing the struggle. But if students assumed that their reasonable attitude would mollify authorities, they were mistaken. On February 20, the government suddenly promulgated an Emergency Law to Maintain Public Order. An Executive Yüan directive followed, outlawing the activities of the Peiping-Tientsin Student Union, which was allegedly controlled by a handful of "agitators." Ch'en Chi-yen, commander of the Peiping Bureau of Public Safety, took this opportunity to announce that he would use "whatever force is necessary" to destroy not only the Union, but other student political activities as well.[101]

He was true to his word. On February 18, even before the Emergency Law had been publicly proclaimed, a score of students were seized in a night raid on Peita and Normal University dormitories. Northeastern was subjected to a painstaking search from 3 A.M. to 8 A.M. on February 21, and 43 students were arrested. Several dozen more were taken into custody in a raid on Chung-kuo College, reportedly after the chancellor had described a student government meeting as Communist-run, and furnished the police with names of campus leaders. Twenty were arrested at Chung-shan Middle School. The suppression even extended to faculty activists: Liu K'an-yüan of Chung-kuo College was apprehended on February 24, and Peita professors Shang Chung-i and Chang Shen-fu and the latter's wife were arrested and imprisoned five days later.[102]

The same day, police oppression reached a dramatic climax at Tsinghua University. Ironically, student radicals had just settled a protracted feud with the faculty by agreeing to sit for examinations that day. These were not held; instead, several hundred police stormed Tsinghua's gates at dawn. The students were prepared, having resumed 24-hour sentry duty when a list of sixteen female activists and a dormitory floorplan were discovered in a girl's quarters. When the alarm sounded, swarms of half-dressed students descended upon the intruders, smashed their vehicles, and chased them from the campus under a barrage of steamed bread intended for the policemen's breakfast.

In response to student protests, Chancellor Mei Yi-Ch'i went into the city to seek an explanation from the mayor. In the meantime the aroused students held an assembly. They had voted to resist any subsequent police violation of campus privacy when the chancellor returned with eight policemen and a list of 47 students wanted by police. Angry students captured the policemen but that evening five hundred more police appeared, reinforced by a regiment of the Twenty-ninth Army. Six hundred students who had retreated to the gymnasium and locked arms were pried apart and individually questioned. Thanks to prior warning, left-wing leaders had fled, but 21 students were jailed, bringing the total number of imprisoned Peiping students to well over a hundred. The same day police attacked Peita, but their fifty suspects there had escaped during the night.[103]

Raids and arrests silenced the Peiping movement for about two weeks. Tsinghua's National Salvation Committee appealed in vain to other schools for assistance. Only the Yenching students dared to protest (after waiting for thirteen days). Pleading for an end to wholesale police terror, the Yenching circular said:

In [the present movement] there are KMT [students], perhaps there are CCP; however, the majority . . . is independent. . . . If there are CCP members and the government believes they are a danger to the republic, let it legally arrest those Communists who are taking part in the patriotic movement. The government has plenty of military police and regular police. Why does it make a big to-do about nothing, sending a thousand men and horses to clamp an iron band around the schools to carry out its searches, without stopping to separate the sheep from the goats?[104]

"The Professionals" Take Over

By March, police had imprisoned or forced underground many of the known student leaders and had frightened their followers into silence. Under such conditions, only the disciplined revolutionary could operate effectively. Thus, student politics became the monopoly of a minority of activists influenced, if not controlled, by the CCP. The situation was reminiscent of the September Eighteenth period in 1931, when after several months of mass action, the student rank and file retired to the sidelines, and the revolutionists came to the fore. It is worth recalling that the leftists who wrecked the *Chung-yang jih-pao* offices in December 1931—a revolutionary vanguard eager to demonstrate but too hostile to petition the government—were led by Peiping students. Suppression during the intervening years had forced Peiping's academic left wing underground, but obviously had not destroyed it.

By mid-March, these revolutionists had partially recovered from the police raids that followed Nanking's Emergency Law. Too battered and embittered to heed the united front's call to moderation, they staged two anti-government demonstrations within a fortnight. On March 18, ten years after the troops of the warlord Tuan Ch'i-jui had shot down anti-Japanese demonstrators in the streets of Peiping, an estimated two thousand students gathered at the Summer Palace near Tsinghua, made invidious comparisons between the warlords and their present rulers, and denounced both for murdering student patriots.[105]

On March 31, leftists held a memorial meeting at Peita for Kuo Ch'ing, a middle school pupil who had died in prison. Following the meeting, participants marched down the avenue four abreast bearing a white-shrouded coffin. More than fifty of them, including the Yenching radical Wang Ju-mei, were arrested after a heated argument with armed motorcycle police who had cordoned the road.[106] Communists attributed the failure of the demonstration to "excessive leftism and reckless action."[107]

The collapse of the Kuo Ch'ing demonstration and the ever-increasing influence of united-front ideology induced the leftists to return to less belligerent tactics. The program of Tsinghua's National Salvation Committee, for example, included meetings, publications, propaganda, and literary activities, but not mass demonstrations. In the words of this group, the goal was "to broaden the salvation front."[108] On a national scale this meant sending Peiping Student Union representatives to the south to hasten the establishment of a national association, while locally the Union sought federation with organizations of women, intellectuals, writers, farmers, and policemen, in a North China People's Front for National Liberation.[109] The effort to bring policemen into the fold reflected a new attitude toward officials. Given the united-front dogma of salvation through good works, who could be consigned to perdition? Even Sung Che-yüan received a personal appeal to redeem himself by turning against the Japanese.[110]

Some school administrators were not eager to be saved. Peita's Chiang Monlin, outraged that his campus had been used for the Kuo Ch'ing meeting, promptly dissolved the school's self-governing association and expelled four of its officers. In response to popular demand, he had the university guarantee the release of all imprisoned Peita students except proven subversives, but he doggedly refused to reinstate them. Other chancellors were more sympathetic; Yenching students were heartened by support from President J. Leighton Stuart, and wholesale arrests at Northeastern University and Chung-shan Middle School brought an enraged Chang Hsüeh-liang to the rescue. By April 15, thanks to this kind of intervention, the majority of the students arrested a fortnight earlier had been liberated; by the first week in May, only four of fifty-four imprisoned Tsinghua students remained in jail.[111]

As the National Salvation Movement developed, increasing numbers of prominent Peiping intellectuals expressed encouragement. Professors Ma Hsü-lun and Tseng Chao-lun addressed the March 18 gathering at Peita; and Ma, Hsü Te-heng, and Dean Chou Ping-lin spoke on May 4. Professors Chang Tung-sun, Lo Lung-chi, Liang Shih-ch'iu, and Ku Chieh-kang expressed their support. The influential *Ta-kung pao* showed a greater respect for youthful political action. Allies were joining the united front.[112] However, there were losses as well as gains. Even as sympathetic an observer as Helen Snow noted that "as soon as the left-wing elements began diluting the movement, it lost élan and vitality."[113] The Tsinghua National Salvation Committee admitted that it was unable to rally student masses and other groups because it had failed to appreciate "the basic nature of the great revolution."[114] The left-wing hegemony that had carried the movement so far had invited official suppression; united-front tactics, too late and too uncertain, could effect no more than a partial recovery. Student leaders had won outside sympathy but had failed to regain mass support in the schools.

During April and May the movement's focus shifted from Peiping to Tientsin. Writing in the *China Weekly Review*, Helen Snow attributed this development to such factors as the augmented police terror in Peiping, the flight of student leaders to Tientsin to avoid arrest, the "accurate application of the united front" by Tientsin's students, the presence in Tientsin of a sizeable proletarian class, the inflammatory effect of Japanese smuggling activities, and the startling discovery of the corpses of three hundred men (presumed to be victims of the Japanese) in the Haiho River near Tientsin.[115]

The importance of another factor, Communist agitation, has become evident since the publication of Helen Snow's *Notes*, which document the activities of Yü Ch'i-wei, later known as Huang Ching.[116] Though still in his early twenties, this revolutionist had a prison record dating from his days as an agitator in Shantung, and had risen to become secretary of the Communist Party's Peiping Bureau.[117] After registering at Peita, Yü went into hiding; he played only a minor role in the December demonstrations, though he mounted a streetcar and gave a speech during a tense moment on December 16.[118] This disciplined Communist, amused at first by the amateurish leftism of student leaders, is said to have later become "the brains of the student movement."[119]

In late March, Yü traveled to Tientsin (and perhaps to Shanghai) to organize the preparatory meeting for a national student union.[120] Shortly after he left Tientsin, the Student Union of that city received a communication from Paris from the World Student Association for Peace, Freedom, and Culture, calling for Chinese participation in an international peace strike. Although some suspected that the document was a Communist forgery, the Union staged a walkout intended to last three days, which was so successful that it was extended to four days throughout the city and a week in two of the larger universities.[121] In Tientsin such efficient mobilization was unprecedented.

Yü revisited Tientsin on May 19. Two days later a congress of the Tientsin Student Union decided to hold a May Thirtieth demonstration.[122] On May 27, Yü wrote the Snows (in English):

I'm now working again for the Tientsin students and plotting for them their recent activities. The Tientsin youths are really very active ones. They are in very high spirits, because they are aroused by the recent occurrences, such as more Jap. troops come to N. China, the "floating corpses," etc., and they have not yet met with those serious injuries such as the Peiping students did in their demonstrations. They are not yet splited [sic] by the fascist traitors, owing to the accurate application of the tactics of the united front by the student leaders.

I think that in a few days, around "5.30," the Tientsin students will hold a monster demonstration, with about 10,000–20,000 students and workers participating. This is not an exaggerated number, I suppose. I think this demonstration will be a very striking fact to the people in China and even the world, and I do think that the Peiping students will be certainly aroused up by this demonstration. This is a direct answer by the students in Tientsin to the Japanese militarists who are intending to occupy N. China by the military forces.[123]

Another letter from Yü, dated May 29, reported the success of the demonstration, which had been staged two days earlier than originally planned. He boasted that ten thousand high-spirited participants had distributed 120,000 pamphlets.[124] But it would be erroneous to interpret this as evidence that Yü was the top Communist in the North China student movement. He appears to have told Helen Snow that he was only second in command.[125] Communist sources state that Liu Shaoch'i was head of the party's North China Bureau, with headquarters in Tientsin, during the December Ninth period. Therefore Yü (who later became Mayor of Tientsin) was probably taking orders from Liu, one of the most astute theorists and skillful agitators in the party (and currently President of the People's Republic of China).

Reorganization and Reappraisal

As Yü Ch'i-wei shuttled back and forth between Peiping and Tientsin, the North China student movement became a cog in the mechanism of the Shanghai-based National Salvation Movement. At an April 12 meeting, delegates voted to add the words "National Salvation" to the name of the Peiping-Tientsin Student Union so as to standardize nomenclature to accord with that used in the south. The Peiping Union followed suit and on April 25 became the Peiping Student National Salvation Union (PSNSU).[126] By June 11, the newly christened body claimed a membership of all Peiping's universities and most middle schools, a total of fifty institutions.[127]

The change in name signified a change in policy. Confessing past errors, the PSNSU announced that it would now concentrate on publicity and on a boycott of Japanese goods. Outside support was assiduously courted. One delegate called on the president of the Peiping Chamber of Commerce; others visited newspaper offices. Appeals to school chancellors included guarantees that coercive methods would be shunned. A PSNSU spokesman assured the public that future actions would be "frank and open," and directed toward the single goal of national salvation. "All patriots" were invited to cooperate in this endeavor and to offer advice and criticism.[128] There was no further mention of demonstrations against Sung Che-yüan's police brutality or against Chiang Kai-shek's appeasement of Japan. The united-front policy was now a reality.

Early in June, the PSNSU's widely publicized willingness to unite with all anti-Japanese groups was put to the test by the separatist Southwest Political Council of Generals Ch'en Chi-t'ang, Li Tsung-jen, and Pai Ch'ung-hsi. Peiping students were amazed when these militarists sponsored large anti-Japanese demonstrations in Kwangtung and Kwangsi and announced a northward expedition to fight the foe. Leftists, uncertain whether they should applaud the southern generals for their patriotism or denounce them for fomenting civil war on the pretext of national salvation, greeted the news warily but felt compelled to make good their offer to support any organization that would oppose Japan. The PSNSU proclaimed that it agreed "most heartily" with the Southwest Council's call for a declaration of war against Japan.[129] But an editorial in the *Yenching Weekly* reflects the uneasiness of the student world:

Even though it is really a warlord battle for power, even though the English and French are pulling the strings behind the scenes, . . . even though the warlords are seeking to turn the masses' high fighting spirits and enthusiasm for resistance to their own advantage, still, that the Southwest is able to break out the "Resist Japan" banner and oppose the traitors is an extraordinary event, at least in the eyes of the masses. . . . Although we do not sympathize with the previous behavior of the Southwest, we do sympathize with this demand for resisting Japan.[130]

Pro-KMT students were less ambivalent. The Peiping-Tientsin-Paoting Union charged that the "Communists cheat and fool the masses [on] the pretext of responding to the Southwest['s] anti-Japanese slogans" and urged classmates to "oppose the Southwest['s effort to destroy] unification!" They shouted "Down with Communists, [violators of] the national front. . . . Support the Central Government. . . . Drive out Japanese imperialism by force!"[131] On the other hand, Communist opinion of the Southwest revolt was divided. The CCP applauded the warlord insurgents; Moscow condemned them. The climate of public opinion created by the student movement was one reason for the bloodless termination of the rebellion. At this hour of national crisis, the thought of civil war had become intolerable.[132]

Meanwhile, Peiping and Tientsin students were encouraging the Twenty-ninth Army to turn its guns against the invader. As a steady stream of enemy reinforcements poured into North China and the Japanese insisted that local troops evacuate the Nanyüan Barracks, student propagandists descended upon the Chinese garrison. Soldiers were reminded of their heroic stand at Hsifengkou three years before, and were urged to heed the masses rather than their spineless commanders.[133] The apostles of national salvation failed in this appeal for mutiny (a vestige of the discredited United Front from Below line), but received a sympathetic reception, especially from the younger officers.

As the school year drew to a close, Peiping's student leaders discovered that the united-front policy was not a panacea. Kuomintang efforts to discredit left-wing leaders, and, more important, the impending examinations and the desire to graduate removed large numbers of undergraduates from active participation.

When it was reported that six thousand Tientsin students had demonstrated and struck to protest Japanese troop build-ups and smuggling, the students of Peiping were too disunited to respond effectively. Only four universities (including Yenching and Tsinghua) and eight middle schools agreed to a sympathy strike.[134] However, the PSNSU did succeed in rallying four thousand marchers on June 13 to support the Southwest Political Council's anti-Japanese program and to persuade Nanking to resist the invader. By this time, student leaders had gained considerable political sophistication. Explaining the absence of anti-civil-war slogans, one of them said: "We do not want Chiang Kai-shek to [use] this slogan against the Southwest while he continues the civil war ... against the Reds."[135] The attitude of Sung Che-yüan's forces showed that the conciliatory united-front approach was finally succeeding. Shouts of support for the Twenty-ninth Army evoked a friendly response from passing soldiers. Sympathetic police apologized to the demonstrators as they reluctantly arrested their leaders, and the leaders were released before sunset.[136]

But Sung Che-yüan could not placate the students without antagonizing the Japanese. Even while students were parading, Major Hamada of the enemy garrison visited the Mayor of Peiping to protest his ambiguous attitude toward the demonstration.[137] The following day, a municipal government representative assured the Japanese Ministry that the student movement would be eradicated. On June 15, Sung Che-yüan urged university chancellors to abolish student political organizations. In protest, wildcat strikes erupted in a number of universities despite objections from the PSNSU and from seniors. The American Minister mentioned reports that KMT elements acting on instruction from Nanking had encouraged the walkout in order to discredit the movement.[138] On June 21, the PSNSU canceled the strike to permit its members to take their final examinations. By then, however, left-wing leaders, who had hoped to mobilize followers for summer activities, had lost control; most students took their examinations and went home.[139]

Interpreting the December Ninth Movement

A sense of outraged nationalism was the emotion underlying the December Ninth Movement. During the silent period, 1933 to 1935, student patriotism was not dead but only dormant. When it was aroused, a generation of students who had been cajoled and coerced into manifest acquiescence suddenly appeared in the streets by the thousands to demand a halt to enemy aggression.

Communist techniques shaped raw nationalism into a purposeful political force. Developments after December Ninth gravitated toward the left, following the pattern of all nation-wide protests since the May Thirtieth Movement. No popular nationalist drive ever retained its spontaneity more than a few weeks. Once the amateur nonpartisan leaders had spent their passion, the professionals were able to turn movements to their own advantage by organization, propaganda, and be-hind-the-scenes manipulation. To the rank and file, demonstrations and strikes were vehicles for expressing patriotism; only revolutionaries had a vested interest in mass movements as such. Except for the CCP, the KMT was the only group with sufficient leadership and experience to mobilize students, but by 1935 the KMT's unpopular foreign policy and its negative attitude toward student politics had all but destroyed its chances to be a serious contender. The KMT's response to December Ninth was very like its reactions to the post-Tsinan and post-Mukden student movements: initial encouragement (though by 1935 it was a very guarded encouragement), then discouragement, and finally suppression.

Why did this approach, which succeeded in 1931, fail in 1936? First, because the December Ninth Movement centered not in Nanking, which the government controlled, but in Peiping, which it did not control. Second, because four years of Japanese aggression had discredited Chiang's foreign policy and had won broad popular support for the student position. Third, because the CCP's violent, exclusive, self-destructive tactics of 1931 had been replaced by a conciliatory united-front approach.

Communist historians proudly emphasize their party's role in the student movement. From their viewpoint, the December 9 demonstration was directly inspired by the Long March, the Red Army's invasion of Shensi, and the August 1 declaration calling for a united front. They claim that not only the CNLV but the Peiping Student Union itself was party-organized. Liu Shao-ch'i is specifically mentioned as the Red mastermind. In effect these scholars admit the truth of the Japanese and KMT accusations of Communist manipulation, which student leaders indignantly denied at the time. On the other hand Edgar and Helen Snow maintain today, as they did in 1935, that the students were spurred to action solely by patriotic impulses and that it was they, the Snows, not Chinese Communists, who provided guidance.[140] Helen Snow suspected (and later confirmed) that Yü Ch'i-wei was a Communist agitator, but she feels that he was uninfluential in the initial stages of the student revival. Edgar Snow states that the demonstration's leaders were "mostly Christian or Christian-trained youths. . . . There was not a Communist among them."[141] In their view, not Communism but liberal nationalism was the critical ideological factor.

In 1935 a controversy raged over the student patriotic campaign. For partisans to concede that there was Communist infiltration would have been political suicide, since young politicians could hope to win national acceptance only as impartial advocates for China's interests. Thus student spokesmen, Communists, and sympathetic foreigners alike interpreted the movement as a spontaneous manifestation of patriotism. Only since 1949 has Mao's regime set out to prove that the CCP led, rather than followed, the mass movement.

A close examination of the writings of Communist historians and the Snows shows them surprisingly close to agreement in their less partisan moments. The Snows, after all, have emphasized the origins of the movement, in which they and Yenching

University undeniably played an important role, while Communists stress the party's role in developing the movement. Mao Tse-tung's admission, which Edgar Snow quotes approvingly, "that the Communist Party was in an utterly defenseless position in all the cultural institutions in the Kuomintang-controlled area," also refers to the situation prior to the December 9 demonstration.[142] Hsiao Wen-lan, the foremost CCP student of the subject, has been reluctant to elaborate on the CCP's initial role,[143] but writes that "without Party leadership, the December Ninth Movement would have been unable to spread so broadly, penetrate so deeply, and maintain itself for so long a time."[144]

It seems impossible to prove or disprove conclusively the charges of Communist subversion. The Snows' denials must be evaluated in the light of Helen Snow's statement that she "did not inquire" about possible Communist affiliation, since it was "one of the things one wanted to be able to say one did not know in those days."[145] Nonetheless, the most reliable contemporary documentation of activities by an individual Communist are Yü Ch'i-wei's letters, preserved in her *Notes*. Although definitive evidence is scarce, CCP sources frequently mention Liu Shao-ch'i (then head of the party's North China Bureau), Li Ch'ang (a Vanguard leader), and other less famous men. Mrs. Snow speculates that Liu's arrival in Peiping may have coincided with the birth of the CNLV.[146] A Kuomintang intelligence report names the prominent Communists Ch'en Po-ta (who allegedly taught at Chung-kuo College under an assumed name), K'o Ch'ing-shih, and Nan Han-ch'en as "backstage manipulators" in the movement.[147] Wang Ju-mei, later well known in the Communist foreign service under the name Huang Hua, was one of the original Yenching organizers, but there is no proof that he or others who went to Yenan or who appeared later as high-level Communists had any connection with the party in 1935. It may have been the student movement that turned them toward the CCP rather than the converse.

There is no sign of external machinations during the initial stage of the student revival. The anguished cry for civil liberties on November 1 was very radical and anti-government, but a petition to the plenary session of a KMT CEC would scarcely have been a logical medium for Communist propaganda at that time. In November 1935, Yenching leaders, desperate for support, pleaded in vain with the Snows to place them in contact with the CCP. The embryonic Peiping Student Union that these students helped to form, with its preponderance of missionary schools, does not resemble a Red organization. Nor does the poorly coordinated December Ninth demonstration bear the earmarks of a professionally planned outbreak.

However, there is circumstantial evidence of growing Communist influence after December 9. The highly organized demonstration of the sixteenth, the January mission to the people, the formation of the Vanguard, the plethora of self-criticism after the Kuo Ch'ing parade, the reorganization of the Peiping and Tientsin unions, and the self-conscious switch to a united-front line seem to have been guided by an invisible hand. This is not to say that the CCP ruled by fiat. Its policy was often poorly implemented, and sometimes left-wing leaders responded slowly to changes in the party line. Nonetheless, Communist influence, already observable in December, was an undeniable reality by April.

The question of direct CCP control is less important than the fact that large numbers of student leaders almost automatically followed the party line because it appeared to be the only road to national salvation. This mode of thinking was also common among the older generation (e.g., the Seven Gentlemen of the National Salvation Movement) and remained an important feature of the political scene until the middle 1950's. Communists learned through the December Ninth Movement how to work with, maneuver, and use China's talented, dedicated left-wing patriots, who in turn became accustomed to leaning on CCP leadership. Of these fellow travelers, only a small number eventually joined the party; the rest remained even more useful for their avowed nonalignment.

The Communists, never satisfied with a movement limited to students, spared no effort to seek other recruits. For ideological reasons, their principal targets were the workers and peasants. Ironically, student efforts to evangelize these groups were least successful; more converts were made among warlord soldiers and city policemen. However, intellectuals dominated the National Salvation Movement. This patriotic drive, utilized by the CCP but initiated by Peiping students, spread to every corner of the land. Chinese politics of 1936 and 1937—the Southwest revolt, the behavior of Chang Hsüeh-liang's troops in Shensi, the Sian Incident, the inexorable drive by the Communists for a united front, and Chiang Kai-shek's increasing implacability toward the Japanese—can be understood fully only in the light of this mounting enthusiasm for a nationwide stand against the aggressor.

None of these results were conceivable to the students who gathered at the Hsin-hua Men on the morning of December 9, 1935. Their object was to protest the campaign for North Chinese autonomy; and the thousands who demonstrated on December 16 sought to prevent the inauguration of the Hopei-Chahar Political Council. Though this body was established, North China remained relatively free of Japanese control until the beginning of the war, for Sung Che-yüan, not the Council, was the real power in the area. The wily general skillfully employed the students as a counterweight against Japanese pressure while Nanking, partly because of student influence, moved toward a united front with the Communists.

By helping to prevent Nanking's short-term appeasement policy from becoming a permanent fixture, these students earned a large share of the credit for frustrating Tokyo's attempt to take over China through diplomacy.[148] Now it was clear to both sides that force would decide the issue.

From the spring of 1936 until after the outbreak of war in the summer of 1937, most student political activity was ancillary to Communist policy. The party had vociferously supported the principal student demand, war against Japan. North China's two most powerful student organizations, the Peiping Student National Salvation Union and the Chinese National Liberation Vanguard, were controlled by or sympathetic to the party; Communists were instrumental in establishing a National Student Association in Shanghai. Strongpoints at Paoan (now called Chihtan), Sian, Peiping, Tientsin, and Shanghai dotted a far-reaching CCP-CY network.

During this period, leaders of left-wing youth organizations stumbled along the tortuous party line that emerged from the CCP's dialogue with the Comintern over the implementation of the united front.[1] The major question was whether Chiang Kai-shek, the slayer of countless comrades, would be an acceptable ally against Japan. In Moscow, the answer was "yes"; but the Chinese party was less certain. The Paoan headquarters urged Nanking military authorities to confederate against the nation's enemy in May but reversed its position in June when the leaders of the Southwest revolt undertook an anti-Japanese, anti-Chiang crusade.[2] On August 25 the party unequivocally invited the Kuomintang to join a united front. However, when Chang Hsüeh-liang kidnapped Chiang Kai-shek on December 12, 1936, the Chinese Communists supported the mutineers.[3] From Chiang's release until the outbreak of war, the CCP tried to rally its followers behind the formerly despised Nanking leader, and bewildered cadres in Peiping schools labored to hold together the even more confused and politically less sophisticated student rank and file.

Though the destiny of the student movement had become inextricably linked to that of the CCP, it had become even more inseparable from the fortunes of the National Salvation Association. This leftist patriotic organization, a by-product of the December Ninth Movement, was attempting to bridge the gap between Chiang and Mao by advocating a broad united front. The National Salvation Movement was centered in Shanghai, where representatives from sixteen cities met on March 28 to lay the groundwork for a National Student Association. There had been no such body since the KMT disbanded the previous one in the fall of 1929. The Peiping delegation included Lu Ts'ui, the heroine of the December 16 demonstration, the Peita leftist Liu Chiang-lin, and perhaps the Communist agitator Yü Ch'i-wei.[4] The Association was launched on May 29. Two days later, in the same city, the All-China Federation of National Salvation Associations (FNSA) was formed. Lu Ts'ui went on to Paris, where she helped to establish another FNSA branch, which was useful in rallying overseas Chinese opinion for a united front, and which facilitated liaison with Comintern agents.

While the National Student Association in Shanghai cooperated with the independent, leftist National Salvation Association, the PSNSU was strongly influenced by the CNLV, an extension of CY. Huang Ch'eng, a Communist, became chairman of the PSNSU in May or June 1936.[5] The CNLV had recovered rapidly after the disastrous Kuo Ch'ing demonstration of March 31, but suffered another setback just before the end of the school year, when two hundred members were expelled for leading wildcat strikes in several Peiping schools. The organization was also torn by internal disagreement over how to apply the united-front principle; the leaders complained that many of their followers were still giving no more than lip service to the idea.[6] Nonetheless, by the beginning of summer vacation, membership (still mostly Peiping students) had increased to twelve hundred.[7] Although this represented only 2 per cent of the city's middle school and college enrollment, it was a dedicated, highly disciplined minority.

For China's students, the summer of 1936 was the most active one in a decade. From Peiping to Kwangsi, their message of national salvation was carried to the people. The National Student Association formulated a program of summer work for affiliated groups, stressing organization, propaganda, and cooperation with school authorities, teachers, staffs, and servants, and even with police. Those leaving for vacation were asked to develop the salvation movement in their home towns and villages and to establish local student unions. Patriotic groups of Kwangsi students, which had only loose ties with the national organization, flourished under the sponsorship of the military leaders Pai Ch'ung-hsi and Li Tsung-jen, who cleverly manipulated the anti-Japanese movement as a weapon in intraparty altercations with Nanking.[8]

Shanghai students were active in boycott and anti-smuggling activities. Members of both the KMT and the CCP campaigned to promote the use of native goods. The former concentrated their energies in the Chamber of Commerce, while the latter employed more violent tactics, such as the July 12 demonstration in the Wing-On Emporium to protest the store's failure to observe the boycott.

Other Shanghai students exploited the theater as an instrument of propaganda that could reach even illiterates. A drama corps staged popular, didactic, left-wing plays. One production portrayed urban factory workers oppressed by greedy bosses while their country cousins died in floods because venal officials pocketed funds intended for the construction of dikes. The play also depicted the arrest of a labor leader and the killing of a family breadwinner in an anti-Japanese demonstration. Survivors wasted no time with mourning; as the curtain fell, they were rushing into the streets to secure the release of their imprisoned comrade.[9]

Leftist students in Peiping, assuming a paternal interest in the work of Shanghai's thespians, offered a formula for successful propagandizing: use a small, tightly knit corps, follow an unchallenged leader, make advance contact with local authorities, and rely on popular support in the event of persecution. The essential ingredient was mass mobilization.[10] The corps tested this advice in an expedition to nearby Sungkiang. Upon arrival, their representatives informed the authorities of the performance and asked them to attend. However, the officials became alarmed when the 66-man troup began to shout slogans, sing, and advertise in the streets. Just before curtain time, detectives and police surrounded the theater. The Chief Magistrate summoned the young actors from dressing rooms and told them, "It is far too hot, and you have already made a deep impression on the people of Sungkiang through your demonstration. We have three trucks for you. Please return to Shanghai for a rest."[11]

Negotiations produced a compromise: the troupe was allowed thirty minutes for the play. At the end of the allotted time, when the theater lights were extinguished, the actors filled the darkened hall with ringing appeals for support against shameless oppression of the patriotic movement; sympathetic spectators howled approval. Townspeople intervened as police cleared the hall and tried to force the students into trucks, but the group finally agreed to leave by train. Hearing of these difficulties, Peiping sympathizers suggested that in the future emphasis be kept on organization and strategy, not on mere numbers. There must be no more than ten men in a group. Upon arrival in a town, they must gather an audience as quickly as possible. Productions must run no more than fifteen minutes. Thus, "a considerable harvest" might be reaped.[12]

Such avuncular advice was not unusual, for even though official student headquarters were in Shanghai, Peiping was the source of inspiration for summertime agitators. There the CNLV's home office, which may have had a hand in drafting letters to the Shanghai troupe, verbally counseled visiting emissaries from national salvation groups. CNLV members returning home for vacations were directed to familiarize themselves with general local conditions, to study existing popular organizations, to investigate possibilities for arming the masses, and to evaluate other projects. Tenets of national salvation were disseminated by means of a rural literacy campaign. CNLV members formed reading and discussion circles; and wall newspapers and a book and periodical exchange provided a ready supply of facts and dogma. Books for general circulation included the writings of Lenin, Dimitrov, and Gorky; but highly illegal Chinese Communist tracts were secretly passed around within the CNLV.[13] In addition, drilling, field maneuvers, and camping prepared the members for difficult days ahead.[14]

In and around Peiping fervent propagandists worked through the summer. A mass meeting in the western suburbs attracted an estimated two thousand peasants. Troops of Sung Che-yüan's Twenty-ninth Army, a prime target of patriotic appeals, were urged to turn their guns against the invader. On June 18, the apprehensive Hopei-Chahar Council banned student assemblies and forbade the creation of new organizations. The CNLV ignored the edict and proceeded with its most ambitious project at an encampment in the Western Hills; there 160 students, three-fifths of them CNLV members, assembled on July 1 for a week's program of daytime guerrilla-warfare exercises and evening political discussions. Before the more than two hundred new recruits could complete the subsequent week's schedule, the camp was forced to disband because of constant harassment by spies and police.[15]

Left-wing guerrillas were not the only summertime military trainees in the Peiping area. Other college students drilled under the auspices of the Twenty-ninth Army at the Nanyüan and Hsiyüan camps, a short distance outside the city.[16] In the Yangtze Valley, many students spent the summer in military camps established by the central government.[17] However, the Nanking regime was still unwilling to commit itself to total preparation for war; Chiang Kai-shek urged young volunteers to use their summer vacations for social service work under the leadership of the schools and the New Life Movement Headquarters. The Kuomintang's Ministry of Training recommended that college and middle school students indoctrinate the citizenry in the Three People's Principles and obedience to party leadership, teach precepts of "common sense" for the emergency period, promote the New Life Movement, analyze the problem of opium smoking, spread literacy, promote the use of Chinese goods, and teach basic principles of sanitation.[18]

Thus, although the government provided military training

for some students, its overall program roused scant enthusiasm since it ignored their principal demands: national unification and mobilization for immediate war. In Shanghai, the nation's second largest university center, only 25 students had volunteered for the rural service program by the beginning of July.[19] The time for village reform had passed; the time for war had arrived.

Once again leftist rivals voiced popular demands that the KMT dared not champion. On July 9, the PSNSU asked a plenum of the KMT CEC to call a national conference on resisting Japan and national salvation, to publicize plans for opposing the enemy, and to energetically prepare for war. The petition also demanded freedom for patriotic movements, the release of political prisoners, the institution of constitutional government, and the addition of student delegates to CEC plenums. The PSNSU warned that if the central committee continued to occupy itself with fighting Chinese instead of Japanese, "it will not be the people who will cast off the government but the government that shall have cast off the people."[20]

Nevertheless, these were mild words compared with the student petition to the November plenum, which had accused the government of torturing, burying alive, and otherwise murdering no fewer than three hundred thousand students. The July document, on the other hand, was fundamentally a call for leadership against the nation's enemy. Its comparatively conciliatory tone revealed how deeply united-front ideas had penetrated in the two-and-a-half months since the words "National Salvation" had been added to the name of the Peiping Student Union.

The Politics of Conciliation

Ignoring the ever-present threat of war in North China, a record number of middle school graduates applied for entrance to Peiping universities in the fall of 1936. The academic year was much quieter than the previous one, partly because many agitators had been expelled during the summer. There were no rumors of transferring schools and libraries to the south, as there had been the previous fall. A spirit of stoic dedication prevailed. Young scholars shunned extremes of panic and heroics, lived simply and frugally, spent less time in the pursuit of pleasure, and borrowed more books from public libraries. Though the enemy stood poised to swallow North China, Peiping students impassively went about their work.[21]

While their classmates pursued knowledge, a radical minority in the CNLV and the PSNSU continued their efforts to save China through mass political organizations. By October, 31 cities had CNLV branches for which the Peiping bureau remained the oracle.[22] Recently formed chapters in Sian, Tientsin, and elsewhere requested rulings on questions ranging from how much secrecy was desirable to how to resolve differences with local student unions. Other salvation groups, which also looked to the CNLV for leadership, reported to its first Enlarged Cadres Conference in Peiping on October 4. The delegates noted that the organization now enjoyed the understanding and sympathy of society; hence it was no longer necessary to maintain the extreme security measures adopted eight months earlier. The small group of hunted radicals had become an established, self-confident organization.[23]

However, the CNLV faced a crisis of morale. Numerous members, including those who had been expelled during the summer, had departed to promote the united front among the soldiers of Yen Hsi-shan in Taiyüan and Chang Hsüeh-liang in Sian, regions contiguous to those occupied by the Red Army. A fortunate few had reached Paoan, the CCP stronghold and a mecca for young revolutionaries. Those remaining behind were impatient. They too wanted to leave for the new frontiers of the radical movement.[24]

Though activists grew restless under the constraints of discipline and the demands of the united front, external conditions dictated continued silence and self-restraint rather than demonstrations. The Peiping student mood was unreceptive to violent action, and the Nanking government was hypersensitive during the delicate negotiations between General Chang Ch'ün and Japanese Ambassador Kawagoe, which lasted from September 15 to December 3. The Hopei-Chahar Council was determined to prevent any disturbances on September 18; students supporting the united front cooperated by joining chancellors and teachers in the school memorial services that quietly marked this fifth anniversary of Japanese aggression. The only significant demonstrations took place in Shanghai and Sian. Nonetheless, police posted at Peiping and Tientsin campus gates several days in advance remained until well after the date had passed.[25]

Congratulating itself on its newfound harmony, the CNLV proceeded with its program to help students solve the problems of postgraduate employment, personal finances, and academic difficulties.[26] Concentration on issues involving the students' self-interest in the wake of the December Ninth Movement was reminiscent of CCP policy after the suppression of the 1931 drive. However this time the goal was not to antagonize the authorities but to conciliate them.

The students' willingness to compromise reached its height on the national holiday, October 10. Peiping and Tientsin leaders abandoned plans for mass demonstrations because of a "keen desire . . . to have no conflict [nor] to embarrass our authorities."[27] The PSNSU announced four goals that typified its conciliatory approach: (1) to establish a broad national united front, (2) to help the central and local governments resist Japan, (3) to encourage students and teachers to cooperate, and (4) "in saving the country, don't forget to seek knowledge."[28] This conspicuous paraphrase of the first half of Ts'ai Yüan-p'ei's maxim characterized the new orthodoxy of this advanced stage of the united-front line. (Hitherto, if student activists invoked Ts'ai's words at all, they stressed the second portion, "In studying, don't forget to save the country.") Leftist students who in January 1936 had urged North China's peasantry to revolt were now doing their utmost to allay the suspicions of officials. A spokesman for the national association said:

Our inexperience and enthusiasm [in last year's movement] led us to make the error of separating ourselves from our school authorities and from the broad masses. We now want to correct this mistake in the light of the lessons we have learned. We can now declare that we have no hatred of our government and will support it in every action it takes to stop the aggressor . . . [and that] nothing will be done to embarrass the Government as long as it follows a policy of defending the country.[29]

However, authorities failed to reciprocate. In mid-October, the Hopei-Chahar Pacification Commissioner—perhaps under pressure from the Japanese military or from Nanking—outlawed all student organizations. As if to emphasize the word "all," the edict specifically marked for extinction self-governing associations (a form of organization once encouraged by Nanking), picket and propaganda corps, "ten-man" propaganda groups, national salvation associations, study, literary, and lecture societies, round-table conferences, and even the KMT's own moral endeavor associations. Although these orders were not strictly enforced in the north, two hundred alleged leftists were expelled from Futan, Chinan, and other Shanghai universities.[30]

When Japanese troops conducted a mock occupation of Peiping on November 3, student leaders, preoccupied with public relations and forced by official suppression to make themselves inconspicuous, were caught unprepared. Not until armored columns were rumbling through the streets did the CNLV assemble hastily in a gymnasium to make plans. But their one-hour protest strike, lowering of school flags to half staff, and plans for city-wide propaganda were incidental beside the martyrdom of a twelve-year-old girl, who reportedly shouted "Down with Japanese imperialism!" as she flung herself under the treads of an enemy tank.[31]

A week later, Japanese-supported Mongolian troops opened an offensive in northern Suiyuan against the forces of Fu Tsoyi. Echoes of the little war reverberated throughout China. Students from as far away as Canton sent delegations bearing supplies for front-line fighters.[32] The PSNSU and the CNLV led a week-long drive to collect funds and clothing for the soldiers. Some students went 24 hours without food and heat to save money for China's defenders, but Northeastern University refugees, who had firsthand knowledge of the conquerors' cruelty, announced they would fast for three days. At Yenching, fifteen students quit school and enlisted with Fu Tsoyi's forces.[33]

Though left-wing students censured the government for its failure to aid Chinese troops, observers noted a new vigor in Chiang's attitude after the Suiyuan invasion. It was commonly believed that "at last the Nanking government was beginning a policy of active resistance to Japanese aggression."[34]

The Suiyuan emergency cemented relations between Peiping student agitators and their chief propaganda target, the Twenty-ninth Army. On November 14, several hundred students from Yenching, Tsinghua, and Peiping Normal universities were guests of the Twenty-ninth at a military review held in P'ang-k'o-chuang, south of Peiping.* These three schools, each raided by police in March 1935, had been the only Peiping universities to sign the November 1, 1935 petition marking the rebirth of the student movement. With an unprecedented camaraderie the delegation presented banners to the commander, then mingled with the soldiers, distributing gifts of towels and fruit.[35]

Feeling renewed confidence, the CNLV increased the size and frequency of its maneuvers. According to the CY leader Li Ch'ang, military instructors were appointed by the CCP's municipal committee. Authorities tried to interfere at first, but gave up when well-rehearsed guerrilla tactics were employed against them. Now more warmly received by the public, the CNLV increased its membership to more than two thousand, and the PSNSU expanded to 54 schools.[36]

However, progress toward a united front in Peiping was obstructed by a crisis in Shanghai. News that seven leaders of the National Salvation Association had been arrested there on November 23 overshadowed celebrations for the Chinese recapture of Pai-ling-miao in Suiyuan. Widespread indignation followed the detention of the Seven Gentlemen, who symbolized the fight for unified resistance to invasion.

As soon as reports of the arrests reached Peiping, student leaders met at Northeastern University and sent a telegram urging the government to release the patriots immediately. Yenching students voted a two-day protest strike, in which they were joined by colleagues in 23 government universities and middle schools. In several instances, liberal professors led discussions of the situation. On November 30, four petitioners,

---

* Another honored guest was Major General Hashimoto, Chief of Staff to the Japanese North China Garrison Commander. Sung Che-yüan evidently was hedging his bets.

who represented the PSNSU and the Yenching student body, were detained by secret police in Nanking and sent home under escort. The CNLV feared that this action and the persecution of the Seven Gentlemen presaged intensified suppression of the salvation movement. Members urged their schoolmates to rouse public opinion and to demand "patriotic freedoms."[37]

The situation called for action. Nearly six months had passed since the last large-scale demonstration in Peiping (June 13, 1936), and the first anniversary of the December Ninth Movement was approaching. Arrests, censorship, and government suppression of anti-Japanese strikes in Shanghai and Tsingtao factories forced left-wing Peiping students to reconsider their conciliatory approach to authorities. Now, in a tactical about-face from its quiescent policy, the CNLV called for "a new, even greater December Ninth." The Vanguard conceded that the "mass base" was smaller than it had been the previous year, but claimed that its powerful organization compensated for this deficiency. Dramatic measures were considered necessary to change the political scene.[38]

Meanwhile, the PSNSU issued a proclamation justifying a demonstration. The statement excoriated the government for blindly maintaining that "diplomatic relations [were] still not hopeless" when enemy troops and planes were slaughtering Chinese in Suiyuan. Thousands of Japanese marines had occupied the port of Tsingtao, surrounded public buildings, and arrested officials and newspaper editors. The union demanded that Nanking promptly break diplomatic relations with the aggressor, send an expedition against the East Hopei puppet regime, recover enemy-held territory in Chahar and the Northeast, support Suiyuan fighters, and aid the Twenty-ninth Army. While critical of the central government, the manifesto was friendly to northern generals Sung Che-yüan, Yen Hsi-shan, Fu Tso-yi, and Chang Hsüeh-liang. It called for an alliance of all factions and parties, but significantly omitted the slogan, "Support the government to resist Japan."[39] Thus, a year after the December Ninth demonstration, the PSNSU had become more sympathetic to Chang Hsüeh-liang, the warlord once vilified for abandoning Manchuria, than to the national leader, Chiang Kai-shek. It is highly relevant that at this time Communists in Shensi were successfully wooing Chang away from his "bandit extermination" duties toward an anti-Japanese alliance.

Student leaders in Peiping, wary of police interference, postponed their demonstration until December 12. The four to five thousand students who answered the call to action that morning did not know that hours earlier in Sian Chiang Kai-shek had been taken prisoner by Chang Hsüeh-liang.[40] The demonstration marked the zenith of leftist influence. Li Ch'ang led the procession, while Yü Ch'i-wei (the high-ranking Communist youth leader) directed proceedings behind the scenes. Hsiao Wen-lan, who later became a Communist historian, distributed red and green leaflets from an automobile hired for the occasion.[41] These pamphlets lauded Shanghai and Tsingtao workers, called upon Nanking to release the Seven Gentlemen, urged popular support for the Twenty-ninth Army's resistance, and reiterated demands for a united front. Police squelched plans for a large-scale procession by breaking up small groups of demonstrators who had gathered at prearranged places outside the schools. Nevertheless, CNLV writers have interpreted proceedings as a successful application of the newly acquired "dispersal and regrouping" tactics of guerrilla warfare.[42]

The same afternoon, some four thousand students assembled on Coal Hill at the request of Mayor Ch'in Te-chun. They cheered him when he asked them to fight shoulder to shoulder with him against the enemy's attack. With Ch'in's permission, the crowd paraded home, shouting anti-Japanese slogans and singing for the first time in the streets of Peiping the stirring words of the *Volunteers' Marching Song,* "Arise! Arise!," and the *National Liberation Song:*

> Workers, peasants, students, soldiers,
>   merchants, rise and arm!
> With spear and sword and hammer march
>   from factory, class, and farm.
> Onward to the battlefront of national
>   salvation,
> Arm in arm we bravely march for China's
>   liberation.[43]

The Sian Incident

Meanwhile, a far more important drama was unfolding in the capital of Shensi province. The roots of the Sian Incident can be traced to: (1) the Japanese invasion of Manchuria, which left Chang Hsüeh-liang and his irredentist followers as a major military force south of the Great Wall; (2) Chiang Kai-shek's decision to use this Northeast Army against (3) the Red Army, which had occupied northern Shensi; (4) the telling effect of Communist propaganda on Chang and his homesick troops; (5) the ambitions of Shensi warlord Yang Hu-ch'eng, caught in the middle of this imbroglio; (6) the influence on all these principals of the National Salvation Association's campaign for an anti-Japanese united front; and (7) the influx of veterans of the Peiping December Ninth Movement into Sian.

The story of the students and Chang Hsüeh-liang ("the Young Marshal") begins directly after the demonstrations of December 1935, when the Peiping Student Union sent agents to solicit aid in other cities. Manchurian exiles who went to Sian to seek Chang's support were welcomed and put to work as propagandists in the Northeast Army. Furthermore, Chang sent word that all anti-Japanese youth, regardless of their political beliefs, would find a haven in the "Western Capital." Some of Peiping's young patriots accepted the invitation and became agitators among the troops and the civilian population. Two of Edgar Snow's Yenching journalism students edited an army newspaper, which became an organ of the anti-Japanese movement in the Northwest.* Students and graduates of Northeastern University, of which Chang Hsüeh-liang was nominally chancellor, were especially active in Sian's political life.** Two hundred Manchurian students formed a special regiment in the Northeast Army and were enrolled in

---

* One of them, Chang Chao-lin, had been president of the Yenching student body during the 1935–36 school year. Early in 1937, he became editor of the *Hsi-ching min-pao*, Sian's largest daily. See Snow, *Journey*, p. 154; Bertram, pp. 167–69, 175, 181.
** The university had moved from Mukden to Peiping after the Japanese attack of September 18, 1931; the College of Engineering had been transferred to Sian in February 1936.

a new political training school under Colonel Sun Ming-chiu, youthful chief of the Young Marshal's bodyguard. From the ranks of this regiment Chang recruited new members for his leadership corps; soon they were displacing older officers.[44]

Sian nationalism was given a radical tinge by the presence of more than two hundred CNLV members as of October 1936, when a Sian branch was formed with the aid of experienced Peiping cadres.[45] The emigrants from Peiping used their experience in mass movements to good advantage. They established peasants' unions, and schools for the illiterate, which disseminated propaganda. In Sienyang, a town west of Sian on the Kansu highway, a correspondent found a team of Peiping student propagandists in a poster-covered room where they worked by day and slept on tables by night.[46] From September 18 to December 9, 1936, six massive demonstrations surged through Sian streets. On October 4, a Northeastern People's National Salvation Association (made up of Manchurian refugees) was formally inaugurated.[47]

Student agitators were a source of conflict between Chang Hsüeh-liang and Chiang Kai-shek. When Chiang Kai-shek accused the Young Marshal of harboring Communists in his military academy, the latter replied that he judged students only by their anti-Japanese sentiments and advised Chiang "not to believe anything the Japanese tell you."[48] On one occasion, Chang Hsüeh-liang's troops broke down the doors of Sian KMT Headquarters to liberate three students who had been kidnapped by local Blueshirts commanded by Chiang Kai-shek's nephew, Chiang Hsiao-hsien, a former nemesis of Peiping radicals.[49] After Chiang Kai-shek's October 1936 visit to Sian, Miao Chien-ch'iu, a fiery political adviser to Chang Hsüeh-liang, told an assembly of cadets that the Nanking leader deserved to be put to death for his appeasement of Japan.[50]

On December 9, 1936, three days before Chiang was kidnapped, thousands of students marched from Sian toward his suburban headquarters at Lin-t'ung to appeal for immediate resistance to Japan and an end to civil war. After police bullets had wounded two students, Chang Hsüeh-liang, fearing further bloodshed, halted the marchers and personally presented their petition. Chiang Kai-shek was furious that his subordinate had dared to side with the demonstrators. In his published diary he recalls, "I severely upbraided him for his acceptance ... of the 'People's Front,' his enlistment of reactionary politicians, and his *laissez faire* attitude toward the activities of the so-called *National Salvation Association*."[51] According to the diary, Chang Hsüeh-liang's resentment of this reprimand impelled him to accept Yang Hu-ch'eng's long-standing proposal of rebellion.[52] Former Peiping students were among Sun Ming-chiu's handpicked regiment, which shot and killed Chiang Hsiao-hsien and captured Chiang Kai-shek at dawn on December 12.[53]

The students' role in this historic event is summarized as follows: (1) student propaganda during 1936 stirred the patriotic sentiments of the Northeast Army and the populace of Sian; (2) a student demonstration on the anniversary of December Ninth precipitated Chang's decision to mutiny; and finally, (3) student-soldiers participated in the actual kidnapping of the nation's leader. But ironically, the student movement was a casualty of the Sian Incident. Campus leftists in Peiping were exultant when they learned of Chiang's arrest. For want of contrary directives from the CCP, CNLV leaders praised the Young Marshal's action, which they regarded as a master stroke that would end the civil war. None of them advocated Chiang's release. As Li Ch'ang recalls:

Early the next morning came the news of the Sian Incident. [CNLV] members ran about, spreading this news, and once again the students were thrown into extreme excitement and joy. How gladdening it was to learn of the arrest of the chief criminal and principal evil-doer who had rebelled against the great revolution and started the 10-year civil war![54]

The jubilant radicals, anticipating encouragement from the Soviet Union, were dumbfounded by Tass reports which reached them four days after the coup. According to *Pravda*, Chang Hsüeh-liang's action had been instigated by "the Japanese military clique" in order to prevent unification under Chiang Kai-shek. *Isvestiya* charged that the move played into the hands of Japanese imperialists.[55] Supporters of the Young

Marshal, especially Manchurian refugees, were aghast. Further confusion followed when the CCP, in open contradiction to Moscow, praised the "patriotic sincerity and zeal" of Sian's leaders and called for a Nanking peace conference at which Chiang's fate would be decided.[56] When Mao Tse-tung changed his tune and joined the Comintern chorus of hallelujahs that greeted Chiang's Christmas Day release, Peiping's young Communists and fellow travelers were stunned. "The situation changed too rapidly and abruptly for [CNLV] members to understand it immediately," Li Ch'ang has written. "Suddenly, they became taciturn and felt disturbed at heart."[57] The faithful could hardly believe what had happened: Mao had betrayed the anti-Japanese patriot Chang Hsüeh-liang to the arch-appeaser, Chiang Kai-shek!

Meanwhile, pro-KMT students were mobilizing. They received support from their classmates, most of whom were shocked by the kidnapping. Since mid-1936, Chiang had been generally recognized as the only conceivable national leader; whatever his shortcomings, he was obviously the one man who could unify China. Furthermore, as long as he remained captive, a frontal assault on the mutineers by Nanking extremists might plunge the nation into a still more disastrous civil war. Before the Sian Incident even the Communists had virtually admitted that only under Chiang's leadership could the country resist Japan. After years of KMT persecution, they could not help but rejoice at Chang Hsüeh-liang's action, but their vindictiveness was not widely shared. A flood of telegrams from campuses in every part of the land demanded that Chiang be liberated and that his captor be punished.

When the Generalissimo was released, young China rejoiced. In Peiping, anti-Communist professors and students joined in the celebration. Politically active Tsinghua led the way with a torchlight parade on the night of December 25; other schools followed suit. More than eight hundred Peita students and teachers assembled to hail the national leader's miraculous release. In a congratulatory telegram, the pro-KMT New Student Union asked Chiang to lead a national alliance against the enemy. This appeal was also expressed in slogans shouted in the streets by joyous students: "Recover Manchuria and North Chahar" and "Recover East Hopei."[58]

Pro-government forces also rallied at Normal University. Chancellor Li Cheng and professors Yang Li-k'uei and Hsiung Meng-fei, whose names were anathema to the left, spoke at a school assembly. Then the student body, followed by pupils of the Associated Middle and Lower Schools, led by university authorities, and protected by police, paraded to the T'ien-an Men. Others joined them, and by 12:30 P.M. an estimated ten thousand had gathered at the traditional meeting place.

Not since 1928 had a pro-government assembly been held at the T'ien-an Men. Only twelve months earlier, this site had been the scene of a massive protest against Nanking's foreign and domestic policies. But events since December 12, 1936, had changed everything. Now exuberant throngs expressed their unanimous support for the Nanking government, denounced the Communists, and urged severe punishment for the Young Marshal. Other resolutions recommended abolition of the "Old Student Union" (PSNSU) and dismissal of "reactionary" professors in the city. Encouraged by school officials, celebrations continued until the Western New Year.[59]

Nanking quickly capitalized on its new popularity. On the eve of Chiang's return to the capital, the official broadcasting station carried an address by a Central University student, who appealed to his colleagues to support the government and oppose all "front organizations." In these extraordinary times, he said, youth throughout the world had realized the necessity of surrendering personal liberties and devoting absolute loyalty to their countries' leaders. China's students must follow the example of youth in Hitler's Germany, Mussolini's Italy, and Stalin's Russia.[60]

In Peiping, while KMT groups and publications proliferated, young radicals were imprisoned and leftist literature was banned. Professors Yang Li-k'uei and Hsiung Meng-fei called for the expulsion of all CNLV members from Normal University. The militantly anti-Communist New Student Union went into action, turning the academic world into a battleground. At Tsinghua, the right-wing School Protection Corps ransacked leftists' dormitory rooms and offices of "subversive" publications. Frenzied raiders, shouting slogans around a bonfire kindled with their literary haul, were put to flight by enraged CNLV stalwarts.[61]

Violence also erupted at Northeastern University, whose six hundred Peiping students split into factions for and against Chancellor Chang Hsüeh-liang—the Young Marshal's partisans outnumbered his foes two to one. When the anti-Chang group supported a move to reorganize the institution under the Nanking government, a bloody free-for-all resulted and three students were wounded seriously enough to require hospitalization. In spite of loud protests, a new chancellor was appointed to replace Chang, who was by then a prisoner in Nanking.* The school was nationalized and moved to Kaifeng, where it reopened in March, 1937.[62]

In Sian, immediately after Chiang Kai-shek's capture, young propagandists had been summoned to explain the event to the people. Three national salvation newspapers had appeared within a fortnight. In addition, students and actors had formed an itinerant theater presenting patriotic drama.[63] James M. Bertram describes one of their productions as follows:

The villain, as usual, [is] a traitor: in this case a chief detective who has ruthlessly suppressed the patriotic movement. The play [is] a study of how his family—wife, son, and daughter—conspire to destroy him. First the son is entrusted with the task, but he hesitates, Hamlet-like. His sister, hearing the issue, condemns him for a faint-heart, and herself volunteers to poison her father. To crown all, the mother comes in and insists that the sacred duty of destroying a traitor must be hers. The poisoning is most ingeniously accomplished, and while the detective writhes around on a sofa, clasping his belly, the woman stands with folded arms—a modern Clytemnestra—and refuses to telephone for a doctor. When the victim finally collapses on the floor, the avenger comes to the footlights and cries: "Women of China, arise! No longer be slaves! Save yourselves, and save China!"

The applause from the students was terrific; but some solid citizens at the back could be heard shouting "Puhao! Disgraceful!" and making a noisy exit.[64]

---

* Having accompanied Chiang back to Nanking, Chang had been sentenced to prison, pardoned, and placed under Chiang's personal custody.

The left-wing nationalistic drive continued to accelerate even after Chang Hsüeh-liang's voluntary return to Nanking with his erstwhile captive, but its days were numbered. The release of Chiang Kai-shek found Sian youth as bewildered as their Peiping comrades.[65] Officers of the Northeast Army split into cliques of moderates seeking to move their forces elsewhere in deference to Nanking's orders and diehards demanding the Young Marshal's release and opposing troop withdrawal. When an attempted coup by radical Sun Ming-chiu failed, the die was cast. The Northeast Army would depart, and the city would be turned over to units loyal to Nanking. Students were dazed; there was nothing to do but leave. Bertram captured the mood of the last days of Sian in an account of a farewell dinner party with former Yenching student leader Chang Chao-lin and others:

We ordered yellow wine, to drink the health of the Young Marshal —still a prisoner at Fenghua. The warm liquor loosened up the talk.

"You must drink first to Chiang Kai-shek," Chang insisted. "United Front, you know! Chiang is our leader now."

He was right; and we drank the toast with a flourish. "Better drink to the Red Army too," a voice said gloomily. "Soon there won't be one—only more Government troops, in a Special Area."

"But the Reds will never give up their army."

"Who can tell, now? They seem to be trying to liquidate themselves, to save Chiang the trouble."

"Never!" someone protested hotly. "The Reds will never give up their army, or their soviet organization. They may change the names, to satisfy Nanking. But that is just tactics—United Front strategy."

"Pretty poor strategy. They'll last just as long as it takes Chiang to isolate them again, and get the Tungpei army out of the Northwest!"

"No; Chiang has really changed. He has become much more democratic. . . ."

. . . There was one last toast that had to be drunk before the party broke up. We stood for it.

"To the unity of China! National Front!"

It was a fine romantic gesture, with the gendarmes outside and the waiters hovering behind the curtain.[66]

As Sian changed hands, scores of students marched north-ward to join the only other openly anti-Japanese force in the area, the Red Army. Soon the Communists' military academy and political training school at Yenan were eagerly admitting veterans of the December Ninth Movement and the Sian Incident.[67]

The Left Sues for Peace

The National Salvation Movement seemed doomed, even as its goals loomed nearer. Its leaders were in jail, its student followers were discredited, and its left-wing counselors were divided between Communists urging support for Chiang Kai-shek and Trotskyites seeking to rally the left around anti-Chiang slogans. The PSNSU, which had once counted its members by the tens of thousands, was reduced to a few thousand by the end of December.[68]

The CNLV, also seriously weakened by numerical losses, began a period of evaluation and self-criticism to absorb the shock of the Sian aftermath. Its leaders were in an embarrassing position. They had to convince their followers that Chiang's release had been correct and that a united front with the government was in the offing. At the same time, members had to be rallied to defense against resurgent and militant campus rightists. Thus, although it was duty-bound to broaden the united front, the group was under constant attack from its prospective allies. No wonder members gave way to confusion, despair, lethargy, and defeatism. Their problem was described in typical jargon as "leftist in outlook, rightist in action."[69]

Under these trying conditions, the first National Vanguard Congress opened in Peiping on February 6. Twenty-four delegates from eighteen CNLV branches and representatives of two major national salvation groups attended. Peiping members supported by comrades from Sian and Tientsin played the leading role, reflecting Peiping's continued dominance of the CNLV's North China nucleus. The congress urged its constituents to rid themselves of negativism and pessimism and to set an example by opening a drive to recruit four thousand new members, bringing total membership to ten thousand in the succeeding year. It proclaimed that the Vanguard was more than a mere promoter of the united front; it was itself a united-front organization, and would welcome to its ranks all who shared its anti-Japanese national salvation views. (A similar declaration had been made by CY in December 1935.) Following the conference, the CNLV reverted to a strategy of restraint, emphasizing internal consolidation and preparation for war against Japan and eschewing spectacular large-scale activities.[70]

A similar posture was adopted by Peiping's "Old Student Union" (the PSNSU), which spent the spring semester ardently wooing the New. The leftist group discovered that "united front" was more easily said than achieved as it tried in vain to make peace with its enemies and to recapture its former preeminence in the academic world. The New Union, remaining adamant, seized the initiative in February by presenting Chiang Kai-shek with a symbolic double-edged sword. The PSNSU responded as best it could by attempting to present a conciliatory banner to the national leader, and by evincing a friendly, temperate attitude toward the government. It praised Chiang's treatment of Chang Hsüeh-liang, blamed the Generalissimo's past misunderstandings with the students on the machinations of Japanese agents, and requested that he carry out the Three People's Principles and resuscitate the foreign policy of Sun Yat-sen's last years (friendship toward the USSR, wariness of Japan).[71]

On February 28, two thousand students attended a leftist-instigated meeting at Chung-kuo College "to celebrate peaceful unification." Its sponsors had hoped that the gathering would inaugurate an era of amity, perhaps even a merger, between the two student unions. However, while an officer of the Old Union was speaking, the assembly was disrupted by shouts that the PSNSU was a "Red bandit" group. Authorities finally dispersed the meeting to prevent a public "misunderstanding" and to avoid antagonizing "our friendly neighbor."[72]

Undaunted by this fiasco, the PSNSU staged a public commemorative meeting on Sun Yat-sen's birthday; only a few hundred attended. Addressing this scant turnout, Yü Ch'i-wei predicted that they would lose popular support unless they joined in a single Peiping union.[73] Failing to gain this ecumenical goal, the leftist group made further efforts to regain its following. In a mid-April congress, it promised to democratize by expelling delegates not properly elected and it reaffirmed its dedication to the interests of its constituents. In accordance with National Student Association policy, there was a rededication to the task of solving young intellectuals' educational and economic problems.[74] Such timeworn declarations had little more than ritual value.

However, a pledge to continue the drive for rapport with the New Union won a favorable response when the New Union expressed willingness to form a joint association under the direction of mutually acceptable professors. Unhappily, negotiations floundered over methods of selecting representatives.[75] The situation deteriorated, and on May 4 the two groups came to blows. Each had planned a public gathering; the PSNSU, ostensibly as a token of good will, had delegated several dozen members to participate in the opposition's meeting. The gesture proved disastrous. After prolonged debate over the choice of a chairman, leftists in the audience raised the martial strains of *Defend Madrid*. The meeting came to a tumultuous end when KMT Boy Scouts attacked the singers with clubs and bricks.[76]

On June 21, the PSNSU made a final overture to its rival by asking for a truce and an alliance under "democratic" conditions. The New Union agreed in principle but restated its irrevocable opposition to subversive elements.[77] The groups were still unreconciled when students dispersed for summer vacation. This situation was typical of the deep rifts beneath the surface of the united front as the nation moved toward war with Japan.

Prewar Youth: A Portrait

In spite of bitter infighting on China's campuses, most prewar students were able to postpone alignment with either the KMT or the CCP; political polarization was yet to come. The Communist appeal for consolidation under Chiang Kai-shek encouraged sentiments of non-partisan patriotism. In the context of a united front it was possible to advocate a national struggle against the enemy without party commitments.

Although Peiping students regarded with interest the altercation between the two unions, only a minority actively participated. Still, the New Student Union had undeniably gained support since the Sian Incident. On the eve of war the organized forces of left and right were deadlocked, a situation which would have been inconceivable a year earlier, when the only important political organizations had been the PSNSU and the CNLV.

Communist blunders at the time of the Sian crisis were partly responsible for this situation. Had the CNLV been more agile in shifting to a pro-Chiang stance, it might have won leadership over Peiping's youth. Yet the situation in Peiping was not a true index of CCP strength in North China; the cream of the radical young intelligentsia had been leaving for Shensi for over a year. CCP and CNLV policy purposefully bled Peiping's manpower to provide qualified leaders elsewhere; students expelled en masse from Peiping schools swelled the ranks of the Red Army officers' academy. Still more arrived in Yenan after the collapse of the Northeast Army's radical wing following the Sian settlement. Finally, after the Marco Polo Bridge Incident, a considerable number, though still a minority, found their way to the northwest or to other Red guerrilla bases as Japanese armies swept over North China.

In July 1937, everybody, even the Communists, conceded that Chiang Kai-shek was the indispensable national leader. Did this mean that the country's youth had become conservative? Did admiration for Chiang extend to his New Life Movement? How many of the vast numbers that followed the government to Hankow and Chungking continued to look to Yenan for guidance? What were the long-range prospects for the Kuomintang among China's young intellectuals?

Kiang Wen-han, Executive Secretary of the Chinese YMCA's Student Division and an experienced analyst of the college scene, observed a "house of opinion divided" in both Christian and government institutions late in 1936. However, "the mental trends of the more thoughtful students" were "radical." His analysis continues:

(1) The outcry for individual development is now changed to one of collective struggle. (2) The worship of idealism and liberalism is

now changed to one of sheer realism and authority. (3) The concern for an individual "way out" is now changed to an actual identification with the masses. (4) The interest in the problem of China is now enriched by a better understanding of the inter-relatedness of the world. (5) The world crisis is no longer interpreted in terms of a recurring cycle, but as the end of an era. (6) Solution is sought no longer for minor adjustments but for a fundamental change.[78]

Kiang's observations find support in a countrywide survey taken by Olga Lang on the eve of the Sino-Japanese War.[79] She characterizes students as:

(1) *Nationalistic*; one problem preoccupied young Chinese: how to save their country from foreign aggression. This concern was especially strong in the North, where the Japanese threat was most immediate, but it extended to every corner of the land. Asked whom they most admired, college youth named Sun Yat-sen, Chiang Kai-shek, Confucius, Yüeh Fei, Ch'in Shih Huang-ti, Feng Yü-hsiang, Ts'ai Ting-k'ai, Fu Tso-yi, and Kuan Kung; and foreigners such as Stalin, Lincoln, Washington, F.D.R., Marx, Lenin, Hitler, Mussolini, Kemal Pasha, and Haile Selassie.[80] To the Westerner, these men represented incompatible ideologies and national interests, but in China all except Confucius were thought of as military heroes and unifiers. Mussolini, the conqueror, was admired because he had infused his country with a resurgent national spirit; his victim, Haile Selassie, because he had defended his native land against foreign imperialism. Student credos covered a wide range, but nationalism was the common denominator.[81]

(2) *Socially conscious*; beyond saving the nation from the immediate Japanese threat, Chinese students were committed to a fundamental social revolution. When asked to state their purposes in life, such phrases as "freedom and liberation of the Chinese people" and "to live and struggle for the masses" flowed easily from their pens.[82] Favorite authors were socially-oriented leftists—Lu Hsün, Pa Chin, Mao Tun, Ting Ling, and Kuo Mo-jo. The most popular non-Chinese writer was Gorky; his revolutionary novel, *Mother,* was the favorite foreign work of fiction. Taste in periodical literature was less radical, but also reflected an interest in social problems and

current affairs. *Tung-fang tsa-chih* (The Eastern Miscellany) and *Kuo-wen chou-pao* (Kuowen Weekly Illustrated) were most widely read. In the nonfiction field, social critics Hu Shih and Lin Yutang (though less outspoken in 1936 than in 1931) were favored over left-wing journalist Tsou T'ao-fen by three to one and two to one margins.[83] Nonetheless, works by Marx, Lenin, and Engels were widely quoted, and Tsou's *Sheng-huo chou-k'an** (Life Weekly), as Kiang Wen-han observed, "appealed to thousands of educated youth."[84]

(3) *Radical*; 34 per cent of the matriculants at non-Christian universities and 12 per cent at Christian institutions were "radical." Since more than 85 per cent of all college youth attended government schools, almost a third of Miss Lang's sample fell into this category. (Radicalism was even more prevalent among students from rural homes, who were not proportionally represented in this sampling.) As she perceived, "the Communist Party was practically the only representative of social-radical thought."[85] One may logically conclude that in 1937 one-third of China's college students were ideologically pro-Communist.

A series of autobiographical sketches by Yenching students entitled "The Post–December Ninth Me" provides further testimony to the penetration of Communist ideas in the academic world. Though the collection follows no party line, most essays are self-critical in the CCP style. A dominant theme is castigation of the pre–December Ninth self as bourgeois and individualistic, and glorification of a mass-oriented post–December Ninth self.[86]

(4) *Rebellious*; more than 40 per cent of college students disapproved of the behavior of their parents, especially their fathers, who were denounced as "reactionary," "conservative," "feudal," and acting "against the trend of the time."[87] However, even the family revolution was translated into nationalistic terms. In the early 1920's, the family, which was then the indisputable focus of power and loyalty, had been lashed by the fury of the May Fourth Movement. By 1937, "children considered themselves primarily citizens and individuals and

* Published as *Ta-chung sheng-huo* after November 1935.

not family members."[88] Many accepted the view of a prominent pamphleteer that the national united front must begin in
the home.[89] China came first.

Thus a rebellious younger generation prepared to defend its
country. The confrontation with the forces of conservatism in
the home and the government was postponed until after the
war. *The Nation Above All*, the title of a popular wartime
drama by Lao She, was the slogan for China's youth. Once the
international crisis had passed there would be time to build a
new world.

Chiang and the Students After Sian

Forces set in motion in Peiping on December 9, 1935, culminated in Sian a year later. The student demonstration had initiated a nationwide movement for war against Japan; Chiang,
kidnapped because he preferred to fight the Communists, was
freed in the hope that he would turn his guns against the foreign invader. During or after his captivity, Chiang came to
terms with the leaders of the Red and Northeast armies, but
he refused to compromise with his civilian critics. Taking
advantage of his increased prestige after he was freed on
Christmas Day, he made the subsequent half year an ordeal
for leaders of the National Salvation Movement. The Seven
Gentlemen languished in jail until after the outbreak of war,
while Peiping's left-wing students were isolated and vilified
by a resurgent right. Thus Chiang enjoyed revenge even
though he was forced to adopt the policies of his enemies.

The Sian Incident had a divisive impact on Peiping's academic world. It occurred just as the PSNSU's campaign for a
united front was reaching its peak. Mayor Ch'in Te-chun's
patriotic speech to the radical nationalists who gathered on
Coal Hill led them to believe that the same authorities who
had scattered their ranks with broadsword and firehose twelve
months earlier were now prepared to turn more formidable
weapons against the Japanese. As demonstrators marched back
to their dormitories singing long proscribed leftist songs, they
had reason to hope that a united, officially sanctioned, pro-
Communist patriotic movement was imminent.

Within twelve hours the news of Chiang's kidnapping changed everything. By publicly displaying vindictive glee at the discomfiture of their leading tormentor, the radicals alienated prospective allies and shattered the united front. The CCP high command, under pressure from Moscow, and for reasons of its own, finally decided to seek Chiang's release, but by the time the new party line reached Peiping, the damage had been done.

We may discount, but may not ignore, Chinese press reports of nearly unanimous nationwide student support for Chiang during his fortnight's detention. In addition to the officially inspired meetings and telegrams calling for his liberation, there was a genuine public desire that the one man who could unify the country live to achieve this goal. Chiang escaped death by a hair's breadth to become the indisputable leader of China for the first time in his tempestuous career.

The Sian Incident had long-range implications for the country's youth. Out of unprecedented pro-Chiang solidarity, totalitarian elements in the KMT created a cult of the Leader that reached its high point during the war. From the same material, imitators of Hitler, Mussolini, and Stalin in the Chinese military fashioned the San-min chu-i Youth Corps, which rallied a younger generation of devout nationalists behind "the highest leader." The ultimate failure of this effort does not obviate its immediate success in the early war years.

Only a fraction of China's youth went to Yenan after the Japanese attack (though many December Ninth leaders were already there). As war enveloped the land, most students followed the government to Wuhan and Chungking. National unity under the Kuomintang seemed within reach. The revolutionary energy of the younger generation was harnessed to achieve a single goal: the expulsion of the invader. Not until war weariness and civil conflict had shattered the fragile united front did long suppressed student radicalism reappear. In July 1937, it would have seemed fantastic to suggest that Chiang Kai-shek's patriotic young supporters would one day be the foundation of a Communist China.

There was no moment of truth for China's prewar students. The political situation was muddled, youthful emotions were confused. Dissatisfied as they were with the Nanking government, students could see no viable alternative. At no time did Chiang Kai-shek control the entire country, yet out of the Kuomintang's first decade in power he emerged as the only serious candidate for command. The forces of Mao Tse-tung presented a much more serious political threat than the epithet Red Bandits implied, but they certainly did not appear to be the imminent conquerors of China.

The students and Chiang were not totally alienated. Gradual erosion, or, more aptly, inner decay, would better describe their relations, for by 1937 the entire nation, including its youth, seemed to be in wholehearted support of the central government.

Student political vicissitudes must be understood in terms of the dominant theme of twentieth-century Chinese history—nationalism. The prevalent variety of nationalism was neither traditionalistic nor aggressive, but anti-imperialist. The concepts of nationalism and anti-imperialism were so closely linked in the minds of students that the words are almost synonymous when used in reference to the student movement.

Modern nationalism evolved slowly. During the half century after the Opium War, foreign encroachment was too gradual to stimulate an immediate patriotic response. At that time many members of the old scholar-gentry class believed it was possible to grant the barbarians privileges on the shores of the

Celestial Kingdom and still keep their ancient cultural heritage intact. It was the Sino-Japanese War of 1894–95 that shocked young China out of its stupor. Japan, an avaricious and ill-mannered newcomer to imperialist society, was eager to swallow in one gulp what England had been nibbling on for 60 years. To the dismay of Japanese expansionists, an equally unruly Chinese nationalism made its debut simultaneously. Every Japanese move on the Asian continent stimulated the development of Chinese anti-imperialism; hence the tragic conflict of 1931–45.

After September 18, 1931, impatient students found themselves at cross-purposes with the wisdom (or folly) of older men. To some officials, immediate resistance seemed suicidal; China's only hope was to gain time to arm. Others, who wishfully entertained a chimera of accommodation with the enemy, argued that Japan's territorial lust would soon be sated. They envisioned a unified China under strong KMT rule, free of Communists and warlords, as a worthy partner for the progressive islanders. A third group felt that books, not guns, were China's salvation—a modern educational system must be created; and since this would be impossible under wartime conditions, a military confrontation had to be avoided at all costs. Young patriots regarded these arguments as apologies for treason.

The classical conflict between impetuous youth and cautious middle age was especially agonizing in the Chinese milieu. Students found discrepancies between learning and reality unbearable. During this era of turmoil, five years of education produced twelve-year-old iconoclasts; another five, rebels of seventeen; five more, revolutionaries of twenty-two. Many who had studied Western political science, philosophy, and economics were met upon returning home (an ordeal which some did their best to avoid) by grandfathers who still smoked opium and fathers who maintained concubines. These tradition-bound elders assumed that their educated progeny would perpetuate a family system that was indefensible in the light of what the students had learned in school. Small wonder that disproportionate numbers of radical young intellectuals came from backward, rural areas. Small wonder that they sought total destruction of the old order and had little enthusiasm for governments that blithely tolerated decadence.

A desire for immediate, uncompromising solutions underlay the students' concept of foreign relations. Here too knowledge was a spark to volatile emotions. Every schoolboy knew that his once-mighty nation had been harnessed in the yoke of foreign imperialism. Every child who could read a newspaper realized that in a world of power politics his homeland must defend itself or die. Such militancy clashed with the Nanking regime's determination to postpone war with Japan. Thus, after the Mukden Incident, the younger generation, already disenchanted by the government's failure to fulfill its revolutionary promises at home, became bitterly critical of its policy of compromise toward foreign aggression.

Students at leading Chinese universities were also at odds with Western-educated teachers, who had returned from industrialized, capitalistic Europe and America to a society that had barely entered the modern world. These men admired much of what they had seen, but brought home no panaceas for China's ills. Experience and education had rendered them unreceptive to the ideological simplicities of Marxism. (The French-trained teachers were notable exceptions.) To bring China "bit by bit, drop by drop" into the modern age implied decades, perhaps centuries, of education. Their less cosmopolitan students, fully aware of the country's backwardness, ubiquitous injustice, and submission to imperialism, sought an all-embracing doctrine that would analyze these evils, place them in a theoretical framework, and prescribe a revolutionary course of action. Such a doctrine was Leninism.

While Hu Shih and Ts'ai Yüan-p'ei were promoting national salvation through education, many students looked to politics. In the early 1920's the May Fourth Movement had divided into two currents: liberal, which advocated gradual experimental reform, and radical, which demanded revolutionary action. Until a popular government unified the nation, the revolution exercised an irresistible appeal. Under the influence of the KMT, the CCP, and the Young China Party, the student movement lost its political naïveté. The violent demonstration of May 4, 1919, had been a thoroughly non-partisan reaction to warlord connivance in foreign aggression. But the equally impassioned May Thirtieth Movement six years later was inextricably entangled in party politics.

A parallel development occurred in literature. During the early Republican period, writers, unmindful of ideological subtleties, had protested against all that was moribund and corrupt in Chinese society. After May Fourth, literature carried a growing political burden; by the time of the Northern Expedition, many authors had begun to regard political and social problems as the only legitimate subjects. In the early 1930's, the League of Leftist Writers forced written social protest into the mold of "proletarian literature."

Throughout two decades of Kuomintang rule the student movement, as well as literature, remained under the shadow of party politics. The anti-Japanese outbursts of 1931 and 1935, though spontaneous in origin, became infiltrated by Communists in their later stages. The artistic contribution of these movements was principally in the didactic theater presented by itinerant student troupes. For the eight years of the Japanese war, virtually all literary talent in both the KMT and CCP zones was enlisted in the war effort. Students, like writers, became the tools of master craftsmen. All major demonstrations from 1945 to 1949 were party-manipulated, one by the KMT, the others by the CCP. After the Communist victory, both youth and literature were turned to the service of state policy.

From the KMT's debate over youth policy in the years 1927–29 to the rise of the CNLV in 1936, the student movement veered steadily to the left. This dramatic transformation is symbolized by the contrast between the KMT-dominated National Student Association crushed by Minister of Training Tai Chi-t'ao in 1929 and the pro-CCP NSA formed in May 1936. When Tai did away with the troublesome but still loyal NSA, he had no way of foreseeing that it would be resurrected in such a monstrous form seven years later.

Nevertheless it would be an overstatement to say that the

younger generation suddenly disowned the Nanking government. As dedicated nationalists, students were reluctant to
abandon hope in the one power capable of uniting the country
against the foe. Kuomintang unification of China, albeit more
in name than in fact, had won an enormous reserve of good
will for the party. The KMT's involvement in chronic civil
war, its suppression of mass movements, and its failure to
effect fundamental changes in Chinese society dampened the
students' enthusiasm but did not destroy their loyalty. Even
the thousands of young warhawks who angrily petitioned
Nanking in the autumn of 1931 still looked to the government
for leadership. Only a radical minority sought to turn the campaign for a dynamic foreign policy into a weapon of civil war.

Not until 1931, when the Kuomintang regime had clearly
demonstrated that it was not prepared to vigorously oppose
the enemy, did youth begin to question the KMT's professed
anti-imperialism. The government's answer to leftist agitation
was a revival of the White Terror, which effectively silenced
revolutionaries, but the victory was superficial. Suppression at
home and appeasement abroad lent plausibility to Communist
propaganda. For the next four years, ideological radicalism
flourished among students under a protective cover of political
caution.

Observers who interpreted the passivity of this generation as
approval of the status quo were mistaken; the quiescent students of the mid-1930's were casting a silent vote of no confidence that they had been unprepared to submit during their
feverish activities of 1931. By 1936 they had become vociferous
champions of a united front, demanding not merely a union
between feuding KMT cliques (as they had in 1931), but an
alliance with the Communists.

The Kuomintang seized power in 1927, and the history of
the subsequent decade reflects KMT failure rather than CCP
success. The ruling party's inability to mold a dynamic, loyal
peacetime youth movement paved the way for Communist victory. Indeed, many believed that the words "loyal" and "youth
movement" were contradictory; until 1938 Nanking based its
policies on the premise that such a movement was neither

necessary nor desirable. Student political action seemed incompatible with academic discipline. Schools were to be incubators no longer for fledgling revolutionaries but for technically skilled, politically indoctrinated citizens.

Circumstances rendered this plan unworkable. Until 1932, political chaos prevented administrative and financial stability. After 1937, the nation's carefully nurtured educational plant was uprooted by war. Officially interpreted Sun-Yat-senism was propagated haphazardly, and failed to provide a framework for ideological unity. It could not survive competition with attractively packaged Marxist doctrines.

Before he died, Sun Yat-sen said, "The revolution is not yet finished." But once in power, Chiang Kai-shek acted as though it were. He regarded himself as a unifier, not as an innovator. He was concerned with fiscal modernization, military consolidation, and the construction of telegraphs, roads, railroads, and airlines. Labor reform and land redistribution failed to interest him; class warfare offended his Confucian sensibilities. The New Life Movement, his single attempt at moral renovation, floundered because it answered neither the economic wants of the masses nor the ideological needs of the intellectuals. Even his triumphs were Pyrrhic victories. He lived to see his roads and railroads become highways for Japanese invasion, his finest university graduates become cadres for Communist armies, his industrial cities become traps for his modern military forces. The dream of national reconstruction of the 1930's turned into a nightmare of civil war in the following decade.

Chiang had scant faith in the power of mass movements. His authoritarian military education and his Confucian ideal of a harmonious social order determined his concept of ruler-subject relationships: the sovereign commanded, the masses obeyed. This imperial frame of mind also explains his obsession with national unity. "First pacify within, then resist without" was a rigid priority.

The students, too, wanted a unified China. They cheered Chiang's victories over the warlords and would probably have protested little against his campaigns to exterminate the "Red

Bandits" had it not been for the threat from abroad. But after September 18, 1931, while youth clamored for the immediate expulsion of the invader, Chiang undertook a long-range program of building a modern army to fight the foe after his enemies at home had been eliminated. Young China's inheritance of ninety years of appeasement and two decades of uninterrupted civil war made Chiang's sense of urgency seem inexcusably misdirected.

Out of these differences arose an unavoidable conflict. Students assumed their familiar role of indignant anti-imperialists, employing tried and tested techniques of mass protest; Chiang, the austere emperor figure, demanded that these self-styled counselors bend to his will. He told petitioners in 1931 that there were only two places for those who wanted to serve their country, a school or the army. He could no more tolerate young nationalists milling around in city streets than he could Communists swarming through country villages.

The youthful explosion set off by the Manchurian crisis destroyed a government policy that sought to disengage youth from politics through legislation, persuasion, and education. The failure of this approach raises the question of whether a more positive youth program could have succeeded. What if the KMT, following the path proposed by Ch'en Kuo-fu instead of that of Ts'ai Yüan-p'ei, had fostered a national student union to tap the young intelligentsia's revolutionary potential? The adoption of Ch'en's ambitious scheme might have retarded, but not halted, the process of disaffection. It is logical to assume that student political leaders, if given an active role under the Nanking government, would have been less receptive to subversive ideas; but a revolutionary program would have been needed to forestall the revolt of the educated elite. The heirs of the May Fourth Movement were radical, and were imbued with an evangelical urge to awaken China's masses. Only a government committed to class struggle, cultural upheaval, and militant anti-imperialism could have won them. Furthermore, even if Nanking had adopted these goals, it would have been forced to deal with intensified pressure for war and social revolution.

However, as the KMT government developed, with its Shanghai-Nanking base, it committed itself to urban modernization in alliance with the treaty-port middle classes, and relinquished rural control to conservative local powers: there was no place for a radical youth movement. Instead, the ruling party tried piecemeal measures. Efforts in the mid-1930's to enlist students in rural reform met with some success, but in aiming to prevent new Communist inroads in the recaptured soviet areas rather than to overhaul the old political and economic structure, they could marshal only limited interest. Military training was received more warmly because it answered the persistent student clamor for preparation to fight Japan. The zeal of Boy Scouts in the urban middle schools of the lower Yangtze proved that military regimentation had considerable appeal for Chinese adolescents. Given time, Chiang might have developed a sizable following of middle school youth.

College students, adopting the roles of scholar-remonstrators, defiant individualists, and revolutionary Marxists, were impetuous and intractable. Yet the same ones who resisted government regimentation were quite capable of regimenting themselves. On December 16, 1935, Peiping's students gave the lie to Chiang Kai-shek's charge that they were unorganized and undisciplined by staging the most highly organized, best disciplined demonstration in the city's history. Officials were baffled. Could these youngsters possibly fail to see the contradiction in demanding measures to resist Japan while rejecting KMT-appointed military instructors?

The explanation lies in a key word of the May Fourth period that remained very much in vogue—*new*. Students would follow only a government that they regarded as "progressive" and "revolutionary." Since the Nanking regime failed to meet these standards, anything it did appeared in an unfavorable light. While Communist discipline was welcomed as "mobilization for national salvation," KMT discipline was denounced as "fascist coercion."

Chiang was born too soon for an age of propaganda and public relations. He suffered from a twofold weakness: insensitivity to public opinion and hypersensitivity to criticism. When the National Salvation Movement became politically embarrassing, he charged its leading spokesmen with abetting the Communists and threw them into prison. That the patriotic momentum of this same movement catapulted him to a pinnacle of popularity after the Sian Incident was but a passing irony, for his prestige waned during the later war years while the Communists were building a solid foundation of mass sympathy. The war postponed the final reckoning and altered the balance of power. V-J Day found Mao Tse-tung in a position to rally support on a scale few would have dreamed possible in July 1937, while Chiang was forced to rely on a crumbling military-bureaucratic coalition incapable of sustaining him.

After the Communists' meteoric postwar ascent to power, it is easy to forget their earlier groping in the dark. Although the KMT lost student leadership by default, the CCP was slow to step into the breach. It too harbored doubts about the young intellectuals, although its skepticism came from a different source. The Kuomintang's was practical: party leaders correctly suspected youth of radicalism, which they believed could be controlled only by suppressing the student movement. Moreover, they appreciated the long-range benefits to be derived from a well-educated younger generation unencumbered by the burden of premature political responsibilities.

The CCP had both practical and theoretical reasons for its ambivalence toward the students. The party of the proletariat felt that it would be inconsistent to rely upon "petit bourgeois" youth, who could not be counted on to act according to "objective" economic conditions as a Marxist social class should have done. Young intellectuals were unpredictable, hence unreliable. Student desertion of CY after the 1927 split with Chiang Kai-shek confirmed these doubts, but political considerations dictated that this element be courted anyway; neither peasants nor workers had the learning and idealism to give direction to a revolution. Theoretical reservations were first dispelled by defining the students as a multi-class compound from which the useful proletarian element could be distilled, and later by the theory that even ingrained bourgeois attitudes could be made proletarian by thought reform. Thus, as students drifted farther and farther from the KMT, the CCP set aside doctrinal scruples to lure them into the fold.

Success came slowly. During the decade of what CCP annals call the "Second Revolutionary Civil War" (1927–37), the history of the party is a dismal record of reckless blunders, painful trial-and-error, and rapid decimation. Urban bases disappeared; soviet areas that had been developed and defended at great cost had to be abandoned. Captured leaders betrayed their comrades or faced firing squads. Contact between CY and its campus sympathizers was all but severed. When Mao urged Chiang to form a united front in 1936, Mao was a supplicant.

Yet the decade in the wilderness had not been spent in vain. The party had learned from its experience in urban schools and in rural villages. While guerrilla warfare had developed in the countryside, techniques for propaganda, mass meetings, and parades had been perfected in the cities. The skillful Peiping demonstration of December 12, 1936, was an enormous improvement over the crude riots that had occurred in Nanking five years before. The subtle art of manipulation that molded the postwar student movement into an efficient fifth column evolved during these critical years. This was accompanied by the emergence of a favorable public image for the CCP. KMT propagandists not only failed to convince the younger generation that the Communists were bandits, but had to labor to strip the CCP of its guise of revolutionary patriotism. Simultaneously, the KMT heard itself called "vacillator," "appeaser," and "reactionary." The distinction between ruler and rebel was thus blurred until the government became the suspected traitor and the Communists the vanguard of national salvation.

Throughout the war, Communist propaganda and Kuomintang corruption undermined the KMT's popularity. Students who had supported the government at the beginning of the war readily switched to the CCP when they saw the ruling party falter. By 1945, the "bandits" had become leading contenders for the loyalty of China's educated youth.

It is difficult to avoid fatalism concerning the outcome of KMT-CCP competition for hegemony over the radical young intelligentsia. Perhaps Chiang Kai-shek was doomed from the moment he broke with the Communists in April 1927. Possibly the predominance of conservatives in the KMT robbed the party of its revolutionary appeal. Perhaps modern Chinese youth have been psychologically driven to seek a "totalistic" ideological orientation that the party of Sun Yat-sen was unequipped to provide.[1] It is quite likely that no government faced with the succession of foreign and domestic crises that plagued the KMT from 1927 to 1949 could have acted to the satisfaction of revolutionary students.

The CCP was fortunate to be out of power during these years. Free to attack the government at its most vulnerable points, alert to the revolutionary potential of the students, and possessing sophisticated techniques for the exploitation of an educated minority, the Communists won the allegiance of an impatient generation.

Abbreviations and Notes

Abbreviations

The following abbreviations are used in the Notes and Bibliography. Publication data not included in the Abbreviations will be found in the Bibliography.

BI   Archives of the Bureau of Investigation, Ministry of Justice, Government of the Republic of China, Ch'ing-t'an, Taipei County, Taiwan.

CCWH   *Chuan-chi wen-hsüeh* (Biographical Literature). Taipei, June 1962–Aug. 1965.

CCYB   *China Christian Year Book.* Christian Literature Society, ed. Shanghai, 1927-37.

CD   Centre de Documentation Chinoise, Paris.

CF   *China Forum.* Shanghai, 1932–34. (HI, WL.)

CIR   *China Illustrated Review.* Tientsin, 1927–29.

CWC   *China Weekly Chronicle.* Peiping, 1935–37.

CWR   *China Weekly Review.* Shanghai, 1927–37.

CWYT   *Chiu-wang yün-tung pao-kao-shu* (Report on the Salvation Movement). Ch'ing-hua ta-hsüeh . . . , ed.

CYB   *China Year Book.* H.G.W. Woodhead, ed. Tientsin, 1927–31; Shanghai, 1932–36.

CYJP   *Chung-yang jih-pao* (Central Daily News). Shanghai, 1928; Nanking, 1929–37.

CYTC   *Chiao-yü tsa-chih* (The Chinese Educational Review). Shanghai, 1928–31; 1934–37.

CYTWYK   *Chung-yang tang-wu yüeh-k'an* (Central Party Affairs Monthly). ?Shanghai, 1928–37. (KMTA.)

EN   "Educational News" section of CYTC.

HI   Hoover Institution on War, Revolution, and Peace, Stanford University.

HY   Chinese-Japanese Library of the Harvard-Yenching Institute, Harvard University.

IECYT   *I-erh chiu yün-tung* (The December Ninth Movement). Jen-min ch'u-pan she, ed.

KMTA   Kuomintang Party Archives, Hsin-chuang, Ts'ao-tun, Nan-t'ou County, Taiwan.

KWCP   *Kuo-wen chou-pao* (Kuowen Weekly, Illustrated). Tientsin, 1927–36; Shanghai, 1936–37.

LNCN	*Lieh-ning ch'ing-nien* (Leninist Youth). ?Shanghai, 1928–33. (BI.)
MC	*Min-chung hsün-lien wei-yüan-hui kung-tso pao-kao* (Report on the Work of the Committee for Training the Masses). KMT-CEC, ed.
NCH	*North China Herald*. Shanghai, 1927–37.
NCS	*North China Star*. Tientsin, June 1935–June 1936.
NCSM	Nym Wales, *Notes on the Chinese Student Movement, 1935–1936*. See Snow, Helen F., in Bibliography.
NYPL	New York Public Library.
NYT	*New York Times.*
PHP-YG	*P'ing-hsi-pao—Yenching Gazette*. Yenching University, Sept. 10–Dec. 12, 1931. (HY.)
SC	Shih Chian (*shih-chien*) Library, Republic of China National War College, Yangmingshan, Taipei County, Taiwan.
SD	United States State Department Archives.
SECTK	*Shih-erh chiu t'e-k'an* (The December Ninth Special). Peiping, 1935–36. (HI.)
SSHP	*Shih-shih hsin-pao* (The China Times). Shanghai, 1929–36.
SW	*Shih-wei—fan-jih yün-tung yü pei-p'ing hsüeh-sheng* (Demonstration—the Anti-Japanese Movement and Peiping's Students). Pei-p'ing hsüeh-sheng k'ang-jih . . . , ed.
SWCK	*Pei-ching ta-hsüeh shih-wei yün-tung chuan-k'an* (Special Issue on the Peking University Demonstration Movement). Kuo-li pei-ching . . . , ed.
TB	Toyo Bunko, Tokyo.
TCSH	*Ta-chung sheng-huo* (Life of the Masses). Shanghai, Nov. 1935–Feb. 1936.
TFTC	*Tung-fang tsa-chih* (The Eastern Miscellany). Shanghai, 1927–37.
TKP	*Ta-kung pao* (L'Impartial). Tientsin, 1931–37.
TLPL	*Tu-li p'ing-lun* (The Independent Critic). Peiping, 1932–37.
WL	Widener Memorial Library, Harvard University.
WMTTW	*Wo-men ti tui-wu* (Our Ranks). CNLV, Tsung-tui-pu, ed.
VOC	*Voice of China*. Shanghai, 1936.
YMCAHL	Historical Library of the Young Men's Christian Association, New York, N.Y.

Full references, including translations of titles,
are provided in the first citations of all items
that are not listed separately in the Bibliography; see prefatory note to the Bibliography,
p. 231. Abbreviations are listed on pp. 197–98.

CHAPTER 1

1. For a brief summary of premodern student movements, see Chow,
pp. 11–12.
2. Lang, pp. 189–92, 287.
3. Chow, p. 358.
4. C. T. Hsia, pp. 101–2, 141.
5. Cheng, pp. 15, 29; C. Y. W. Meng, "Reconstruction Through Education," *CWR*, 74:8 (Oct. 26, 1935), 270–71.
6. Kiang Ying-cheng, pp. 178, 58.
7. Computations are based on Lang, pp. 273 and 88. For a discussion
of the urban middle and upper classes, see Lang, pp. 92–101.
8. The returned student may be treated as a separate problem. See
works by Wang and Brandt on aspects of this subject.
9. Wang Shih-chieh, "Education," in *The Chinese Year Book, 1935–36*,
p. 471.
10. Lang, p. 365.
11. Kiang Ying-cheng, p. 58.
12. Lifton, p. 469.

CHAPTER 2

1. *Jen-min t'uan-t'i fa-kuei hui-pien*, p. 344.
2. Yang Chia-ming, pp. 115–16.
3. Chapman, pp. 11–13. For warlord atrocities against students, see
Loh, pp. 237–38.
4. Finch, p. 143.
5. Kuo Jung-sheng, in answer to my questionnaire.
6. George Sokolsky, "The Kuomintang," in *CYB* 1928, p. 1348.
7. Isaacs, *Tragedy*, p. 112.
8. P'ing Hsin, "San-shih-nien lai ti ch'ing-nien yün-tung" (The Past
Thirty Years of the Youth Movement), *Hsüeh-sheng tsa-chih*, 21:1 (Jan.
1941), 30.
9. Chapman, p. 25.

10. Hu Ch'iu-yüan, *passim.*

11. "T'ang Chien t'ung-chih ti ssu" (The Death of Comrade T'ang Chien), *LNCN,* 1:2 (Nov. 1928), 49.

12. Y. T. Wu, "The Revolution and Student Thought," *CCYB* 1928, p. 225.

13. T. Z. Koo, Letter to friends, ?Shanghai, Dec. 30, 1927, in YMCAHL.

14. " 'Wu-ssu' chiu-chou chi-nien chih chung-yao hsüan-yen" (Important Proclamations in Commemoration of the Ninth Anniversary of May Fourth), *CYTC,* 20:6 (June 1928), EN 18.

15. Comrade Schüller, "Report on the Activity of the Young Communist International," *International Press Correspondence,* 8:42 (Aug. 1, 1928), 744.

16. Brandt, *Stalin's Failure,* pp. 47–49.

17. Rafail Moiseyarick Khitarov, "From the Second to the Fifth Congress of the Young Communists' International, 1921–1928" (Moscow-Leningrad, 1931); translated in SD 893.00B/881, Riga, Latvia, 1932. CY was further weakened by internal acrimony over the relationship between party and corps; see T'uan Chin, "Chung-kuo kung-ch'an chu-i ch'ing-nien-t'uan tsui-chin nei-pu ti fen-hua" (The Most Recent Internal Rift in the Chinese Communist Youth Corps), *Hsing-ch'i,* no. 2 (Apr. 22, 1928), pp. 25–28.

18. Khitarov, (*op. cit,* note 17).

19. *Komsomolskaya Pravda,* no. 214 (Sept. 18, 1928), quoted in SD 861.00, Riga, Latvia, 1928.

20. Pao, *Chung-kuo kung-ch'an-tang . . . ,* p. 18.

21. CY-CEC, ed., *Chung-kung. . . .*

22. Chu Meng-shih, "T'an chung-hsüeh-sheng yü she-hui yün-tung" (A Discussion of Middle School Students and Social Movements), *I-pan,* 2:3 (Mar. 1927), 341; P'an Shih-hsüan, "Tui-yü hsüeh-sheng ju tang chih i-nan" (Doubts about Students Entering the Party), in Wang Chien-hsing, p. 7.

23. Ts'ai Yüan-p'ei, "Tu-shu yü chiu-kuo" (Study and National Salvation), *Chih-nan chou-k'an,* no. 2 (Mar. 12, 1927), pp. 6–8.

24. From my interview (Kowloon, Aug. 1959) with Hu Chia-t'ing, former principal of the Fourth Anhwei Middle School in Paocheng.

25. Letter written by T. Z. Koo, ?Shanghai, Oct. 19, 1927, in YMCAHL. Also see Chester S. Miao and Frank W. Price, "Religion and Character in Christian Middle Schools," *Educational Review,* 21:4 (Oct. 1929), 384–85.

26. Eugene E. Barnett, "Progress and Problems in Nationalist China: General Observations on Situation in Cities in Yangtse Valley, October–November, 1928," Shanghai, 1928, in YMCAHL. A teacher at one Christian school told Barnett that 80 per cent of the students were infected by "Bolshevik" ideas. Such a high estimate must be regarded with skepticism.

27. *CWR,* 40:11 (May 14, 1927), 304.

28. For examples, see *CYJP,* Aug. 28 and Sept. 16, 1928.

29. Y. T. Wu, "Movements among Chinese Students," *CCYB* 1931, p. 261.

30. Wu Jung-chih, pp. 163, 170–72.

31. *CYJP*, Feb. 24, 26, 1928.

32. H. C. Tsao, "The Nationalist Movement and Christian Education," *CCYB* 1928, p. 184.

33. Allen B. Linden, "The Promising Years, 1924–1928," draft chapter in a forthcoming Columbia University Ph.D. thesis on politics and education in prewar China, pp. 89–90 and *passim*. Also see *MC*, Preface, p. 1; and KMT, Chung-yang hsüan-ch'uan pu, pp. 7–10.

34. *CYJP*, Apr. 20, 22, 28, 1928.

35. *CYJP*, May 7, 1928.

36. *NCH*, Apr. 28, 1928.

37. See above, p. 16.

38. *CYJP*, May 11, 1928.

39. *CIR*, June 2, 1928.

40. *CYJP*, May 5, 1928.

41. *CYJP*, May 9, 1928.

42. *CYJP*, June 6, 1928.

43. *CYJP*, May 9, 1928.

44. *CYJP*, May 24, 1928.

45. "Jih-pen pao-hsing fa-sheng hou chih ch'üan-kuo chiao-yü chieh" (The National Educational World since the Outbreak of Japanese Barbarism), *CYTC*, 20:6 (June 1928), EN 14–15; *CYJP*, May 6, 1928.

46. *CIR*, May 12, 1928.

47. *CIR*, June 2, 1928.

48. *NCH*, June 2, 1928. Italics mine.

49. Kawai, pp. 144ff.

50. For examples of the student demands, see *CYJP*, May 8, 11, 12, 1928.

51. See *CYJP* May 8, 11, 12, and June 10, 1928.

52. SD 893.00 PR Shanghai/7, July 13, 1928.

53. "Jih-pen pao-hsing ...," p. 15 (*op. cit.*, note 45).

54. KMT, Ho-pei-sheng ..., p. 114.

55. Shih Ts'un-t'ung, "Chung-kuo ko-ming yü hsüeh-sheng yün-tung" (The Chinese Revolution and the Student Movement), *Ko-ming p'ing-lun*, no. 18, p. 10.

56. *CYJP*, May 19, 1928. See also Kennedy, pp. 179–80.

57. *MC*, p. 3; *MC* Preface, p. 2.

58. Wang Tao-yü et al., pp. 76–78.

59. Linden, p. 52 (*op. cit.*, note 33).

60. Chung-hua min-kuo ta-hsüeh-yüan, Sec. D, p. 2.

61. *Ibid.*, Sec. A, pp. 71–72.

62. Hu Han-min, "Ko-ming yü ch'iu-hsüeh" (Revolution and Seeking Learning), *Chung-yang pan-yüeh-k'an*, 2:2 (Oct. 15, 1928), 4–11.

63. Tai Chi-t'ao, pp. 10–11.

64. KMT-CEC, "Min-chung hsün-lien chi-hua ta-kang" (Outline of Plans for Training the Masses), *CYTWYK,* no. 1 (Aug. 1928).

65. KMT-CEC, "Min-chung hsün-lien chi-hua ta-kang (hsiu-cheng an)" (Outline of Plans for Training the Masses [Revised Version]), *CYTWYK,* no. 2 (Sept. 1928).

66. The involved history of these proposals is summarized in "Yang Hsing-fo t'an ch'ing-nien yün-tung" (Yang Hsing-fo Discusses the Youth Movement), *CYJP,* Aug. 5, 1928. The National Academy's outline is printed in KMT, Chung-yang mi-shu ch'u, pp. 145–50; the Kwangtung-Kwangsi plan follows on pp. 150–52. Other pertinent documents in this volume are the Fourth Plenum's resolution on education, pp. 144–45, and the National Educational Conference's proposed "Resolutions for Student Self-Governing Associations," pp. 152–54.

67. Linden, pp. 78–84 (*op. cit.,* note 33).

68. KMT Chung-yang mi-shu ch'u . . . , p. 143; Sun, p. 141.

69. KMT Chung-yang mi-shu ch'u . . . , p. 143; Sun, p. 142.

70. "Ch'ü-hsiao ch'ing-nien yün-tung chih lun-cheng" (The Argument over Abolishing the Youth Movement), *CYTC,* 20:9 (Sept. 1928), EN pp. 5–6.

71. *CYJP,* May 5, 1928.

72. "Ch'ü-hsiao . . . ," p. 6 (*op. cit.,* note 70).

73. *MC,* p. 4.

74. *CYJP,* July 27, 1928.

75. *CYJP,* Mar. 13, 1928.

76. *CYJP,* May 28, 1928.

77. "Ch'ü-hsiao . . . ," p. 6 (*op. cit.,* note 70).

78. *NCH,* Aug. 4, 1928; *CYJP,* July 20, 1928.

79. *CYJP,* Aug. 30, 1928.

80. Y. T. Wu, "Movements . . . ," p. 261 (*op. cit.,* note 29).

81. *CYJP,* Sept. 4, 1928.

82. *CYJP,* Sept. 6, 1928.

83. *CIR,* Apr. 20, 1929; *CYJP,* Aug. 9, 1929.

84. See telegrams from Chiang Monlin and Ts'ai Yüan-p'ei to the Peita students in *Chiao-yü pu kung-pao,* 1:1 (Jan. 1929), 118. See also Li Shu-hua, pp. 38, 109–10.

85. *CYJP,* Apr. 23, July 9, 1928.

86. D. Willard Lyon, "Education and Religion," *CCYB* 1929, p. 282; Corbett, pp. 172–75; Scott, p. 46.

87. See *CIR,* Dec. 12, 1928, Jan. 5, 1929; and "Shou-tu hsüeh-sheng chih ai-kuo yün-tung—fan-jih ta shih-wei" (The Patriotic Movement of Students in the Capital—the Great Anti-Japanese Demonstration), *CYTC,* 21:1 (Jan. 1929), 177; *CYJP,* Feb. 16, 20, 26, 28, Mar. 2, 3, 28, 1929; and *LNCN,* 1:7 (Dec. 25, 1928), 30–33.

88. *Chiao-yü pu kung-pao,* 1:3 (Mar. 1929), 57–58; *CIR,* Feb. 23, 1929.

89. SD 893.00 PR, Shanghai/14, Apr. 10, 1929.

90. See *CIR*, May 18, 1929, and "Shang-hai san-hsiao chih ch'a-feng—ta-lu, hua-nan, chien-hua" (The Official Shutdown of Three Shanghai Schools—Ta-lu, Hua-nan, and Chien-hua), *CYTC*, 21:6 (June 1929), 175–76.

91. "Order of the National Government Regarding Discipline of Students," *Educational Review*, 21:2 (Apr. 1929), 197.

92. KMT, Tang-shih-liao, Sec. E, p. 54.

93. "Chung-kuo kuo-min-tang chung-yang chih-hsing wei-yüan-hui hsün-mien ch'üan-kuo hsüeh-sheng t'ung-tien" (Circular Telegram from the KMT CEC to Guide and Exhort the Nation's Students), *CYTWYK*, 2:9 (Apr. 1929).

94. SD 893.00 PR, Shanghai 1/14, Apr. 10, 1929.

95. "Shang-hai hsüeh-sheng yün-tung chih wei-sheng" (The Last Sound from the Shanghai Student Movement), *CYTC*, 21:6 (June 1929), 176.

96. *Ibid.*, and "Shang-hai hsüeh-sheng yün-tung ti fen-jao" (Chaos in the Shanghai Student Movement), *CYTC*, 21:7 (July 1929), 119; *CIR*, May 18, 1929.

97. See "Chung-kuo kuo-min-tang chung-yang chih-hsing wei-yüan-hui tsu-chih hsi-t'ung t'u" (Diagram of the Organizational Structure of the KMT CEC), *CYTWYK*, 2:10 (May 1929); "Chung-yang hsün-lien pu ch'i-yüeh-fen kung-tso pao-kao" (Work Report of the Central Training Ministry for July), *CYTWYK*, 2:13 (Aug. 1929); and *MC*, p. 24.

98. *Ti-san-chieh san-chung ch'üan-hui....*

99. "Principles of Organization for Student Groups" and "Outline of Organization for Student Self-Governing Associations," in KMT-CEC Hsüan-ch'üan pu, pp. 118–24.

100. *Ibid.*, pp. 132–36.

101. *CYTWYK*, no. 28 (Nov. 1930), pp. 170–71; *CYTWYK*, no. 30 (Jan. 1931), p. 7; KMT, Tang-shih-liao, Sec. E., pp. 67–68.

102. A guarantor system had been widespread in 1927–28; see above, p. 16.

103. *CYTWYK*, no. 22 (May 1930), p. 107.

104. *CYTWYK*, no. 23 (June 1930); no. 24 (July 1930).

105. *CYJP*, Apr. 26, 1931.

106. *CYJP*, June 12, 1931.

107. *CYJP*, Apr. 15, May 4, 1930.

108. Daniel C. Fu, director, "The 1930 Special Study of the Young Men's Christian Association of China" (Shanghai, 1930), III, 64, in YMCAHL. See also Miao and Price, pp. 424–25 (*op. cit.*, note 25).

109. *Survey of International Affairs, 1929*, p. 299.

110. *Ibid.*

111. *Survey of International Affairs, 1930*, p. 334.

112. *Ibid.*

113. *Ibid.*, p. 333.

114. Eugene E. Barnett, "Conference with Mr. Gerald W. Birks" (Dec. 22, 1930), in YMCAHL. See also *CYJP*, Feb. 3, 1931, and Ko Cheng-tung,

"Shih-chieh hsüeh-ch'ao p'eng-p'ao chih shih-i yüeh" (The Worldwide Roar of Student Tides in November), *Chung-kuo hsüeh-sheng,* 2:11 (Nov. 1930), 2–3.

115. Fu, "The 1930 Special Study . . . ," III, 23 (*op. cit.,* note 108).

116. Fu, "The 1930 Special Study . . . ," III, 33; Timothy Tingfang Lew, "Readjustments of Christian Educational Work in China to Day [sic] in View of the Changing Social and Intellectual Conditions," *The Chinese Recorder,* 61:8 (Aug. 1930), 488; Y. T. Wu, "Movements . . . ," pp. 264ff (*op. cit.,* note 29).

117. Fu, "The 1930 Special Study . . . ," III, 21 (*op. cit.,* note 108).

118. Li Li-san, "The New Revolutionary Rising Tide and Preliminary Successes in One or More Provinces" (June 1930), in Brandt, Schwartz, and Fairbank, p. 199.

119. Y. T. Wu, "Movements . . . ," p. 264 (*op. cit.,* note 29); T. Z. Koo, Letter to a friend, ?Shanghai, Nov. 30, 1929, in YMCAHL.

120. Lew, "Readjustments . . . ," p. 489 (*op. cit.,* note 116).

121. W. E. Wilkinson, "Christian Students," *The Chinese Recorder,* 61:8 (Aug. 1930), 490.

122. Fu, "The 1930 Special Study . . . ," III, 22 (*op. cit.,* note 108). In another study, students asked to rate the value of different professions to society ranked "official" next to last, just below "soldier," and superior only to "pastor." See Lennig Sweet, "Student Research," *Educational Review,* 23:1 (Jan. 1931), 35.

123. *CYJP,* Feb. 25, 1931.

124. See *SSHP,* Nov. 29, 1930, and *CYJP,* Feb. 25, 1931, for the situation at National Central University; *CYJP,* Dec. 19, 25, 26, 30, 1930, *SSHP,* Dec. 20, 1930, and SD 893.00 PR Canton/37, Feb. 10, 1931, for Sun Yat-sen University; and *CYJP,* Mar. 14, June 3, 1931, and June 8, 1931, and Lo Chia-lun, *Tsui-chin . . . ,* for Tsinghua.

125. Wang Ching-wei, "Ch'ing-nien yün-tung ti ts'o-wu," (The Mistakes of the Youth Movement), in KMT T'ien-chin . . . , p. 27. See also Wang Tao-yü et al., p. 33.

126. For examples, see Y. T. Wu, "Movements . . . ," pp. 262–63 (*op. cit.,* note 29); Shrader, pp. 199–200; Barnett, "Conference . . . ," (*op. cit.,* note 114); and Fu, "The 1930 Special Study . . . ," III, 28 (*op. cit.,* note 108).

127. T. A. Hsia, pp. 70–76.

128. *Hung-ch'i jih-pao,* Oct. 14, 18, 20, 1930; Chung-kung chiang-nan sheng-wei (CCP Southern Kiangsu Provincial Committee), ed., "Chia-chin hsiao-nei huo-tung cheng-ch'ü ko-ming hsüeh-sheng ch'ün-chung ts'an-chia kung-nung min-chu ko-ming" (Intensify School Intramural Activities to Get the Revolutionary Student Masses to Participate in the Workers' and Peasants' Democratic Revolution) (?Shanghai, 1930), in BI.

129. "The Chinese Communist Party and Its Activities in Shanghai," and "The Shanghai Youths Anti-Imperialistic League of the Chinese Communist Party" (Shanghai, 1929), Jay Calvin Huston Collection in HI.

130. See Ch'en Pu-lei, *Hui-i-lu,* pp. 23–24.

131. CY Kiang-su sheng-wei-hui (CY Kiangsu Provincial Committee), ed., "Chin-chi t'ung-chih—kuan-yü pi-mi kung-tso" (Emergency Communiqué—Regarding Secret Work) (?Shanghai, Jan. 5, ?1931), in BI.

132. Sung Yen, "Jan-shao ti hsin" (Heart Aflame), *Hung-ch'i p'iao-p'iao,* II, 139; reprinted in *Kung-ch'ing-t'uan . . . ,* p. 232.

133. For reports on the situation in Szechwan's educational institutions, see "Hsüeh-hsiao tang-yü chih man-yen" (The Spread of School Party-prisons), *CYTC,* 22:9 (Sept. 1930), 119–20; *CYJP,* Aug. 22, 1930, Dec. 13, 1930, Jan. 30, 1931; and L. S. Tao, "The White Terror in China," *International Press Correspondence,* 11:50 (Sept. 24, 1931), 914.

134. *TKP,* Dec. 12, 1930.

135. Chung-kung chiang-nan sheng-wei, "Chia-chin . . ." (*op. cit.,* note 128).

136. *Ibid.*

137. *Ibid.* On the "united front from below," see Colm, *passim,* Van Slyke, pp. 44–54.

138. Sung Yen, "Jan-shao ti hsin," *passim* (*op. cit.,* note 132).

139. *Ibid.*

140. "Ho-chi kung-ch'ao chung chih shou-tu hsüeh-sheng shih-wei yün-tung" (The Student Demonstration Movement in the Capital in Connection with the Ho-chi Labor Trouble), *CYTC,* 22:4 (Apr. 1930), 121–22. The Communists took credit for having led this outburst. See *LNCN,* 2:11 (Apr. 10, 1930), 2.

141. *Chinese Affairs,* no. 108–9 (Dec. 15, 1930), pp. 4–5; "Hsün-cheng shih-ch'i chih ch'üan-kuo hsüeh-feng wen-t'i" (The Problem of the Nationwide School Environment During the Tutelage Period), *CYTC,* 23:1 (Jan. 1931), 175.

142. *Chinese Affairs,* no. 108–9 (Dec. 15, 1930), pp. 1–4; "Hsün-cheng shih-ch'i . . . ," pp. 175–76 (*op. cit.,* note 141); Berkov, p. 128. For other government pronouncements on the same subject, see *CYJP,* Apr. 29, Dec. 30, 1930.

143. Morin, pp. 134–35.

144. Gourlay, p. 129.

CHAPTER 3

1. *SSHP, CYJP,* Sept. 22–Sept. 25, 1931, *passim.*

2. *SSHP, CYJP,* Sept. 22–Sept. 25, 1931, *passim.*

3. *PHP-YG,* Sept. 22, 1931.

4. *PHP-YG,* Oct. 4, 1931.

5. *PHP-YG,* Sept. 22, 1931.

6. W. W. Lockwood, Letter to New York YMCA Office, Shanghai, Oct. 8, 1931, in YMCAHL.

7. Kawai, p. 148.

8. *SSHP,* Sept. 25, 1931; "Hsüeh-sheng ai-kuo yün-tung chih fang-chen chi tsu-chih" (The Aim and Organization of the Student Patriotic Move-

ment), *CYTC*, 22:11 (Nov. 1931), 111–13; and *CYTWYK*, no. 38 (Sept. 1931), pp. 1046–48. For examples of local authorities carrying out these orders, see Kawai, pp. 167–68.

9. Kawai, pp. 166–67.

10. *CYTWYK*, no. 38 (Sept. 1931), pp. 1046–48.

11. *CYJP*, Sept. 23, 1931; *SSHP*, Sept. 25, 1931.

12. *SSHP*, Nov. 26, 1931.

13. See "Pao-jih jou-lin-hsia chih tung-pei liang ta-hsüeh" (Two Northeast Schools under the Heel of a Cruel Japan), *CYTC*, 21:11 (Nov. 1931), 113–14.

14. Yü Meng-yen (Nancy Yü-Huang) in an interview with me, Taipei, Mar., 1960. Formerly a pupil at Nankai Girls' Middle School, Mrs. Huang is now the publisher of the Taipei English-language daily, *The China Post*.

15. Wei Ch'ing, "Pei-p'ing hsüeh-sheng fan-jih yün-tung ti kuo-ch'ü ho hsien-tsai" (The Past and Present of the Peiping Students' Anti-Japanese Movement), *SW*, pp. 45–46.

16. Though left-wing leaders found the International Settlement and the French Concession of Shanghai safer than Peiping, the universities of Shanghai did not have the prestige of Peita, Tsinghua, and Yenching; see Grieder, pp. 308–9. Isolation from the party hierarchy may have made Peiping's Communist students more self-reliant, hence more adaptable to changing circumstances.

17. *PHP-YG*, Sept. 29, 1931.

18. Wei Ch'ing, "Pei-p'ing hsüeh-sheng . . . ," p. 48 (*op. cit.*, note 15).

19. *Ibid.*, pp. 48–49.

20. "Pei-ching ta-hsüeh nan-hsia shih-wei-t'uan tai-piao-t'uan pao-kao" (Report of the Representative Committee of the Peking University Southbound Demonstration Corps), *SWCK*, pp. 15–16.

21. *CWR*, 58:5 (Oct. 3, 1931), 178; *SSHP*, Sept. 29, 1931; *NYT*, Sept. 28, 1931.

22. Yü Chi-chung, interview with me, Taipei, Nov. 15, 1961. Mr. Yü is now the publisher of the newspaper *Cheng-hsin hsin-wen* in Taipei.

23. *Ibid.*; and *CWR*, 58:5 (Oct. 3, 1931), 178; *SSHP*, Sept. 29, 1931; *NYT*, Sept. 28, 1931; and Li Shu-hua, p. 45.

24. *NYT*, Sept. 28, 1931.

25. Yü Chi-chung, interview (*cit.*, note 22).

26. *SSHP*, Sept. 29, 1931; *Shen Pao*, Sept. 29, 1931; *NYT*, Sept. 30, 1931.

27. *CYJP*, Oct. 8, 1931.

28. *CYJP*, Oct. 2, 3, 8, 1931.

29. *CYJP*, Oct. 14, 1931.

30. Wu Yu-i, "Fu-ching ch'ing-yüan ti ching-kuo" (The Experience of Going to the Capital to Petition), *Sheng-huo*, 6:43 (Oct. 10, 1931), 962.

31. *Ibid.*

32. *CYJP*, Oct. 19, 1931; *PHP-YG*, Oct. 20, 1931.

33. *PHP-YG,* Oct. 1, 1931.

34. C. Y. W. Meng, "Nanking Orders All Students to Undergo Rigid Military Training," *CWR,* 69:6 (July 7, 1934), 226–29; *KMT, Tang-shih-liao,* Sec. E, pp. 59–60; *CYTWYK,* no. 38 (Sept. 1931), p. 1046–48; Pao Tsun-p'eng, *Chung-kuo ch'ing-nien* ..., pp. 133–34; *SSHP,* Oct. 9, 1931; *PHP-YG,* Oct. 8, 1931. The debate over the proper role of the student-citizen crystallized about the time of the Fifth Plenum of the KMT's Second CEC in August 1928.

35. *NYT,* Oct. 1, 1931; *PHP-YG,* Oct. 1, 1931.

36. Hua Chen-chung and Chu Po-kang, p. 373.

37. *CYJP,* Oct. 1, 1931.

38. Meng, "Nanking Orders ...," p. 226 (*op. cit.,* note 34); *NYT,* Oct. 1, 1931; *The Shanghai Evening Post and Mercury,* Oct. 9, 1931; *CYJP,* Oct. 20, 1931.

39. *NYT,* Oct. 1, 1931.

40. Wu Yu-i, "Fu-ching ch'ing-yüan ...," p. 964 (*op. cit.,* note 30).

41. *PHP-YG,* Oct. 13, 1931.

42. *PHP-YG,* Oct. 25, 1931.

43. *CYJP,* Oct. 20, 1931; *SSHP,* Oct. 10, 1931.

44. Unidentified clipping from an English-language newspaper dated "Wusih, Dec. 2, 1931," in Wales Collection at HI.

45. *CYJP,* Oct. 21, 1931.

46. SD 893.00/11753, Nanking, Dec. 24, 1931.

47. See Remer, pp. 160ff.

48. W. W. Lockwood, Letter to New York YMCA Office, Shanghai, Oct. 12, 1931, in YMCAHL.

49. Personal interview (Taipei, Nov. 1961) with Yang Pi-li, formerly a student at Provincial Wusih University, now a government functionary in Taipei. Also see Remer, pp. 163, 170–71.

50. "Kuo-nei-wai chiao-yü chieh chih k'ang-jih chiu-kuo yün-tung" (The Resist Japan National Salvation Movement Inside and Outside the Country), *CYTC,* 23:11 (Nov. 1931), 110–11; *TFTC,* 28:23 (Dec. 10, 1931), 111; *CYJP,* Oct. 11, 1931.

51. SD 893.00 PR Shanghai/41, Nov. 10, 1931.

52. Remer, p. 155.

53. *CYJP,* Oct. 7, 1931.

54. *CYJP, SSHP,* Oct. 7–Nov. 10, 1931, *passim.*

55. *SSHP,* Nov. 8–11, 1931, and personal interview with Feng Yung, Feb. 1961, near Taipei. Feng said that his small private institution (registration approximately 300) had been the first in the northeast to carry out student military training. The day after the Mukden Incident, he was arrested by the Japanese, but escaped and organized his Youth Corps.

56. *SSHP,* Nov. 16, 1931.

57. *SSHP,* Nov. 21, 1931.

58. *SSHP,* Nov. 22, 1931; SD 893.00 PR Shanghai /42, Dec. 8, 1931.

59. *SSHP,* Nov. 21, 1931, says that plans for a second petitioning were discussed at an emergency assembly of the University Students' RJNSA, but Shen Yün-lung stated in a personal interview (Taipei, Sept. 15, 1961) that the second petition movement was not under the auspices of the regular Student Union, which many students considered too subservient to the KMT. Names of the second petitioning's leaders, Chou Hsiao-po, Shen Yün-lung, and Yü Kang, appeared in the press for the first time at the end of November. This fact supports Shen's version. Mr. Shen was, and still is, a member of the Young China Party. He is now with the Institute of Modern History of the Academia Sinica in Taiwan.

60. According to Shen Yün-lung, Chou had no evident political connections at the time of the movement, but was appointed an adviser to the Executive Yüan upon graduation from college. After the Sian Incident of December 1936 was settled, H. H. Kung sent him to Sian as a liaison agent. Following the outbreak of the Sino-Japanese War, Wang Ching-wei's followers found him in Shanghai, destitute from gambling losses. At the war's end, he still had friends in Chungking to testify that he had joined Wang's government for espionage purposes, and he was never punished. However, Chou Hsiao-po's political opportunism finally led to his downfall. In 1949, while in Canton, seeing that a Red victory was imminent, he made contact with the Communists. He was caught by the Nationalists and summarily executed.

61. *SSHP,* Nov. 25, 1931.

62. *Ibid.*

63. *SSHP,* Nov. 27, 1931, and personal interview with Shen Yün-lung, Feb. 5, 1960 (*cit.,* note 59).

64. Personal interview (Taipei, Nov. 1961) with Fang Chih, who was then an official in the Ministry of Propaganda, and is now Secretary-General of the Free China Relief Association.

65. See Ch'en Pu-lei, *Hui-i-lu,* p. 27.

66. Interview with Yang Pi-li, one of the Wusih petitioners (*cit.,* note 49).

67. *SSHP,* Nov. 29, 1931; Wen Chi-tzu, "Chiu-i-pa shih-tai shang-hai hsüeh-sheng k'ang-jih yün-tung ti p'ien-tuan hui-i" (Fragmentary Recollections of the Shanghai Students' Resist Japan Movement of the September Eighteenth Period), *Hung-ch'i p'iao-p'iao,* VI, 34; reprinted in *Kung-ch'ing-t'uan . . . ,* p. 207. Wen states that the grounds and the auditorium of the Military Academy were covered by machine guns during Chiang's speech and that the students were sent back to Shanghai by armed police, but other sources provide no corroboration.

68. Personal interview (Hong Kong, Aug. 1959) with Huang Chung-fu (Jack Huang), one of the Tsinghua contingent. Mr. Huang is now an employee of Pan-American Airways.

69. The above description is based upon *SSHP* and *Shen Pao,* Nov. 28, 1931; C. Y. W. Meng, "Chinese Demand War with Japan," *CWR,* 59:1

(Dec. 5, 1931), 12–14; and interviews with Shen Yün-lung (Feb. 5, 1960, Sept. 15, 1961). Chiang's handwritten message to the students is reproduced in *CYJP,* Nov. 29, 1931, and is also quoted in full in *Shen Pao,* Nov. 28, 1931. A translation appears in *CWR,* 51:1 (Dec. 5, 1931), 12, but the one on p. 63 is my own. The *CYJP* version is a single page in size and contains 103 ideographs, although Shen says that Chiang took half an hour to compose his answer, which was four pages long. Some sources, including Shen, claim that Chiang made a definite commitment to go north to fight the Japanese; all agree that he advised the students to return to their books. For a Kuomintang version of the encounter, see Tong, II, 334–35. For a Communist account, see Wen Chi-tzu, "Chiu-i-pa shih-tai . . . ," pp. 35–36 (*op. cit.,* note 67).

70. Wen Chi-tzu, "Chiu-i-pa shih-tai . . . ," p. 34 (*op. cit.,* note 67).

71. *SSHP,* Nov. 26, 1931.

72. *SSHP,* Nov. 27, 1931; Dec. 4, 1931.

73. *PHP-YG,* Oct. 18, 1931.

74. *Ibid.*

75. Eugene E. Barnett, Letters to Dr. Mott and Col. Birks, Shanghai, Oct. 3, 1931, in YMCAHL.

76. O. R. Magill, Letter to friends, Shanghai, Mar. 18, 1932, in YMCAHL.

77. *CYJP,* Dec. 1, 2, 3, 1931.

78. Telegram of Dec. 3, 1931, reported in *CYJP,* Dec. 4, 1931.

79. *PHP-YG,* Oct. 10, 1931.

80. Wei Ch'ing, "Pei-p'ing . . . ," pp. 52–54 (*op. cit.,* note 15); *PHP-YG,* Nov. 12, 1931.

81. *SSHP,* Nov. 26, 1931; *Pei-p'ing ch'en-pao,* Nov. 27, 1931.

82. "Pei-ching ta-hsüeh . . . pao-kao," p. 16 (*op. cit.,* note 20).

83. *Ibid.*

84. "Pei-ching ta-hsüeh shih-wei yün-tung ti i-i chi ch'i ch'ien-t'u" (The Meaning of the Peking University Demonstration Movement and Its Future), *SWCK,* p. 11.

85. "Pei-ching ta-hsüeh . . . pao-kao," pp. 16–17 (*op. cit.,* note 80).

86. *Ibid.,* p. 18.

87. "Pei-ching ta-hsüeh . . . pao-kao," pp. 18–19 (*op. cit.,* note 20); *CYJP,* Dec. 9, 1931.

88. *CYJP,* Dec. 4, 1931.

89. "Pei-ching ta-hsüeh . . . pao-kao," p. 20 (*op. cit.,* note 20).

90. *Ibid.,* pp. 21–22.

91. *Ibid.,* pp. 22–25.

92. *Ibid.,* pp. 26–27.

93. *CYJP,* Dec. 6, 1931; *Pei-p'ing ch'en-pao,* Dec. 6, 1931; *NYT,* Dec. 6, 1931.

94. "Pei-ching ta-hsüeh . . . pao-kao," pp. 29–30 (*op. cit.,* note 20).

95. *NYT,* Dec. 8, 1931.

96. *CYJP,* Dec. 6, 1931.

97. SD 893.00/11753, Nanking, Dec. 24, 1931.

98. *CYJP,* Dec. 8, 1931.

99. *I-shih pao,* Dec. 8, 1931.

100. *Foreign Relations of the United States, 1931,* III, 686.

101. *CYJP,* Dec. 9, 10, 1931; Tong, II, 335.

102. My reconstruction of the Peita student's entrance is based upon "Pei-ching ta-hsüeh . . . pao-kao," pp. 49–50 (*op. cit.,* note 20).

103. *Ibid.*

104. *Ibid.,* pp. 50–51; Shih Fan, "Tz'u-tz'u hsüeh-sheng ch'ün-chung wei-k'un shih-cheng-fu hsing-tung chih i-i" (The Significance of This Action of the Student Masses Surrounding the City Government), *Hung-ch'i chou-pao,* no. 27 (Dec. 17, 1931), p. 28.

105. For details of the Shanghai drama, see Pei-ching ta-hsüeh . . . pao-kao, pp. 50–53 (*op. cit.,* note 20); Shih Fan, "Tz'u tz'u . . . ," pp. 28–30 (*op. cit.,* note 104); *SSHP,* Dec. 11, 1931; and *NYT,* Dec. 10, 11, 1931.

106. See *CYJP,* Dec. 8, 1931.

107. Ch'ing I, "Pei-p'ing hsüeh-sheng ti nan-hsia shih-wei yün-tung" (The Peiping Students' Southbound Demonstration Movement), *SW,* pp. 6–13; Ch'ien Tan, "Pei-p'ing shih-wei ti i-mu" (One Act in the Peiping Demonstration), *SW,* pp. 39–40; *Pei-p'ing ch'en-pao* and *TKP,* Dec. 5–8, 1931, *passim.* Ch'ing I says that the train departed at 7 A.M.; *NYT* reports noon.

108. Ch'en Chi, "Kung-ch'ing-t'uan-yüan chan-tou tsai nan-ching" (CY Members Do Battle in Nanking), *Hung-ch'i p'iao-p'iao,* II, 151.

109. *CYJP,* Dec. 12, 1931.

110. O. R. Magill, Letter to friends, Shanghai, Mar. 18, 1931, in YMCAHL.

111. "Pei-ching ta-hsüeh . . . pao-kao," p. 54 (*op. cit.,* note 20).

112. Ch'ing I, "Pei-p'ing hsüeh-sheng . . . ," pp. 16–17 (*op. cit.,* note 107).

113. *CYJP,* Dec. 13, 1931.

114. Ch'ing I, "Pei-p'ing hsüeh-sheng . . . ," pp. 17–18 (*op. cit.,* note 107); *CYJP,* Dec. 15, 1931.

115. Ch'ing I, "Pei-p'ing hsüeh-sheng . . . ," p. 18 (*op. cit.,* note 107); *CYJP,* Dec. 16, 17, 1931; *North China Daily News,* Dec. 17, 1931, clipping in Wales Collection in HI.

116. Li Shu-hua, pp. 45–46; Ch'en Pu-lei, p. 27.

117. SD 893.00/11753, Nanking, Dec. 24, 1931; Kao Yin-tsu, p. 362.

118. *CYTWYK,* no. 41 (Dec. 1931), p. 2675.

119. *CYJP,* Dec. 16, 1935.

120. *I-shih pao,* Dec. 16, 1931.

121. Sources differ widely on the details of the incident, in particular concerning the Communist flag episode. Fang Chih told me that he per-

sonally pulled the incriminating banner from the pocket of a naïve girl student who was unwittingly serving the Communists. The suspicious credit line on the *CYJP* photograph, "Art Section of the Central Propaganda Ministry," may or may not merely reflect the Ministry's share in capturing and photographing the flag. Student indignation at the alleged forgery was largely responsible for the sack of the *CYJP* offices two days later.

According to left-wing students, the demonstrators kidnapped Ts'ai and Ch'en only when attacked by "gangsters," who rushed out at them from Party Headquarters, armed with clubs and knives. In the *I-shih pao* story, the students were reportedly the ones who used clubs and guns, and the two men were rescued by "officials and police," who fired blank cartridges only. Interviewed by an *I-shih pao* reporter, Ts'ai made no mention of student arms; see *I-shih pao*, Dec. 16, 1931. The best pro-student account of the incident is by Ch'ing I (*op. cit.*, note 107); another good one is by Ch'en Chi (*op. cit.*, note 108). Versions sympathetic to the government are found in *CYJP* and *I-shih pao*, Dec. 16, 1931. Also see *NYT*, Dec. 16, 1931; *Foreign Relations of the United States, 1931*, III, 684–86; SD 893.00/11753, Nanking, Dec. 24, 1931; Berkov, p. 140; and Li Shu-hua, p. 46.

122. SD 893.00/11753, Nanking, Dec. 24, 1931; *CYJP*, Dec. 17, 1931; Yü Chi-chung, interview (*cit.*, note 22).

123. At this time, there were an estimated fifteen thousand Nanking students and five thousand outsiders in the capital.

124. This youngster, the only recorded martyr of the 1931 student movement, was enrolled at Hui-wen English School in Shanghai. According to Wen Chi-tzu he was a CY member. ("Chiu-i-pa shih-tai . . . ," p. 40, *op. cit.*, note 67.)

125. Ch'ing I, "Pei-p'ing hsüeh-sheng . . . ," pp. 24–27 (*op. cit.*, note 107). Chen Po-shing, "Student Congress Called to Solve National Problems, *CF* 1:1 (Jan. 13, 1932), 2; SD 893.00/11753, Nanking, Dec. 24, 1931; Wen Chi-tzu, "Chiu-i-pa shih-tai . . . ," pp. 39–40 (*op. cit.*, note 67); *CYJP*, Dec. 18, 1931; Ch'en Chi, "Kung-ch'ing-t'uan . . . ," p. 161 (*op. cit.*, note 108).

126. *CYJP*, Dec. 18, 1931.

127. Ch'ing I, "Pei-p'ing t'ung hsüeh . . . ," pp. 28–30 (*op. cit.*, note 107); *CYJP*, Dec. 19, 1931; Ch'en Chi, Kung-ch'ing-t'uan . . . ," pp. 162–63 (*op. cit.*, note 108); *NYT*, Dec. 18, 19, 1931.

128. *CYJP*, Dec. 18, 20, 1931.

129. *CYJP*, Dec. 19, 1931.

130. SD 893.00/11753, Nanking, Dec. 24, 1931.

131. *The Shanghai Evening Post and Mercury*, Dec. 21, 1931, cited in Isaacs, *Five Years*, p. 79. Also see statement of Soong Ching-ling in *CWR*,

59:4 (Dec. 26, 1931), 128. For American refutation, see SD 893.00/11788, Nanking, Jan. 23, 1932.

132. For examples, see *SSHP*, Dec. 23, 1931, and *CYJP*, Dec. 25, 1931.

133. There were 3,000 from Shanghai, 3,500 from Peiping, 3,000 from Tsinan, 2,500 from Hangchow, 1,300 from Süchow (Kiangsu), 150 from Tsingtao, 150 from Hankow, 3,000 from other places. Figures in SD 893.00 PR Nanking/47, Jan. 12, 1932.

134. Wen Chi-tzu, "Chiu-i-pa shih-tai ...," p. 34 (*op. cit.*, note 67).

135. Among the alleged "Kuomintang illusions" was a student affinity for Shanghai Mayor Chang Ch'ün (who had resigned under student pressure!). See Po Ku (pseudonym for Ch'in Pang-hsien), "Lun hsüeh-sheng yün-tung mu-ch'ien ti hsing-shih" (On the Present State of the Student Movement), *Hung-ch'i chou-pao*, no. 27 (Dec. 17, 1931), p. 21.

136. *Ibid.*, pp. 26–27.

137. *CYJP*, Jan. 7, 17, 1932; SSHP, Jan. 10, 13, 1932.

138. *CYJP*, Jan. 12, 20, 1932.

139. SD 893.00 Shanghai/44, Mar. 8, 1932; Chen Po-shing, pp. 1–2 (*op. cit.*, note 125); *CF*, 1:2 (Jan. 20, 1932), 1; 1:3 (Jan. 27, 1932), 2; *SSHP*, Jan. 18, 1932.

140. *SSHP*, Jan. 11, 1932.

141. *SSHP*, Jan. 10, 1932; Hsüeh Ni, "T'i-i tao ch'üan-kuo t'ung-hsüeh mien-ch'ien" (Resolution Presented before the Nation's Students), *SWCK*, pp. 1–3.

142. *SSHP*, Jan. 14, 1932.

143. Kao Wei, "Ching chih-wen hsüeh-lien-hui" (Respectful Inquiries to the Student Union), *SSHP*, Jan. 23, 1932.

144. Chung-yang fen-chü ([Northwest Anhwei] Branch Bureau of the [CCP] Central [Executive Committee]), ed., *Lun hsüeh-sheng yün-tung mu-ch'ien ti hsing-shih* (On the Present State of the Student Movement), Northwest Anhwei, Jan. 23, 1932, in BI. This incorporates Po Ku's article of the same title (*op. cit.*, note 135).

145. Hua Chen-chung and Chu Po-kang, pp. 425–32.

146. O. R. Magill, Letter to friends, Shanghai, Mar. 18, 1932, in YMCAHL.

147. Interview with Yü Chi-chung, one of the three (*cit.*, note 22).

148. This account is based on Hua Chen-chung and Chu Po-kang, ed., article by Hsin-yü, "Chi fu-tan i-yung chün" (Recollections of the Futan Volunteer Army), p. 401–4, and "Hsüeh-sheng i-yung chün sui-ying hsün-lien pan ti-i tui-chang p'eng p'ei-liang pao-kao shu" (Report of the First Regimental Commander, P'eng P'ei-liang, of the Student Volunteer Army Training Group Attached to [the Nineteenth Route Army]), pp. 404–35.

149. "Hsüeh-sheng i-yung chün ...," p. 423 (*op. cit.*, note 148).

150. O. R. Magill, Letter to friends, Shanghai, Mar. 18, 1932, in YMCAHL.

151. Chen Po-shing, p. 2 (*op. cit.*, note 125).

152. Morin, p. 194.

CHAPTER 4

1. "Students Suffering from Major Calamities in China at Present" (Shanghai, May 21, 1932), in YMCAHL.

2. Lang, p. 94.

3. Andrew T. Roy, "Chinese Kaleidoscope," *The Intercollegian and Far Horizons*, 53:2 (Nov.–Dec. 1935), 31–32.

4. *CYJP*, July 4, 1932.

5. Chang Pin, "Ch'üan-shih tsung-pa-k'o kuang-ta fan-kuo-min-tang fa-hsi-ssu-ti yün-tung" (The Citywide General Strike to Expand the Movement Against Kuomintang Fascism), *Pei-fang hung-ch'i*, no. 4 (June 12, 1932), pp. 10–18; Kuang Ho, "Fan-tui pai-se k'ung-pu" (Against the White Terror), *LNCN*, July 1932, pp. 8–16.

6. Wu Ching-hsien, "I-chiu san-erh . . . ," p. 19; Shen Yün-lung interview, Feb. 5, 1960.

7. See the following in the Harold Isaacs Collection (in HI) for leftist attacks: *Chiao-yü chieh, Chiao-yü hsiao-hsi, Hua-pei chiao-yü hsin-wen, Pei-fang ch'ing-nien, Pei-fang lieh-ning ch'ing-nien, Pei-ta lun-t'an, Pei-ta p'ing-lun.* See *Tu-li p'ing-lun* and *Kuo-wen chou-pao* for replies by Hu Shih, V. K. Ting, and others.

8. K'ai Feng (pseudonym for Ho K'o-ch'üan), "Mu-ch'ien hsüeh-sheng yün-tung ti chuang-k'uang yü t'uan ti jen-wu" (The Present State of the Student Movement and the Corps' Responsibility), *Hung-ch'i chou-pao*, no. 29 (Jan. 15, 1932).

9. *The China Journal*, 17:5 (Nov. 1932), 255.

10. *TKP*, June 18, 1933.

11. Kiang Ying-cheng, p. 32.

12. Wang Shih-chieh, "Education," in *The Chinese Year Book 1935–1936*, pp. 479–80; *NCSM*, p. 97; Louis E. Wolferz, Christmas letter to friends, Dec. 13, 1935, Yenching University file in the office of the United Board for Christian Missions in the Far East, New York, N.Y.

13. SD 893.00/12320, Nanking, Feb. 23, 1933.

14. Wu Ching-hsien, p. 19.

15. *Hua-pei chiao-yü hsin-wen*, Oct. 15, 1932.

16. Varg, pp. 235–36.

17. *TKP*, Nov. 12, 13, 1934.

18. *TKP*, May 3, 1935; translation in *Summaries of Leading Articles in the Chinese Press*, 3:24 (June 3, 1935), 9.

19. "Hsiu-cheng min-chung t'uan-t'i tsu-chih fang-an" (Plan for Reforming Mass Organizations), *CYTWYK*, no. 49 (Aug. 1932), pp. 407–10.

20. *CYTWYK*, no. 52 (Nov. 1932), pp. 801–3.

21. KMT-CEC, Min-chung yün-tung . . . ; Shang-hai-shih, vol. 1, Sec. E, p. 11.

22. Mark J. Ginsbourg, "Hupeh's Propaganda Schools," *CWR*, 71:3 (Dec. 15, 1934), 94.

23. In addition to Ginsbourg, see Percival Finch, "Rehabilitating For-

mer Red Territory," *NCH,* Jan. 4, 1933; Downs, pp. 423–25, and Jen-chi Chang, pp. 31–35.

24. Ta-kung-pao hsi-an fen-kuan, pp. 9–10. This statement was made in 1931 at the height of the Manchurian crisis. For evidence that Chiang's views were the same four years later, see *Hsin-wen pao,* Nov. 13, 1935.

25. P'an Kung-chan, p. 21.

26. A dispatch from Berlin in *NYT,* May 22, 1934, reported that a delegation of young Chinese officers was visiting Italy, Germany, and the USSR to study Fascist and Communist techniques. The correspondent observed, "Because of the revolutionary activities among the Chinese younger generation, notably students, the methods whereby Chancellor Hitler has turned the revolutionary enemy in Germany to his own purposes are of particular interest to the Nanking authorities."

27. *TKP,* Dec. 4, 6, 11, 1934.

28. Helen F. Snow, "Is Youth Crushed . . . ."

29. Wolferz, Christmas letter (*op. cit.,* note 12).

30. Dwight W. Edwards, "1934–35 Annual Report," Peiping, Aug. 22, 1935, in YMCAHL.

31. *TKP,* Jan. 14, 1933; *The Yenching News,* Mar. 19, 1935; *The China Journal,* 18:3 (Sept. 1933), 160.

32. T'ao Hsi-sheng, "Pei-p'ing erh-san shih" (Events in Peiping), part 1, *CCWH,* 1:6 (Nov. 1962), 8–9.

33. *Cultural Monthly* (?*Wen-hua yüeh-k'an*), Nov. 15, 1932; cited in Helen F. Snow, "Is Youth Crushed . . . ."

34. "How Chinese Students Are Persecuted," *Student Review,* 11:7 (May 1933), 14–15.

35. Nym Wales (pseudonym for Helen F. Snow), "Fascism in China," cited in *NCSM,* pp. 9, 24.

36. Helen F. Snow, "Is Youth Crushed . . . ."

37. S. C. Leung, "Preliminary Draft of Ten-year Policy of the National [Chinese YMCA] Committee," Shanghai, Apr. 26, 1935, in YMCAHL; also see *TKP,* June 11, 1934.

38. Leung, "Preliminary Draft . . ." (*op. cit.,* note 37).

39. *The Chinese Year Book, 1935–1936,* p. 546.

40. Gregg, p. 147.

41. Roy, "Chinese Kaleidoscope," p. 32 (*op. cit.,* note 3).

42. Ching Po, "K'ai-fang tang-chin yü chen-pa ch'ing-nien" (Cast Off Party Restraints and Rescue Youth), *Ch'ing-hua chou-k'an,* 38:12 (Jan. 14, 1933), 1225.

43. See Nomura, p. 20.

44. For published declarations of CCP student policy, see (1) Chang Pin, "Ch'üan-shih tsung-pa-k'o . . . ," pp. 10–18 (*op. cit.,* note 5); (2) Kuang Ho, "Fan-tui pai-se . . . ," pp. 8–16 (*op. cit.,* note 5); (3) Chung-kuo kung-ch'an ch'ing-nien-t'uan ho-pei-sheng wei-yüan-hui, "Yüan-chu kung-hsüeh-yüan pa-k'o hsüan-yen" (Proclamation in Support of the [National

Peiping University] College of Engineering Strike), *LNCN,* July 1932, pp. 38–40; (4) K'ai Feng, Mu-ch'ien hsüeh-sheng yün-tung . . ." *(op. cit.,* note 8); (5) Chia-chin tui-yü hsüeh-sheng tou-cheng ti ling-tao" (Intensify Leadership in Regard to the Student Struggle), *LNCN,* Oct. 15, 1932, pp. 15–16; (6) Sheng wei.

45. Lang, pp. 317–18.

46. Translation from *Summary of Leading Articles,* 3:20 (Apr. 2, 1935), 2.

47. Leung, "Preliminary Draft" *(op. cit.,* note 37).

48. Lyman Hoover, "Annual Administrative Report," Peiping, June 1933, in YMCAHL.

49. *Yen-ching ta-hsüeh hsiao-k'an,* June 8, 1934; Everett M. Stowe, "Interest of Middle School Youth," *Educational Review,* 27:1 (Jan. 1935), 52.

50. O. R. Magill, "Annual Administrative Report," ?Shanghai, Aug. 1933, in YMCAHL.

51. Edgar Snow, "How Rural China Is Being Remade," *CWR,* 67:5 (Dec. 30, 1933), 303. Similar statements about college youth of that period have been made in my personal interviews with former students of various political persuasions.

52. *TKP,* Mar. 3, 9, 14, 24, Apr. 17, May 31, June 9, 1932; *CF,* 1:17 (June 11, 1933), 11–12; Remer, p. 166.

53. *CWR,* 63:8 (Jan. 21, 1933), 355.

54. Hoh Chih-hsing, "Are Chinese Students Demoralized in the Present Crisis?" *CWR,* 63:8 (Jan. 12, 1933), 351.

55. Fu Ssu-nien, "Chung-kuo-jen tso jen ti chi-hui tao-le" (The Time Has Come for Chinese to Act Like Men), Fu Meng-chen hsien-sheng pien-chi wei-yüan-hui, ed., *Fu Meng-chen . . . ,* V, 49.

56. "How Chinese," pp. 14–15 *(op. cit.,* note 34).

57. Lennig Sweet, "Administrative Report," Peiping, June 10, 1933, in YMCAHL.

58. Ralph M. Hogan, "Annual Administrative Report," Shanghai, June 1, 1933, in YMCAHL.

59. Lyman Hoover, "Annual Administrative Report," Peiping, June 1933, in YMCAHL; also see *Yü-kuan . . . ,* pp. 261–62; *TKP,* Jan. 19, 20, 1933.

60. Hoover, "Report" *(op. cit.,* note 59).

61. Liu Hsiu-ju, one of the original founders of the Shanghai union, answered my questionnaire and I interviewed him in Taipei, Apr. 18–19, 1960. According to Mr. Liu, he and his colleagues accepted the Three People's Principles and had faith in Nanking's determination to fight Japan, but were "rather dissatisfied with the bureaucratic manner of a small number of men" within the party. Though they hated the Communists' "cruel and inhuman methods and principles of organization," they sympathized with the CCP's championship of the underdog. "Thus," he concluded, "we stood on the extreme left wing of the Kuomintang."

62. Liu Hsiu-ju, interview (*cit.*, note 61); Pao Tsun-p'eng, *Chung-kuo ch'ing-nien* . . . , pp. 134–36; Shang-hai-shih, vol. 1, Sec. E, pp. 10–11.

63. Shang-hai-shih, vol. 1, Sec. E, p. 11.

64. KMT, Tang-shih-liao, p. 89; Shang-hai-shih, vol. 1, Sec. E, pp. 10–11.

65. Magill, "Report," (*op. cit.*, note 50).

66. *Yen-ching hsin-wen—The Yenching News*, Feb. 21, 1935.

67. Magill, "Report" (*op. cit.*, note 50).

68. Hoover, "Report" (*op. cit.*, note 59).

69. Magill, "Report" (*op. cit.*, note 50).

70. Kiang Wen-han, "Secularization of Christian Colleges in China," *The Chinese Recorder*, 68:5 (May 1937), 305.

71. Varg, pp. 215–16, 235. Also see Stowe, p. 52.

72. Kiang Wen-han, "Secularization . . . ," p. 305.

73. Lawrence Todnem, "Annual Report," Hankow, Aug. 25, 1934, in YMCAHL.

74. *CYJP*, Sept. 2, 1935.

75. Sanetō, pp. 128–29.

CHAPTER 5

1. *NCS*, Oct. 16, 1935.

2. *NYT*, Nov. 3, 1935.

3. *CWR* 74:11 (Nov. 16, 1935), 369, 375; cited in Bisson, *Japan*, p. 89.

4. Bisson, *Japan*, p. 91; Freyn, p. 16.

5. Interview with James T. C. Liu, Apr. 1, 1957. Now a Princeton professor, Dr. Liu was a student in the Hui-wen Middle School in Peiping at the time of December Ninth. He entered Tsinghua University in the fall of 1936. Compare the revolt against military education in Dec. 1934; see above, p. 98.

6. Chiang Nan-hsiang, "In Memory of Comrade Yang Hsüeh-cheng," in Chiang Nan-hsiang et al., pp. 147–48.

7. Quoted in Yang Chün-ch'en, "I-erh chiu yün-tung ti hui-i" (Recollections of the December Ninth Movement), in *IECYT*, p. 52.

8. Pi Yün-ch'eng, "Fan-men ch'ing-nien ti i-pan hu-sheng" (The General Cry of Anguished Youth), *TCSH*, 1:3 (Nov. 30, 1935), 68.

9. *NYT*, Mar. 13, 1935; *Peiping Chronicle*, Mar. 16, 1935; *Yen-ching hsin-wen—The Yenching News*, March 19, 1935.

10. X. A. N. (pseudonym), "Shih-erh chiu hui-i-lu" (Reminiscences of December Ninth), in Yen-ching ta-hsüeh hsüeh-sheng tzu-chih hui, p. 2; Ying (pseudonym), "Reminiscences from a Diary," *VOC*, 2:1 (Jan. 1, 1937), 8.

11. X. A. N., "Shih-erh chiu . . ." (*op. cit.*, note 10); Ying, "Reminiscences" (*op. cit.*, note 10); *NCSM*, p. 13.

12. *NCSM*, p. 16.

13. *Ibid.*, pp. 13–14.

14. X. A. N., p. 2 (*op. cit.*, note 10).

15. *NCSM*, p. 1; also see Edgar Snow, *Journey*, p. 141.

16. *NCSM*, p. 194.

17. In *NCSM*, p. 12, Helen Snow tells how Chang Chao-lin pleaded with her to put him in contact with the Communists.

18. X. A. N., pp. 5–7 (*op. cit.*, note 10); Ying, pp. 8–9 (*op. cit.*, note 10).

19. X. A. N., pp. 7–9.

20. *Ibid.*, p. 9.

21. *Ibid.*, pp. 9–10.

22. Pei-p'ing shih hsüeh-sheng lien-ho hui, pp. 15–16; Ying, p. 9 (*op. cit.*, note 10).

23. Translation made available through the courtesy of Edgar Snow.

24. Chiang Monlin, pp. 204–5; *TKP*, Dec. 2, 1935.

25. *Hsien-tai chih-shih*, no. 1 (Jan. 25, 1936), p. 74.

26. Ying, p. 9 (*op. cit.*, note 10); X. A. N., pp. 5–7 (*op. cit.*, note 10).

27. Letter from Edgar Snow to "Friend"; quoted in *NCSM*, p. 194.

28. Personal interview (Taipei, Mar. 24, 1960) with Chü Hao-jan, who was a student at Tsinghua during the 1930's. Today he is a teacher on Taiwan.

29. X. A. N., p. 11 (*op. cit.*, note 10).

30. *Ibid.*, pp. 11–12; also see Ying, pp. 9, 22 (*op. cit.*, note 10).

31. X. A. N., pp. 12–13; "I-erh chiu yün-tung ch'ien ti cheng-chih hsing-shih" (The Political Situation before December Ninth), in *IECYT*, p. 9; "Ts'ung i-erh chiu tao ch'i-ch'i ti pei-p'ing hsüeh-sheng yün-tung" (The Peiping Student Movement from December Ninth to July Seventh), in *IECYT*, p. 12.

32. Students collected no official statistics for the December 9 demonstration. Estimates of the number gathered in front of the Chü-jen T'ang range from eight hundred to six thousand; one source claims that marchers numbered nearly ten thousand later in the demonstration. Excluding the Yenching-Tsinghua group outside the Hsi-chih Men, Helen Snow states, "We had guessed that about two thousand students participated on December 9th, but the students later revised this to about 800." (*NCSM*, p. 26.) This last figure is probably the most reliable, since it represents a revised estimate by the students, who were not inclined to minimize their own strength. There were perhaps eight hundred to nearly a thousand in the Yenching-Tsinghua contingent.

33. "Pei-p'ing hsüeh-sheng 'i-erh-chiu' shih-wei" (The Peiping Student Demonstration of December Ninth), *"I-erh chiu" yü ch'ing-nien* (1948), reprinted in *IECYT*, pp. 30–43; Pu Ch'eng, Hsüeh-sheng lien-ho ch'ing-yüan hou ti i-ko ts'an-chia-che ti pao-kao" (The Report of a Participant after the Students' United Petition), *SECTK*, no. 2 (Dec. 17, 1935), pp. 5–8; "Further Developments in the Peiping Student Movement," *CWR* 75:4 (Dec. 28, 1935), 130–33; Packard, pp. 16–18; *NCSM*, pp. 29–30, 161–62; Ch'in Te-chun, "Chi-ch'a cheng-wei-hui shih-ch'i ti hui-i" (Reminis-

censes of the Period of the Hopei-Chahar Political Council), *CCWH*, 2:1 (Jan. 1963), 20; personal interview (Apr. 30, 1957) with William Hung, a former Yenching professor.

34. *NCS*, Dec. 11, 14, 1935; *CWYT*, p. 18.

35. My interview with Mr. Snow, Palisades, N.Y., Mar. 22, 1957.

36. *CWYT*, p. 20; Packard, pp. 38, 87; some of the Tsinghua propaganda materials are in the Wales Collection at HI.

37. *SECTK*, no. 3 (Dec. 20, 1935), p. 12. Other estimates vary between 6,500 and 7,700. The source quoted here is the only one that provides a school-by-school breakdown. After an exhaustive survey of estimates of the number of demonstrators on May 4, 1919, Chow Tse-tsung has determined the figure three thousand to be most reliable. See Chow, pp. 384–85.

38. "Pei-p'ing hsüeh-sheng erh-tz'u shih-wei chi" (Record of the Peiping Students' Second Demonstration), originally appeared in the *Ta-mei wan-pao*, Dec. 19, 1935; reprinted in *IECYT*, p. 47.

39. "Pei-p'ing hsüeh-sheng erh-tz'u . . . ," pp. 44–50; Helen F. Snow, "The Peiping Student Movement" (signed P.F.S.—"Peg" F. Snow), *CWR*, 75:4 (Dec. 28, 1935), 127–29; *SECTK*, no. 3 (Dec. 20, 1935), *passim*; Packard, pp. 20–25; *NCSM*, pp. 32–34, 44, 106, 110–11, 128, 162.

40. Snow, *Journey*, p. 145; Bisson, *Japan*, pp. 107–8.

41. Ang (pseudonym), "Chiu-kuo yün-tung shih fan-tung ma?" (Is the National Salvation Movement Reactionary?), *SECTK*, no. 3 (Dec. 20, 1935), pp. 1–2.

42. "Peiping Students Stage Demonstration Against Autonomy Move," *CWR*, 75:3 (Dec. 21, 1935), 100; Edgar Snow, "The Genesis of the Students' Movement," *CWR*, 75:5 (Jan. 4, 1936), 163; *NCS*, Dec. 12, 18, 1935; *NCH*, Dec. 25, 1935; *NYT*, Dec. 10, 11, 17, 1935.

43. Chung-kuo kung-ch'an chu-i ch'ing-nien t'uan chung-yang wei-yüan-hui (*CY, CEC*), ed., "Wei k'ang-jih chiu-kuo kao ch'üan-kuo ko-hsiao hsüeh-sheng ho ko-chieh ch'ing-nien t'ung-pao hsüan-yen" (A Proclamation to the Entire Nation's School Students and Various Circles of Young Countrymen on Resisting Japan and Saving the Nation), *IECYT*, pp. 136–39. Also quoted in Pao, *Chung-kuo ch'ing-nien . . .*, p. 157, from original in *Ch'ün-chung* (The Masses), vol. VIII: nos. 20–21.

44. Li Wen, "Nan-ching hsüeh-sheng yün-tung ti fu-huo" (The Rebirth of the Nanking Student Movement), *TCSH*, 1:8 (Jan. 4, 1936), pp. 195–96; reprinted in *IECYT*, pp. 129–35.

45. SD 893.00 PR Tientsin/91, Jan. 14, 1936; Chiang Ling, "Hua-pei hsüeh-sheng ti lien-ho chan-hsien (North China's Students' United Front), *TCSH*, 1:13 (Feb. 8, 1936), 323–25; reprinted in *IECYT*, pp. 98–102, and Chiao-tung ch'ing lien, pp. 29–30.

46. *IECYT*, pp. 80–90; *NCSM*, p. 58.

47. Shang-hai hsüeh-sheng fan-jih shih-wei chi fu-ning ch'ing-yüan" (The Shanghai Students' Anti-Japanese Demonstration and Petition to

the Capital), *Chiu-kuo shih-pao* (Paris), Jan. 29, 1936; reprinted in *IECYT*, pp. 103–6. See also *IECYT*, p. 82.

48. "Shang-hai ... ch'ing-yüan," pp. 103–6 (*op. cit.,* note 47); Shang-hai-shih vol. 1, Sec. L, pp. 38–39; Packard, p. 30; P'an Kung-chan, personal interview, Rego Park, N.Y., July 14, 1965. Mr. P'an, representing Shanghai KMT headquarters, persuaded the students to return home. Other officials were Ko Cheng-lun, the Nanking Military Police head, and Lei Chen, from the Ministry of Education.

49. Packard, pp. 33–34.

50. *IECYT*, p. 89.

51. Li Wen, "Nan-ching ... fu-huo," *passim,* and personal interviews with Yang Pi-li (see Chapter 3, note 49) and Shih Chien-sheng, who was a middle school student in Nanking in the 1930's and is today the Dean of the College of Law, National Taiwan University (Taipei, Nov. 1961).

52. Hsiang Tzu, "Wu-ch'ang hsüeh-sheng ta shih-wei chi-shih" (A Factual Record of the Great Wuchang Student Demonstration), *TCSH*, 1:8 (Jan. 4, 1936), 197; *IECYT*, pp. 121–24; SD 893.00/13329, Peiping, Dec. 31, 1935; SD 893.00 PR Hankow/104, Jan. 8, 1936; Nu Ch'ao, "Kuang-chou hsüeh-sheng ti nu-ch'ao," *Tu-shu sheng-huo,* 3:8 (Feb. 25, 1936); reprinted in *IECYT*, pp. 116–20.

53. For example, see issues of *SECTK* and *Chiu-wang san-jih k'an* in Wales Collection at HI.

54. "Chinese Students Under Fire," *The Student Advocate,* 1:2 (Mar. 1936), 12–13.

55. Hatano, p. 388; *NCSM*, p. 43; R. Knailes, "The Students Fight!" *VOC*, 1:1 (Mar. 15, 1936), 3–4.

56. Hua-pei wen-hua lao-tung-che hsieh-hui (North Chinese Cultural Workers' Alliance), *Wei shih-chü kao ch'üan-kuo jen shu* (A Declaration to the Nation's People Concerning the Present Situation), leaflet, Wales Collection in HI; *Pei-p'ing fu-nü,* no. 1 (Mar. 1, 1936), *passim; NCSM,* pp. 79–80, 88, 166.

57. *Pei-p'ing ch'en-pao,* Dec. 10, 1935.

58. Quoted in *NCSM*, p. 31.

59. *Ibid.,* pp. 85–87.

60. *TKP,* Dec. 11, 1935; *CYJP,* Dec. 20, 1935.

61. Hu Shih, "Wei hsüeh-sheng yün-tung chin i-yen," *TKP,* Dec. 15, 1935.

62. Wei Li, "Hu shih-chih tsui-chin ti huang-liao yen-lun ti ch'ing-suan" (A Final Evaluation of Hu Shih-chih's Most Recent Absurd Discussion), *Hsien-tai chih-shih,* no. 1 (Jan. 25, 1936), pp. 48–59; Mo Ning, "Tu-le hu shih ti 'wei hsüeh-sheng yün-tung chin i-yen' " (After Reading Hu Shih's "A Word on the Student Movement"), *SECTK,* no. 3 (Dec. 20, 1935), pp. 2–4. Since the latter was a student publication, the author was probably a student.

63. Mo, p. 4 (*op. cit.,* note 62).

64. *NCSM*, p. 161.

65. *Ibid.*, p. 174; *CWC*, 7:1, (Dec. 30–Jan. 5, 1936), 30.

66. Chang I-ku and Wang Hsiao-feng, "P'ing-chin hsüeh-sheng lien-ho-hui k'uo-ta hsüan-ch'uan-t'uan hsia-hsiang hsüan-ch'uan" (The Peiping-Tientsin Student Union's Propaganda Corps Goes to the Country to Disseminate Propaganda), *IECYT*, p. 62; based on letters in *Ta-chung sheng-huo*, 1:11, 12 (Jan. 25, Feb. 1, 1936), 272–74, 305–7.

67. *Ta-jen, nü-jen, hsiao-hai-tzu-men* (Men, women, children . . .), leaflet in Wales Collection in HI. For an example of the use of traditional story-telling techniques, see Freyn, pp. 40–42, or *Lao-pai-hsing* (The Common Folk), pamphlet in Wales Collection.

68. Freyn, p. 46.

69. *CWC*, 7:2 (Jan. 12, 1936), 39.

70. R. Knailes, "The Students Fight!" p. 4 (*op. cit.*, note 56).

71. Freyn, p. 39. See also Freyn, p. 46 and *IECYT*, p. 58.

72. Freyn, pp. 47–48.

73. *Ibid.*, p. 50.

74. Letter from Li Min to Edgar Snow, Jan. 11, 1936, quoted in *NCSM*, p. 150.

75. Freyn, p. 50.

76. Li Min, letter to the Snows, Jan. 16, 1936, quoted in *NCSM*, p. 151.

77. For the final phase of the pilgrimage, see *IECYT*, pp. 15, 59, 67–69, 73; Freyn, pp. 50–52; *NCSM*, p. 151.

78. Chiang Ling, "Hua-pei . . . ," (*op. cit.*, note 45).

79. Chang I-ku and Wang Hsiao-feng, "P'ing-chin . . . ," p. 69 (*op. cit.*, note 67).

80. Li Min, letter to Helen Snow, Jan. 18, 1936, quoted in *NCSM*, p. 151. Miss Li added parenthetically, "secret, don't publish this."

81. *WMTTW*, pp. 7–8; *IECYT*, pp. 72–79.

82. *WMTTW*, pp. 15, 24; *IECYT*, p. 76.

83. Freyn, pp. 54–55. For a premature report that the Peiping Union would send delegates, see *NCS*, Dec. 25, 1935.

84. Interview with Yang Lien-sheng (Cambridge, Mass., Apr. 26, 1957), who was appointed by Tsinghua chancellor Mei Yi-ch'i; and interview with Yang Hsi-k'un (Taipei, Apr. 18, 1960), who was one of two students chosen by Chiang Monlin at Peita. Yang Hsi-k'un went. (He is presently Vice-Minister of Foreign Affairs and Director of the Department of African Affairs in the Republic of China's Foreign Ministry.) Yang Lien-sheng remained in Peiping. (He is now a professor at Harvard University.)

85. *CWC*, 17:3 (Jan. 13–19, 1936), 3.

86. Freyn, p. 54.

87. "Chiang yüan-chang chao-chien ko hsüeh-hsiao tai-piao" (Chairman Chiang Summons School Representatives), *Fu-hsing yüeh-k'an*, vol.

IV, nos. 6–7 (Mar. 1936); *CWC,* 17:3 (Jan. 13–19, 1936), 3–4; C.Y.W. Meng, "General Chiang and the Professor-Student Conference in Nanking," *CWR,* 75:8 (Jan. 25, 1936), 272–73; Freyn, p. 54; Tong, II, 371.

88. Interview with Yang Hsi-k'un (*cit.,* note 84).

89. Liu Chien-ch'ün, "Hsüeh-ch'ao hui-i yu-kan" (Sentiments on Recollecting Student Disturbances), *CCWH,* 4:6 (June 1964), 35–42; "The Propaganda War and Afterward," *CWR,* 75:12 (Feb. 22, 1936), 404; *NCSM,* p. 49.

90. *Li-hsing-she she-chang* (Constitution of the Endeavor Society), leaflet, Wales Collection in HI. Also see Yen T'ieh, "Na-ch'i ch'iang-kan tou ko-ming" (Take Up Your Guns to Fight the Revolution), in Li Ch'ang et al., p. 156.

91. *International Press Correspondence,* 16:19 (Apr. 18, 1936), 507.

92. See *Ch'ing-hua p'ing-lun,* "Fan-kung chiu-kuo t'e-k'an" (Special Anti-Communist National Salvation Issue), Feb. 14, 1936, and regular issue of Mar. 29, 1936; also see *NCSM,* pp. 106–7.

93. *Ch'ing-hua p'ing-lun,* Feb. 14, 1936, quoted in NCSM, p. 106.

94. *Ch'ing-hua p'ing-lun,* Feb. 14, 1936. My translation is based upon NCSM, p. 50.

95. Hsiao Wen-lan, "Tsou-kuo ti tao-lu" (The Road [We Have] Traveled), *Chung-kuo ch'ing-nien,* no. 211 (Dec. 1, 1952), p. 4.

96. Quoted in Ssu-li pei-p'ing yen-ching ta-hsüeh ch'üan-t'i hsüeh-sheng (Yenching University Student Body), ed., *Wei yao-ch'iu chiu-kuo tzu-yu kao ch'üan-kuo t'ung-pao* (A Proclamation to Countrymen of the Entire Nation in Regard to Demanding Freedom to Save the Nation), Mar. 13, 1936, leaflet in Wales Collection in HI.

97. Pao, *Chung-kuo kung-ch'an-tang . . . ,* p. 37; Lo Chia-lun, *Wen-hua . . . ,* pp. 155–59; *CYTWYK,* no. 91 (Feb. 1936), pp. 125–27.

98. "Lüeh t'an hsüeh-hsiao nei-pu ti kung-tso" (A Brief Talk on Intramural Work in the Schools), *TCSH,* 1:14 (Feb. 15, 1936), 339.

99. Pei-p'ing-shih . . . , p. 13. Further revisions were made subsequently; see "The Propaganda War and Afterward," *CWR,* 75:12 (Feb. 22, 1936), 403–4.

100. *NCS,* Feb. 1, 1936; Freyn, p. 61.

101. *NCS,* Feb. 22, 1936.

102. *NCSM,* pp. 49–51, 131, 153–54, 163. Chang also taught at Tsinghua.

103. *CWYT,* pp. 33–36; "On the Peiping Student Front," *CWR,* 76:3 (Mar. 21, 1936), 107, quoted in *NCSM,* p. 50; *VOC,* 1:1 (Mar. 15, 1936), 15; see also *NCSM,* pp. 88, 107, 128.

104. Ssu-li pei-p'ing yen-ching . . . , *Wei yao-ch'iu . . . (op. cit.,* note 97); the partial translation in *NCSM,* p. 51, is inaccurate.

105. *CWYT,* p. 38; *San-i-pa chi-nien t'e-k'an* (March Eighteenth Memorial Special), Wales Collection in HI.

106. *IECYT*, pp. 17–18; *NCSM*, p. 101. Wang Ju-mei's account of his arrest and imprisonment is given in *NCSM*, pp. 112–17. He was released on Apr. 17, 1936.

107. Hsiao Wen-lan (under pseud. Yang Shu), *Hua shih-tai . . .*, p. 23; also Hsiao Wen-lan, "Ts'ung 'i-erh chiu' tao 'ch'i-ch'i' ti pei-p'ing hsüeh-sheng yün-tung," in *IECYT*, p. 18. The CNLV alleged that Kuo Ch'ing was one of its members, see CNLV, *San-nien-lai. . . .* (Cf. Chapter 3, note 124.)

108. *CWYT*, p. 41.

109. *NCSM*, p. 167.

110. *Ibid.*

111. Freyn, pp. 76–80; *NCSM*, pp. 56, 59, 93; *CWYT*, p. 41.

112. Hsiao Wen-lan, *Hua shih-tai . . .*, p. 23 (*op. cit.*, note 108).

113. *NCSM*, p. 43.

114. *CWYT*, p. 51.

115. "On the Peiping Student Front," *CWR*, 77:2 (June 13, 1936), 72.

116. *NCSM*, pp. 36–41.

117. *Biographical Service*, no. 43. (Nov. 22, 1956).

118. *NCSM*, p. 40. The photograph of Yü Ch'i-wei speaking from a streetcar possibly first appeared in *TCSH* and has been reprinted in Chung-hua ch'üan-kuo . . . ed., p. 24, and in Li Ch'ang et al., fourth page of photographs.

119. *NCSM*, p. 38.

120. *Ibid.*, pp. 196, 197.

121. SD 893.00/13510, Tientsin, May 7, 1936.

122. SD 893.00/13655, Tientsin, July 8, 1936.

123. *NCSM*, p. 39.

124. *Ibid.*, p. 40; SD 893.00/13581, Tientsin, May 28, 1936, estimates that seven to eight thousand students participated, and includes two hand-bills, one addressed "To Our Brethren of the Military and the Police."

125. *NCSM*, p. 37.

126. *VOC*, 1:6 (June 1, 1936), 11; *NCSM*, pp. 42, 90; Freyn, p. 98.

127. United Press dispatch, Peiping, June 11, 1936, quoted in *NCSM*, p. 90. The total was still below that reached before the intensified official suppression that began in Feb. 1936. At that time the Union had embraced 64 schools, representing 24,537 students; see *CWR*, 75:12 (Feb. 22, 1936), 403.

128. *VOC*, 1:6 (June 1, 1936), 11.

129. *NCSM*, p. 90.

130. "Hsi-nan yeh yao k'ang-jih!" (The Southwest Also Wants to Resist Japan!), *Yen-ta chou-k'an*, 7:5 (June 6, 1936), 4.

131. *NCSM*, p. 62.

132. Bisson, *Japan*, p. 43.

133. *Wei jih-pen tseng ping hua-pei kao erh-shih-chiu chün shu* (A Declaration to the Twenty-ninth Army on the Japanese Increase of Troops

in North China), leaflet, Wales Collection in HI; *NCSM*, pp. 63, 182; Bisson, *Japan*, pp. 137–38.

134. Freyn, pp. 92–95; *NCSM*, p. 156.

135. *NCSM*, p. 64.

136. *Ibid.*, pp. 64–65, 118–20; SD 893.00/13551, Peiping, June 15, 1936; Freyn, p. 25.

137. Freyn, p. 103.

138. SD 893.00/13551, Peiping, June 15, 1936.

139. Fei Pai, p. 21.

140. For a fuller discussion of the CCP line on the December Ninth Movement, see my article "The December Ninth Movement: A Case Study." Mr. Snow's comment about his current views appears in *The China Quarterly*, no. 26 (Apr.–June 1966); my reply is in no. 27 (July–Sept. 1966).

141. Snow, *Journey*, p. 142.

142. *Selected Works of Mao Tse-tung*, III, 149, quoted in Snow, *Journey*, p. 146.

143. Israel, "The December Ninth Movement: A Case Study," pp. 154, 158.

144. Hsiao Wen-lan (under pseud. Tzu Fang), "Chi i-erh chiu" (In Remembrance of Dec. 9), *Chung-kuo ch'ing-nien*, no. 53–54 (Dec. 9, 1950), p. 25, reprinted in Hu Hua, p. 345.

145. *NCSM*, p. 36; see Li Min, letter to Helen Snow, *NCSM*, p. 151, (*cit.*, note 80), which virtually acknowledges that the CNLV had Communist connections.

146. *NCSM*, p. 46.

147. Chung-yang tiao-ch'a t'ung-chi chü, pp. 6b-7, 11. I am indebted to Professor Lyman P. Van Slyke for bringing this source to my attention.

148. James T. C. Liu, "Sino-Japanese Diplomacy," p. 218.

CHAPTER 6

1. Thomson, "Communist Policy . . . ," *passim*.

2. Nomura, p. 63. Nomura's research complements Thomson's by its use of Japanese studies. A broader historical survey of the CCP's united front is available in Van Slyke; see especially pp. 56–108.

3. Thomson, "Communist Policy . . . ," pp. 134–37, argues that the CCP reversed itself because of pressure from Moscow. Van Slyke disagrees (pp. 92ff).

4. *NCSM*, pp. 61, 109, 117.

5. Shih Li-te, "A Tribute to Huang Cheng," Chiang Nan-hsiang et al., p. 161. Translated from Li Ch'ang et al., pp. 187–88.

6. *WMTTW*, pp. 12–17.

7. CNLV, *San-nien lai.* . . .

8. Earnest Liang, "Our Summer Vacation," *VOC*, 1:9 (July 15, 1936),

8–9, 16–17; Mei Chung-fu, "The Widening Front," *VOC,* 1:11 (Aug. 15, 1936), 14–16; Hatano, pp. 385ff.

9. "The Way to Life," *VOC,* 1:11 (Aug. 15, 1936), 2–4, 20–22.

10. Nozawa, "12·9 go . . . ," pp. 88–89.

11. Li Pai, "A Dramatic Pilgrimage," *VOC,* 1:11 (Aug. 15, 1936), 9–10.

12. *Ibid.,* p. 10; Nozawa, "12·9 go . . . ," p. 89.

13. Li Ch'ang, "Recollections," (no. 297), p. 29.

14. *WMTTW,* pp. 18–20.

15. Hatano, *Chugoku* . . . , p. 728; Fei Pai, p. 22; *CWR,* 77:8 (July 25, 1936), 292; SD 893.00/13683, Tientsin, July 29, 1936; *WMTTW,* pp. 19–20; CNLV, *San-nien lai* . . . ; Li Ch'ang, "Recollections," (no. 297), pp. 28–29.

16. Ch'in Te-chun, then mayor of Peiping, states that by the outbreak of war, there were more than a thousand student trainees, many of whom were killed in the July 28, 1937 fighting at Nan-yüan. See Ch'in's "Chi-ch'a cheng-wei-hui shih-ch'i ti hui-i," (Reminiscences of the Period of the Hopei-Chahar Political Council), *CCWH,* 2:1 (Jan. 1963), 21.

17. Day, p. 79.

18. *SSHP,* June 2, 1936; *CYTWYK,* no. 95 (June 1936), pp. 558–59.

19. *CWC,* 8:2 (July 9–15, 1936),8.

20. SD 893.00/13683, Tientsin, July 29, 1936.

21. Ch'ing-nien hsüeh-sheng ch'i-chih chih chuan-pien" (Changes in the Temperament of Young Students), *TKP,* Sept. 19, 1936; reprinted in *KWCP,* 13:38 (Sept. 28, 1936); Hsü Yün-shu (pseudonym for Hsü Kao-yüan), Hsüeh-sheng yün-tung ti chien-t'ao" (A Survey of the Student Movement), *KWCP,* 13:38 (Sept. 28, 1936); "Chung-kuo ti ch'ing-nien hsin-li" (The Psychology of China's Youth), *TKP,* Oct. 26, 1936; reprinted in *KWCP,* 13:43 (Nov. 2, 1936).

22. Li Ch'ang, "Recollections," (no. 297), p. 30.

23. *WMTTW,* pp. 23–27, 38–39.

24. Li Ch'ang, "Recollections," (no. 297), p. 30.

25. Bisson, *Japan,* pp. 145–46, 159; Hsiao Wen-lan, *Hua shih-tai* . . . , p. 25; Kwang Lu and Wen Woo-nien, "September Eighteenth in Shanghai," *VOC,* 1:14 (Oct. 1, 1936), 11–13; *K'ung-ch'ien ti chin-chang hsing-shih ho wo-men ti p'o-ch'ieh jen-wu—wei shih-hsien i-ko hsin ti keng wei-ta ti "i-erh chiu" tou-cheng!* (The Unprecedented Tense Situation and Our Pressing Responsibility—to Struggle to Bring About a New, Even Greater, December Ninth!), Peiping, 1936, leaflet in BI, filed with other CNLV leaflets under the folder title, "Min-tsu chieh-fang hsien-feng-tui tui shih-chü hsüan-yen."

26. Hsiao Wen-lan, "Chi i-erh chiu," p. 25.

27. Mei Lo, "To Prove Our Sincerity," *VOC,* 1:17 (Nov. 15, 1936), p. 5.

28. Hsiao Wen-lan, *Hua shih-tai* . . . , p. 25.

29. Mei Lo, "To Prove," pp. 4–5 (*op. cit.,* note 27).

30. *CWR,* 78:8 (Oct. 24, 1936), 279; also see *CWC,* 8:19 (Nov. 5–11, 1936), 29.

31. *WMTTW,* pp. 29–30. CNLV, *San-nien lai* ... ; *VOC,* 1:18 (Dec. 1, 1936), 12, 17–18.

32. Bertram, *First Act,* p. 35.

33. *WMTTW,* pp. 28–29; Chung-yang tiao-ch'a ... ed., *Jen-min* ... , p. 53; *CWC,* 8:20 (Nov. 12–18, 1936), 31–32.

34. Bertram, p. 18.

35. Lu Chiang-mei, "The Army and the Students," *VOC,* 1:18 (Dec. 1, 1936), 11, 17; *CWC,* 8:20 (Nov. 12–18, 1936), 33.

36. Lu, "The Army," p. 11 (*op. cit.,* note 41); Fei Pai, p. 22; *WMTTW,* pp. 28–31; CNLV, *San-nien lai* ... ; Li Ch'ang, "Recollections," (no. 296), p. 35, and (no. 297), p. 29; *Kao shih-min shu* (Declaration to the City's People) and *Pei-p'ing-shih hsüeh-sheng chiu-kuo lien-ho-hui ch'ing-chu kuo-chün shou-fu ta-miao ping ch'ing cheng-fu shou-fu shih-ti tui-jih chüeh-chiao hsüan-yen* (Proclamation of the PSNSU, to Congratulate the National Army on Recovering Ta-miao and to Request the Government to Recover the Lost Territories and to Sever Relations with Japan), leaflets, Wales Collection in HI.

37. *CWC,* 8:21 (Nov. 19–25, 1936), 23; *CWC,* 8:22 (Nov. 26–Dec. 2, 1936), 21; *NCSM,* 158–60; Tsung-tui-pu (Central Headquarters), *Chin-chi t'ung-chih* (Emergency Communique), Nov. 30, 1936, leaflet in CNLV collection in BI (see note 25 for folder title).

38. *K'ung-ch'ien ti chin-chang* ... ; "Students March Again," *VOC,* 2:1 (Jan. 1, 1937),10, 16.

39. Pei-p'ing-shih hsüeh-sheng chiu-kuo lien-ho-hui (PSNSU), ed., *Pei-p'ing-shih ch'üan-t'i hsüeh-sheng shih-wei hsüan-yen* (Demonstration Proclamation of the Peiping Student Body), leaflet in Wales Collection in HI; see *NCSM,* p. 70, for partial translation.

40. KMT educator T'ao Hsi-sheng, who was teaching at Peita during this period, has recently asserted that Communist leaders of the PSNSU timed the demonstration to coincide with the Sian Incident. He presents no evidence for this or for his allegation that the Communists attracted participants by giving each a pair of ice skates. See his "Pei-p'ing erh-san shih" (Events in Peiping), Part 3, *CCWH,* 2:1 (Jan. 1963), 8.

41. Li Ch'ang, "Recollections," (no. 296), p. 35. Hsiao Wen-lan has written a book on the December Ninth Movement, *Chi i-erh chiu,* which has appeared in six editions between 1955 and 1961; some sections had previously appeared in *IECYT.* Though the demonstration was quite clearly run by leftists, we have only Li Ch'ang's account of these colorful details.

42. Li Ch'ang, "Recollections," (no. 296), pp. 35–36; *WMTTW,* pp. 31–32.

43. Songs in Chung-kuo hsin min-chu ... ed., pp. 1, 16–17. For accounts of the demonstration, see Bertram, pp. 8–16; Li Ch'ang, "Recollections," (no. 296), pp. 35–36; *WMTTW,* pp. 31–32; *CWC,* 8:24 (Dec. 10–16, 1936), 31; *NCSM,* pp. 68–70; and "Students March Again," *VOC,* 2:1 (Jan. 1, 1937), 10, 16. Ch'in Te-chun gives his account of the Coal Hill meeting

in "Chi-ch'a . . . ," pp. 20–21, where it is incorrectly presented as an episode in the demonstration of Dec. 9, 1935 (*op. cit.*, note 16).

44. Bertram, p. 108; Snow, *Red Star*, pp. 22; Bisson, *Japan*, p. 160; *VOC*, 2:3 (Feb. 1, 1937), 5–6.

45. *NCSM*, p. 7; Snow, *Journey*, p. 145; Snow, *Red Star*, pp. 20–21; *WMTTW*, p. 45.

46. Bertram, p. 238.

47. Bisson, *Japan*, pp. 159–60.

48. Smedley, p. 137.

49. *Ibid.*

50. Snow, *Random Notes*, p. 5; Bertram, p. 37.

51. Chiang Kai-shek, *A Fortnight*, p. 91. For other accounts of the demonstration, see Li Lien-pi, "Ku-ch'eng nu-huo," in Li Ch'ang et al., pp. 109–14; *NCSM*, pp. 69, 209; Bisson, *Japan*, pp. 165–66; Smedley, pp. 139–40; Snow, *Red Star*, p. 403; Bertram, pp. 114–15.

52. Chiang Kai-shek, *A Fortnight*, p. 90; Selle, pp. 323–24. For an analysis of other events after Dec. 9, 1936, leading to the mutiny of Dec. 12, see Bertram, pp. 115–16.

53. Bisson, *Japan*, p. 167.

54. Li Ch'ang, "Recollections," (no. 297), p. 31.

55. Dallin, p. 69; also see *NCSM*, p. 72; Snow, *Journey*, p. 410; Bertram, pp. 26–27; Thomson, "Communist Policy," pp. 135–36.

56. Mao Tse-tung et al., *China*, pp. 122–23.

57. Li Ch'ang, "Recollections," (no. 297), p. 31.

58. *CWC*, 8:26 (Dec. 24–31, 1936), 27; *TKP*, Dec. 27, 1936.

59. *TKP*, Dec. 27, 1936; *CYJP*, Dec. 17–27, 1936, *passim*; Hsiao Wen-lan, *Hua shih-tai . . .*, p. 27; *Ta-wan pao*, Dec. 28, 1936, translated in *NCSM*, p. 105; Li Ch'ang, "Recollections," (no. 297), pp. 21–32; *CWC*, 9:1 (Jan. 6, 1937), 24.

60. *CYJP*, Dec. 25, 1936; and see Chapter 4, note 26.

61. Li Ch'ang, "Recollections," (no. 297), p. 32; *WMTTW*, p. 34; *NCSM*, p. 74; *CWC*, 9:1 (Jan. 6, 1937), 24; 9:3 (Jan. 20, 1937), 10; 9:4 (Jan. 27, 1937), 30; 9:5 (Feb. 3, 1937), 31.

62. *CWC*, 8:26 (Dec. 24–31, 1936), 28; 9:3 (Jan. 20, 1937), 12; 9:4 (Jan. 27, 1937), 30; Tsang Ch'i-fang, "Kuo-li tung-pei ta-hsüeh" (National Northeastern University), in Chang Ch'i-yün, II, 296–97.

63. Chung-yang tiao-ch'a . . . , ed., *Jen-min . . .* , p. 69; Smedley, p. 147.

64. Bertram, pp. 190–91.

65. Li Lien-pi, "Ku-ch'eng . . . ," in Li Ch'ang et al., p. 116.

66. Bertram, pp. 278–79.

67. *Ibid.*, p. 300, and Snow, *Red Star*, p. 432; Helen Snow, *Inside*, pp. 81–82, 213; Li Lien-pi, "Ku-ch'eng . . . ," in Li Ch'ang et al., p. 116.

68. Hsiao Wen-lan, *Hua shih-tai . . .* , pp. 27–28. (For earlier figures, see Chapter 5, note 127.)

69. *WMTTW*, p. 57. Recently, CNLV leader Li Ch'ang has character-

ized the dissenting faction as "right capitulationist." Li has censured these mavericks for having advocated "unconditional unity" with other groups. His analysis, keyed to present-day ideological exigencies, ignores the problems of ultra-leftism, which seemed more serious to CNLV organizers at the time; compare "Recollections," (no. 297), p. 33, with *WMTTW,* pp. 49, 57.

70. Tsung tui-pu (Central Corps Headquarters), *Han-chia kung-tso ta-kang* (Outline of Winter Vacation Work), Peiping, Jan. 1937, in CNLV collection in BI (see note 25); *WMTTW,* pp. 34, 40; CNLV, *San-nien lai. . . .*

71. Hsiao Wen-lan, *Hua shih-tai . . . ,* p. 29; *Pei-p'ing-shih hsüeh-sheng chiu-kuo lien-ho-hui shang chiang wei-yüan-chang chi san-chung ch'üan-hui shu* (PSNSU Declaration to Chairman Chiang and the Third Plenum of the CEC), leaflet, Wales Collection in HI; *CWC,* 9:6 (Feb. 10, 1936), 30–31; *CWC,* 9:7 (Feb. 17, 1936), 17; "True to their Past," *VOC,* 2:4 (Feb. 15, 1937), 7–8.

72. "Peaceful Unification Hailed," *VOC,* 2:7 (Apr. 1, 1937), 11.

73. Fei Pai, "I-nien lai . . . ," p. 22; Hsiao Wen-lan, *Hua shih-tai . . . ,* p. 29; and Chang Nan.

74. Hsiao Wen-lan, *Hua shih-tai . . . ,* p. 30; Li Hsüeh-sen, "Our First Anniversary," *VOC,* 2:11 (June 1, 1937), 9.

75. Hsiao Wen-lan, *Hua shih-tai . . . ,* p. 30.

76. *Ibid.; TKP,* May 5, 1937; Pao, *Chung-kuo kung-ch'an-tang . . . ,* p. 38; Li Ch'ang, "Recollections," (no. 297), 34.

77. Pao, *Chung-kuo kung-ch'an-tang . . . ,* p. 42.

78. Kiang Wen-han, "Secularization . . . ," p. 303.

79. See Lang, Chapter XX (Chinese Youth), section on "Students," pp. 269–323, and "Appendix," Tables I–XIX, pp. 348–68.

80. *Ibid.,* pp. 277–79.

81. *Ibid.,* p. 316.

82. *Ibid.,* p. 279.

83. *Ibid.,* pp. 363–64.

84. Kiang, "Secularization . . . ," p. 304.

85. Lang, p. 316.

86. Yen-ching ta-hsüeh hsüeh-sheng tzu-chih hui, ed., *Shih-erh chiu . . . ,* pp. 46–61.

87. Lang, p. 286.

88. *Ibid.,* p. 287.

89. *Ibid.,* p. 294.

CHAPTER 7

1. Lifton, pp. 367–77, and Parts Three and Four, *passim.*

Bibliography

Bibliography

This is a selective bibliography that excludes (1) general background works not specifically related to the student movement, except those mentioned in footnotes; (2) individual articles from major periodicals and newspapers; (3) pamphlets, leaflets, and handbills, such as those in the Nym Wales Collection at Stanford's Hoover Institution and in the Bureau of Investigation on Taiwan; (4) unpublished letters and reports in the YMCA Historical Library in New York; (5) all items from the United States State Department Archives and (6) periodicals listed in Abbreviations. For examples of works in these categories, the reader is referred to the Notes.

Rare items are identified by the library where they were consulted (though many doubtless exist elsewhere as well). Libraries are indicated by abbreviations in parentheses (see Abbreviations, pp. 197–98).

Ai Fen. "Kuan-yü hsüeh-sheng ti t'ao-wang," *Pei-p'ing wen-hua*, no. 2 (June 1, 1933), p. 11.

Berkov, Robert. Strong Man of China: The Story of Chiang Kai-shek. Boston, 1938.

Bertram, James M. First Act in China: The Story of the Sian Mutiny. New York, 1938. The British edition is *Crisis in China* (London, 1937).

Biographical Service (Union Research Service), no. 43, Kowloon, Nov. 27, 1956.

Bisson, T. A. "Chinese Student Uprising Blocks Japan," *Foreign Policy Bulletin*, vol. 15 (Jan. 3, 1936), p. 10.

———. Japan in China. New York, 1938.

———. "Nanking Bows to Japan in North China," *Foreign Policy Bulletin*, vol. 14 (Jan. 25, 1935), p. 13.

Brandt, Conrad. "The French-Returned Elite in the Chinese Communist Party." In E. F. Szczepanik, ed., *Symposium on Economic and Social Problems of the Far East* (Hong Kong, 1961), pp. 229–38.

———. Stalin's Failure in China. Cambridge, Mass., 1958.

Brandt, Conrad, Benjamin Schwartz, and John K. Fairbank. A Documentary History of Chinese Communism. Cambridge, Mass., 1952.

Chang Ch'i-yün, ed. Chung-hua min-kuo ta-hsüeh chih (Annals of the Republic of China's Universities). 2 vols. Taipei, 1954.

Chang, Jen-chi. Pre-Communist China's Rural School and Community. Boston, 1960.

Chang Nan. "I-erh chiu i Huang Ching t'ung-chih" (A December Ninth Recollection of Comrade Huang Ching), *Shang-hai wen-hui pao,* Dec. 9, 1958.

Ch'ang-ch'eng (The Great Wall). Shanghai, 1934–35.

Chapman, Herbert Owen. The Chinese Revolution, 1926–27: A Record of the Period under Communist Control as Seen from the National Capital, Hankow. London, 1928.

Ch'en Ch'i-t'ien (under pseud. Ming Chih). *Fan-o yü fan-kung* (Against Russia and Against the Communists). ?Shanghai, 1928.

Ch'en Chüeh. *Chiu i-pa hou kuo-nan t'ung-shih tzu-liao* (Materials on the Painful History of the Post–September-Eighteenth National Crisis). 5 vols. Peiping, 1932–33.

Ch'en, Jack. "Young China's United Front," *Asia,* 38:7 (July 1938), 414–15.

Ch'en-pao. See Pei-p'ing ch'en-pao.

Ch'en Pu-lei. "Fu-ch'i tzu-jen wei-hu chiao-yü chih-hsü chih an-ting" (Bear the Responsibility of Maintaining the Stability of the Educational Order), *Chung-yang chou-pao* (Central Weekly), no. 287 (Dec. 4, 1933), section 3, pp. 7–8.

———. Hui-i-lu (Memoirs). Shanghai, 1949.

Cheng, Ronald Yu-soong. The Financing of Public Education in China: A Factual Analysis of Its Major Problems of Reconstruction. Shanghai, 1935.

Chiang Kai-shek. A Fortnight in Sian: Extracts from a Diary. Shanghai, 1937. Bound in one volume with Mayling Soong Chiang, *Sian: A Coup d'Etat.*

Chiang Monlin. Tides from the West. New Haven, Conn., 1947.

Chiang Nan-hsiang et al. The Roar of a Nation—Reminiscences of the December 9th Student Movement. Peking, 1963. (A partial translation of *I-erh chiu hui-i-lu,* by Li Ch'ang et al., which is listed below.)

Chiao-tung ch'ing-lien (The Chiaotung Youth League), ed. I-erh chiu yü ch'ing-nien (December Ninth and Youth). Chiaotung, 1945.

Chiao-yü chieh (Educational Circles), no. 1. Peiping, July 10, 1933. (HI.)

Chiao-yü hsiao-hsi (Educational News), no. 14. Peiping, Mar. 14, 1933. (HI.)

Chiao-yü pu kung-pao (Ministry of Education Gazette). Nanking, 1929–36.

Chih-nan chou-k'an (The Knowledge-Is-Difficult Weekly). Shanghai, 1927–29.

The China Journal. Shanghai, 1932.

China Today. New York, 1934–37.

The China Year Book. H. G. W. Woodhead, ed. Tientsin, 1927–31; Shanghai, 1932–36.

Chinese Affairs. Nanking, 1928–34.

The Chinese Recorder. Shanghai, 1927–37.

The Chinese Year Book. Kwei Chungshu, ed. Shanghai, 1935–37.

Ch'ing-hua (Tsinghua). Peiping, 1930. (HI.)

Ch'ing-hua chou-k'an (Tsinghua Weekly). Peiping, 1933.

Ch'ing-hua p'ing-lun (Tsinghua Critic). Peiping, Feb. 14 and Mar. 9, 1936. (HI.)

Ch'ing-hua ta-hsüeh hsüeh-sheng tzu-chih-hui chiu-kuo wei-yüan-hui (National Salvation Committee of the Tsinghua University Student Self-Governing Association), ed. Chiu-wang yün-tung pao-kao-shu (Report on the Salvation Movement). Peiping, May 9, 1936. (HI.)

Chiu-kuo k'ang-jih yüeh-k'an—The Young Chinese. Berkeley, Calif., 1936. (HI.)

Chiu-kuo pan-yüeh-k'an (National Salvation Semimonthly), no. 1. Canton, May 1935. (HI.)

Chiu-kuo shih-pao (Giu Guo Sh Bao; Au Secours de la Patrie). Paris, Jan. 29, Feb. 4, and July 25, 1936. (CD.)

Chiu-wang pao-tao (Salvation Report), no. 4. Peiping, Dec. 9, 1936. (HI.)

Chiu-wang san-jih k'an (Tri-Daily Salvation Magazine). Peiping, Dec. 28, 1935. (HI.)

Chow Tse-tsung. The May Fourth Movement: Intellectual Revolution in Modern China. Cambridge, Mass., 1960.

Chu, Samuel. "The New Life Movement, 1934–1937." In John E. Lane, ed., *Researches in the Social Sciences on China* (Columbia University East Asian Institute Studies No. 3, New York, 1957).

Chung-kuo ch'ing-nien (China Youth). Peking, 1952–60.

Chung-kuo hsin min-chu chu-i ch'ing-nien t'uan pei-ching-shih wei-yüan-hui (Peiping Committee of the Chinese New Democratic Youth Corps), ed. Chung-kuo hsüeh-sheng yün-tung ko-ch'ü hsüan (Selected Songs from the Chinese Student Movement). Peking, 1956.

Chung-kuo hsüeh-sheng (Chinese Student). Shanghai, 1929–31.

Chung-kuo kung-ch'an-tang ti-liu-tz'u ch'üan-kuo ta-hui i-chüeh-an (Resolutions of the Sixth National Congress of the Chinese Communist Party). N.p., ?1928. (HI.)

Chung-t'ung-chü. See Chung-yang tiao-ch'a t'ung-chi-chü.

Chung-yang min-chung yün-tung chih-tao wei-yüan-hui. See KMT-CEC, Min-chung . . . .

Chung-yang pan-yüeh-k'an (Central Semimonthly). Nanking, 1928.

Chung-yang tiao-ch'a t'ung-chi chü (Central Bureau of Investigation and Statistics), ed. Chung-kung tsu-chih shih-k'uang (The Actual State of Chinese Communist Organization). ?Nanking, ?1937. (BI.)

———. Jen-min chen-hsien ti t'ou-shih (The People's Front Exposed). ?Nanking, ?1937. (BI.)

CNLV (Chung-hua min-tsu chieh-fang hsien-feng-tui), ed. Min-tsu chieh-fang hsien-feng-tui tui shih-chü hsüan-yen (Proclamations on the Current Situation by the CNLV). ?Nanking, ?1937. Folder title of collection of pamphlets and leaflets. (BI.)

――――. San-nien lai ti min-hsien (The CNLV During the Past Three Years). ?Yenan, 1938. My personal unpaginated version is a handwritten copy of the original in BI.

――――, Tsung-tui-pu (Central Headquarters of the CNLV), ed. Wo-men ti tui-wu (Our Ranks). ?Peiping, 1937. (BI.)

Colm, Peter W. Chinese Communist Tactics: The "United Front from Below" and the "United Front" (1931–1938). Regional Studies Paper, Harvard University, 1951.

Corbett, Charles Hodge. Shantung Christian University (Cheeloo). New York, 1955.

CY Chih-wei-hui (Chinese Communist Youth Corps Executive Committee), ed. Chung-kung ch'ing-nien-t'uan wu ch'üan ta-hui chüeh-i-an (Resolutions of the Fifth National Congress of the CY). N.p., 1928. (BI.)

Dallin, David J. Soviet Russia and the Far East. New Haven, Conn., 1948.

Day, Clarence Burton. Hangchow University. New York, 1955.

Downs, S. W. "Experimental Research and Experiments in Canton, China," *School and Society*, 40:1031 (Sept. 29, 1934), 423–25.

Educational Review. Shanghai, 1927–37.

The Faculty and Students of Tsing Hua University, ed. The Tsinanfu Crisis. Peiping, 1928. (WL.)

Fan-kung chiu-kuo t'e-k'an (Anti-Communist National Salvation Special), premier issue. Peiping, Feb. 9, 1936. (HI.)

Fei Pai. "I-nien lai pei-p'ing hsüeh-sheng yün-tung ti hui-ku" (A Retrospective Look at the Peiping Student Movement During the Past Year), *Chieh-fang* (Liberation), 1:4 (May 24, 1937), 21–23.

Finch, Percy. Shanghai and Beyond. New York, 1953.

Foreign Relations of the United States, 1931. Washington, 1946, 3 vols.

Freyn, Hubert. Prelude to War: The Chinese Student Rebellion of 1935–1936. Shanghai, 1939.

Fu-hsing yüeh-k'an (Regeneration Monthly). Shanghai, 1936.

Fu Meng-chen hsien-sheng pien-chi wei-yüan-hui (The Fu Ssu-nien [Meng-chen] Editorial Committee), ed. Fu Meng-chen hsien-sheng chi (Collected Works of Fu Ssu-nien). 6 vols. Taipei, 1952.

Gourlay, Walter E. "Yellow Unions in Shanghai: A Study of Kuomintang Technique in Labor Control," *Papers on China*, vol. 7 (1953), pp. 103–35.

Gregg, Alice H. China and Educational Autonomy: The Changing Role of the Protestant Educational Missionary in China, 1807–1937 Syracuse, N.Y., 1946.

Grieder, Jerome Bailey. Hu Shih and Liberalism: A Chapter in the Intellectual Modernization of China. Ph.D. thesis, Harvard University, 1962.

Hatano Ken'ichi. Chūgoku kyōsantō sen-kyū-hyaku-sanjū-roku-nen shi (History of the Chinese Communist Party for 1936). Tokyo, 1937.
———. Gendai shina no seiji to jimbutsu (Politics and Personalities of Contemporary China). Tokyo, 1937.
"How Chinese Students Are Persecuted," *Student Review*, 2:7 (May, 1933), 14–15.
Hsia, C. T. A History of Modern Chinese Fiction. New Haven, Conn., 1961.
Hsia, T. A. Enigma of the Five Martyrs, A Study of the Leftist Literary Movement in Modern China. Berkeley, Calif., 1962.
Hsiao Wen-lan (under pseud. Yang Shu). Hua shih-tai ti i-erh chiu (The Epoch-making December Ninth). Hankow, 1937. (BI.)
——— (under pseud. Yang Shu). Chi i-erh chiu (Memory of December Ninth). Peking, 1954.
——— (under pseud. Tzu Fang). Chi i-erh chiu (Memory of December Ninth). Peking, 1955.
——— (under pseud. Yang Shu). Chi i-erh chiu (Memory of December Ninth). Peking, 1961. (A revised and enlarged edition of the two preceding works.)
Hsien-tai chih-shih (Xiandai Zhsh; Contemporary Knowledge). Premier issue. Shanghai, Jan. 25, 1936. (HI.)
Hsien-tai hsüeh-sheng (Contemporary Student). Shanghai, 1930–31.
Hsin-ch'en-pao ts'ung-shu shih (The New Peiping Morning Post Series Press), ed. Pei-p'ing ko ta-hsüeh ti chuang-k'uang (The State of Peiping's Universities). Peiping, 1929. Revised edition, 1930. (HY.)
Hsin-chü (The New Typhoon), no. 6. ?Shanghai, June 30, 1932.
Hsin-sheng (New Life). Shanghai, 1934–35.
Hsin shih-tai pan-yüeh-k'an (New Age Semimonthly), no. 2. Wuchang, Sept. 1, 1932.
Hsin-wen-pao (The News). Shanghai, scattered issues, 1931–35.
Hsing-cheng-yüan she-chi wei-yüan-hui (Planning Committee of the Executive Yüan), ed. Kung-fei ch'ing-nien yün-tung chih yen-pien yü p'ou-hsi (The Evolution of the Communist Bandit Youth Movement and an Analysis). Taipei, 1953.
Hsing-ch'i (The Weekly), no. 2. Shanghai, Apr. 22, 1928. (TB.)
Hsü Li-ch'ün. "I-erh chiu yün-tung ti-ssu chou-nien" (The Fourth Anniversary of the December Ninth Movement), *Tu-shu yüeh-pao* (The Reader Monthly), 1:10 (Sept. 1, 1939), 453–54.
Hsüan-ch'uan-che (The Propagandist), no. 7. Shanghai, Apr. 4, 1931.
Hsüeh-sheng chou-pao (Xyoshengzhoubao; Student Weekly). Peiping, 1936.
Hsüeh-sheng tsa-chih (Students' Magazine). Shanghai, 1927–31; Hong Kong, 1941.
Hu Ch'iu-yüan. "Pei-fa shih-ch'i" (The Period of the Northern Expedition), *Min-chu ch'ao* (Current Democracy; Democratic Current), 9:21

(195) (Nov. 1, 1959), 10–15; and 9:22 (196) (Nov. 16, 1959), 12–16. (The English title "Current Democracy" appears on the cover; however the correct translation of the Chinese title is "Democratic Current.")

Hu Hua, ed. Chung-kuo hsin min-chu chu-i ko-ming shih ts'an-k'ao tzu-liao (Reference Materials for the History of China's New Democratic Revolution). Shanghai, 1951.

Hu I-kuan. "Ch'ing-nien yün-tung ti li-lun ho shih-chi" (The Theory and Actuality of the Youth Movement), *Hsin sheng-ming* (New Destiny), 1:6 (June 1, 1928).

Hua Chen-chung and Chu Po-kang. Shih-chiu-lu chün k'ang-jih hsüeh-chan shih-liao (Historical Materials on the Nineteenth Route Army's Bloody War to Resist Japan). Shanghai, 1933.

Hua-pei chiao-yü hsin-wen (North China Education News). Peiping, 1932. (HI.)

Huang Ti, " 'Wu-ssu' i-lai chih chung-kuo hsüeh-ch'ao" (China's Student Storms since May Fourth), *She-hui-hsüeh chieh* (The Sociological World), vol. 6 (June 1932), pp. 287–303.

Hung-ch'i chou-pao (Red Flag Weekly). Scattered issues, 1931–34. (HI.)

Hung-ch'i jih-pao (Red Flag Daily). Shanghai, Oct. 1930. (HI.)

Hung-ch'i p'iao-p'iao (Red Flag Waving). 12 vols. Peking, 1957–58.

I-pan (In General). Shanghai, 1927–28.

I-shih pao (Yi shih pao; Social Welfare). Tientsin, Dec. 1931.

International Press Correspondence, English edition. Vienna, Berlin, London, 1927–35.

Isaacs, Harold R., ed. Five Years of Kuomintang Reaction. Reprinted from the Special May Edition of the *China Forum,* Shanghai, May 1932.

———. The Tragedy of the Chinese Revolution. Second revised edition, Stanford, Calif., 1961. (First edition, 1938.)

Israel, John. The Chinese Student Movement, 1927–1937. Ph.D. thesis, Harvard University, 1963.

———. The Chinese Student Movement: 1927–1937: A Bibliographical Essay Based on the Resources of the Hoover Institution. Stanford, Calif., 1959.

———. "The December Ninth Movement: A Case Study in Chinese Communist Historiography," *China Quarterly,* no. 23 (July-Sept. 1965), pp. 140–69.

———. The Student Movement of December 9, 1935. Regional Studies Paper, Harvard University, 1957.

Iwamura Michio. Chūgoku gakusei undō-shi (History of the Chinese Student Movement). Tokyo, 1949.

Jen-min ch'u-pan she (People's Publishing House), ed. I-erh chiu yün-tung (The December Ninth Movement). Peking, 1954.

Kao Yin-tsu, ed. Chung-hua min-kuo ta-shih chi (Chronology of Major Events of the Chinese Republic). Taipei, 1957.

Kawai Shingo. Kokumintō Shina no kyōiku seisaku—toku ni sono minzokushugiteki keikō o chūshin to shite (Kuomintang China's Educational Policy—with Special Reference to its Nationalistic Orientation). Tokyo, 1941.

Kennedy, Melville Talbot, Jr. The Kuomintang and Chinese Unification, 1928–1931. Ph.D. thesis, Harvard University, 1958.

Kiang Wen-han. The Chinese Student Movement. New York, 1948.

Kiang Ying-cheng. The Geography of Higher Education in China. Ph.D. thesis, Columbia University, 1955.

KMT, Chung-yang hsüan-ch'uan pu (Central Ministry of Propaganda), ed. Chung-kuo kuo-min-tang ti-erh-chieh chung-yang chih-hsing wei-yüan ti-ssu-tz'u ch'üan-t'i hui-i hsüan-yen ping i-chüeh an hsüan-ch'uan ta-kang (Outline for Propagandizing the Proclamations and Resolutions of the Fourth Plenum of the Members of the Chinese Kuomintang's Second Central Executive Committee). Nanking, 1928. (HI.)

———, Chung-yang mi-shu ch'u (Central Secretariat), ed. Chung-kuo kuo-min-tang ti-erh-chieh chung-yang chih-hsing wei-yüan ti-wu-tz'u ch'üan-t'i hui-i chi-lu (Record of the Fifth Plenum of the Members of the Chinese Kuomintang's Second Central Executive Committee). Shanghai, 1928. (HY.)

———, Ho-pei-sheng tang-wu cheng-li wei-yüan-hui (Hopei Provincial Party Affairs Reform Committee of the KMT), ed. Jen-min t'uan-t'i fa-kuei hui-pien (Collection of Regulations on Popular Organizations). Peiping, ?1930.

———, Tang-shih-liao pien-chi wei-yüan-hui (KMT Editorial Committee for Materials on Party History), ed. Min-kuo erh-shih-san-nien chung-kuo kuo-min-tang nien-chien (The 1934 KMT Yearbook). ?Nanking, 1934. (SC.)

———, Ti-san-chieh san-chung ch'üan-hui chung-yang hsün-lien pu kung-tso kai-k'uang pao-kao (Report of the Third Plenum of the Third [KMT] CEC on the General State of the Training Ministry's Work). ?Shanghai, 1930. (KMTA.)

———, T'ien-chin t'e-pieh-shih chih-hsing wei-yüan-hui hsüan-ch'uan pu (Propaganda Bureau of the Tientsin Special City Executive Committee of the Chinese Kuomintang), ed. Ko-ming ch'ing-nien ti shih-ming (The Destiny of Revolutionary Youth). Tientsin, 1929. (KMTA.)

KMT-CEC (Chung-kuo kuo-min-tang chung-yang chih-hsing wei-yüan-hui), ed. Min-chung hsün-lien wei-yüan-hui kung-tso pao-kao (Report on the Work of the Committee for Training the Masses). ?Shanghai, 1929. (KMTA.)

———, Hsüan-ch'uan pu (Ministry of Propaganda), ed. Ko-ming ch'ing-nien (Revolutionary Youth). ?Shanghai, 1930. (SC.)

———, Hsün-lien wei-yüan-hui (Training Committee), ed. Chung-kuo kuo-min-tang li-tz'u hui-i hsüan-yen chi chung-yao chüeh-i-an hui-pien (Collection of Proclamations and Important Resolutions of Successive Conferences of the KMT). 3 vols. Chungking, 1941. (SC.)

———, Min-chung yün-tung chih-tao wei-yüan-hui (The Mass Movements Guidance Committee), ed. Chung-kuo kuo-min-tang ch'üan-kuo min-chung yün-tung kung-tso t'ao-lun-hui pao-kao-shu (Report of the Colloquium on the KMT's National Mass Movements). ?Nanking, June 1934. (SC.)

———, ———. Ch'üan-kuo jen-min t'uan-t'i t'ung-chi (Statistics on the Nation's Popular Organizations). Nanking, 1935. (HI.)

———, ———. Min-chung yün-tung fa-kuei fang-an chi-lan (A General Survey of Regulations and Plans for Mass Movements). ?Nanking, July 1933. (HY.)

———, ———. Min-chung yün-tung fa-kuei fang-an hui-pien (Collection of Regulations and Plans for Mass Movements). 2 vols. ?Nanking, June 1934. (SC.)

Ko-ming p'ing-lun (Revolutionary Critic). Shanghai, 1928. (HI.)

Kuang-hua ch'i-k'an (Kuanghua Monthly). Shanghai, 1929. (HI.)

Kuang-hua chou-pao (Kuanghua Weekly). Shanghai, 1927. (HI.)

Kuei ch'ao (Kwangsi Tide). Shanghai, Jan. 1932. (HI.)

Kung-ch'ing-t'uan wo-ti mu-ch'in (My Mother, the Communist Youth Corps). Chung-kuo ch'ing-nien ch'u-pan-she (China Youth Publishers), ed. Peking, 1958. Reprinted from issues of *Hung-ch'i p'iao-p'iao*.

Kuo-fang wen-i (National Defense Literature). Peiping, 1936. (HI.)

Kuo-li pei-ching ta-hsüeh fei-ch'ang hsüeh-sheng hui (Extraordinary Student Association of National Peking University), ed. Pei-ching ta-hsüeh shih-wei yün-tung chuan-k'an (Special Issue on the Peking University Demonstration Movement). Peiping, 1932. (HI.)

Kuo-min p'ing-lun (The Citizen Critic). Shanghai, 1931–32.

Lang, Olga. Chinese Family and Society. New Haven, Conn., 1946.

Li Ch'ang. "Recollections of the National Liberation Vanguard of China." In *Selections from China Mainland Magazines,* no. 296 (Jan. 15, 1962), pp. 27–36, and no. 297 (Jan. 22, 1962), pp. 28–43. Translated from an article in *Chung-kuo ch'ing-nien* (China Youth), no. 22 (Nov. 16, 1961), pp. 6–16. Also appears in Li Ch'ang et al., listed below.

Li Ch'ang et al. "I-erh chiu" hui-i-lu (Memoirs of December Ninth). Peking, 1961.

Li Shu-hua. The Reminiscences of Li Shu-hua as Told to Minta Chou Wang, August 17, 1960, to February 22, 1961. Mar. 1961. Columbia University Chinese Oral History Project. Typed manuscript in the Special Collections Library, Butler Library, Columbia University.

Lifton, Robert Jay. Thought Reform and the Psychology of Totalism. New York, 1961.

Ling-tang (The Bell). Tientsin, 1932–36. (HI.)

Liu Ch'ün. Hsien tai hsüeh-sheng ti ken-pen wen-t'i (Basic Questions About Contemporary Students). Shanghai, 1936.

———. Kao p'ang-huang chung ti chung-kuo ch'ing-nien (To the Perplexed Youth of China). Shanghai, 1936.

Liu, James Tze-chien. Sino-Japanese Diplomacy During the Appeasement Period. Ph.D. thesis, University of Pittsburgh, 1950.

Lo Chia-lun. Tsui-chin i-nien chih ch'ing-hua (Tsinghua in the Past Year). ?Peiping, ?1929.

———. Wen-hua chiao-yü yü ch'ing-nien (Culture, Education, and Youth). Taipei, 1952.

Loh, Pichon P. Y. The Popular Upsurge in China: Nationalism and Westernization, 1919–1927. Ph.D. thesis, University of Chicago, 1955.

Ma Hsiang-po. I-jih i-t'an (A Talk a Day). Shanghai, 1936.

Ma Hsü-lun. Wo tsai liu-shih sui i-ch'ien (My Life Before Age Sixty). Shanghai, 1947.

Mao Tse-tung. Selected Works. 5 vols. London, 1954.

Mao Tse-tung et al. China: The March Toward Unity. New York, 1937.

Mao Tun. See Shen Yen-ping.

Min-hsien-tui. See CNLV.

Min-tsu chieh-fang chan-hsien (Liberigo de Cina Popolo; National Liberation Front). Peiping, Dec. 1935. (HI.)

Ming Chih. See Ch'en Ch'i-t'ien.

Mo-teng ch'ing-nien (Modern Youth), no. 1. ?Shanghai, 1929.

Montell, Sherwin. The New Life Movement. Regional Studies Paper, Harvard University, 1952.

Morin, Relman. East Wind Rising: a Long View of the Pacific Crisis. New York, 1960.

Mu-tan-chiang-shih ch'ing-nien t'uan chou-pei wei-yüan-hui (Mutankiang City Youth Corps Preparatory Committee), ed. Wei-ta ti i-erh-chiu yün-tung (The Great December Ninth Movement). Mutankiang, 1948.

Nan-feng (South Wind), 2:3. Canton, Nov. 1, 1935.

Nei-cheng-pu nien-chien pien-chi wei-yüan-hui (Ministry of Interior Yearbook Editorial Committee), ed. Nei-cheng nien-chien (Ministry of Interior Yearbook). 4 vols. Shanghai, 1936.

Nomura, Tomohide. Some Aspects of the United Front in China, 1931–36. M.A. thesis, Columbia University, 1961.

Nozawa Yutaka. "12·9 zengo—kō-nichi minzoku tōitsu sensen no keisei katei" (The December Ninth Period—The Process of the Formation of the National United Front to Resist Japan), Rekishi hyoron (Historical Critic), no. 41 (Jan. 1953), pp. 116–27.

———. "12·9 go no chūgoku gakusei undō no kō-nichi kyūkoku undō" (The Chinese Students' Resist Japan National Salvation Movement After December Ninth), Rekishi hyoron (Historical Critic), no. 44 (Apr. 1953), pp. 84–91.

———. "Tōitsu sensen to intelligentsia" (The United Front and the Intelligentsia). In Sekai-shi ni okeru asia; rekishigaku kenkyūkai 1953 nendo taikai hō koku (Asia in World History; Report of the 1953 Meeting of the Historical Research Society), Tokyo, 1953, pp. 133–43.

Packard, Ruth L. The Chinese Student Movement, 1935–1936. M.A. thesis, University of Chicago, 1941.

P'an Kung-chan. Hsüeh-sheng ti hsin sheng-huo (The Student's New Life). Nanking, 1935.

Pao Tsun-p'eng. Chung-kuo chin-tai ch'ing-nien yün-tung shih (History of the Modern Chinese Youth Movement). Taipei, 1953.

——. Chung-kuo ch'ing-nien yün-tung shih (History of the Chinese Youth Movement). Taipei, 1954.

——. Chung-kuo kung-ch'an-tang ch'ing-nien yün-tung shih lun (A Discussion of the History of the CCP Youth Movement). Nanking, 1947.

——. Hsiao-mieh t'a hai-shih pei t'a hsiao-mieh—kung-fei p'o-hai ch'ing-nien shih-lu (Kill or Be Killed—The True Story of the Communist Bandits' Persecution of Youth). Taipei, 1953.

——. Our Incoexistible Foe. Taipei, 1953. A translation of *Hsiao-mieh* . . . , listed above.

Peake, Cyrus H. "Manchurian Echoes in Chinese Nationalism," *Pacific Affairs,* 7:4 (Dec. 1934), 406–14.

——. Nationalism and Education in Modern China. New York, 1932.

Pei-fang ch'ing-nien (Northern Youth), nos. 3–7. Peiping, Apr. 20–May 30, 1932. (HI.)

Pei-fang hsiao-pao (The Little Northern Newspaper). Peiping, May 1, 1932. (HI.)

Pei-fang hung-ch'i (Northern Red Flag). Peiping, 1932–33. (HI.)

Pei-fang lieh-ning ch'ing-nien (Northern Leninist Youth), no. 1. Peiping, July 1932. (HI.)

Pei-p'ing ch'en-pao (The Peiping Morning Post). Peiping, 1931–36.

Pei-p'ing fu-nü (Peiping Woman). Premier issue, Peiping, Mar. 1, 1936. (HI.)

Pei-p'ing hsüeh-lien jih-pao (Peiping Student Union Daily), no. 6. Peiping, Jan. 29, 1936. (HI.)

Pei-p'ing hsüeh-sheng k'ang-jih chiu-kuo lien-ho hui (Peiping Student Resist Japan National Salvation Union), ed. Shih-wei—fan-jih yün-tung yü pei-p'ing hsüeh-sheng (Demonstration—the Anti-Japanese Movement and Peiping's Students). Peiping, 1932. (HI.)

Pei-p'ing-shih hsüeh-sheng lien-ho-hui (Peiping Student Union), Pao-kao-shu (Report). Peiping, Jan. 28, 1936. (HI.)

Pei-ta chou-k'an (Peita Weekly). Peiping, 1935–36. (HI.)

Pei-ta hsin-wen (Peita News). Peiping, May-July 1932. (HI.)

Pei-ta lun-t'an (Peita Forum). Peiping, Jan. 6, 1933. (HI.)

Pei-ta p'ing-lun (Peita Critic), no. 2. Peiping, May 11, 1933. (HI.)

P'ing-hsi-pao—The Yenching Gazette. Yenching University, Sept. 10–Dec. 12, 1931. (HY.)

Purcell, Victor. Problems of Chinese Education. London, 1936.

Remer, C. F. A Study of Chinese Boycotts. Baltimore, 1933.

Rosinger, Lawrence K. China's Wartime Politics, 1937–1944. Princeton, N.J., 1944.

Roy, Andrew T. "Chinese Kaleidoscope," *The Intercollegian and Far Horizons,* 53:2 (Nov.-Dec. 1935), 31–32.

Sanetō Keishū. Chūgoku-jin nihon ryūgaku-shi (History of Chinese Students in Japan). Tokyo, 1960.

Scott, Roderick. Fukien Christian University: A Historical Sketch. New York, 1954.

Selle, Earl Albert. Donald of China. New York, 1948.

Shanghai Evening Post and Mercury. Shanghai, scattered issues, 1930–36.

Shang-hai-shih t'ung-chih kuan (Gazetteer Office of the City of Shanghai), ed. Chung-hua min-kuo erh-shih-wu-nien shang-hai-shih nien-chien (The City of Shanghai Yearbook, 1936). 2 vols. Shanghai, 1936.

She-hui yü chiao-yü she (Society and Education Association), ed. Ta-hsüeh tsa-ching (College Scenes). Shanghai, 1932.

Shen-pao (The Shun Pao). Shanghai, 1931–37.

Shen Yen-ping (under pseud. Mao Tun). Huan-mieh (Disillusioned). Shanghai, 1930.

Sheng-huo (Life). Shanghai, 1931–33.

Sheng-wei (Shensi Provincial Committee of the CCP), ed. Hsüeh-sheng yün-tung ti chüeh-i (Resolution on the Student Movement). Shensi, ?1933. (BI.)

Shih Ts'un-t'ung, ed. Mu-ch'ien chung-kuo ko-ming wen-t'i (Present Problems of the Chinese Revolution). ?Shanghai, 1928.

Shrader, Ralph Raymond. Some Adjustment Problems of Chinese High School Students. M.A. thesis, University of Chicago, 1933.

Shu Chih. "Tsai ch'ing-nien ch'ün-chung mien-ch'ien ti lu" (The Road Before the Youthful Masses), *Yü-chou chih kuang* (Cosmic Light), no. 1 (Sept. 18, 1932), pp. 17–18.

Smedley, Agnes. Battle Hymn of China. New York, 1943.

Snow, Edgar. Red Star Over China. New York, 1938.

———. Random Notes on Red China (1936–1945). Cambridge, Mass., 1957.

———. Journey to the Beginning. New York, 1958.

Snow, Helen F. (under pseud. Nym Wales). Is Youth Crushed Again in China? Manuscript, Peiping, 1935. (HI.)

———. Inside Red China. New York, 1939.

———. Notes on the Chinese Student Movement. Madison, Conn., 1959. Mimeographed.

———. My Yenan Notebooks. Madison, Conn., 1961. Mimeographed.

Ssu-fa hsing-cheng-pu tiao-ch'a chü (Bureau of Investigation of the Ministry of Justice), ed. Kung-fei hsüeh-yün kung-tso ti p'ou-shih (The Communist Bandits' Student Movement Work Exposed). Taipei, 1961.

Ssu-ma Lu. Tou-cheng shih-pa nien (Eighteen Years of Struggle). Hong Kong, 1952. With an introduction by Hu Ch'iu-yüan.

Stuart, John Leighton. Fifty Years in China. New York, 1946.

Student Advocate. New York, 1936.

The Student World. Geneva, 1936.

Su-lien yin-mo wen-cheng hui-pien (Collection of Documentary Evidence of the Soviet Conspiracy). Peking Metropolitan Police Headquarters, Inspection Bureau, Commission for Translation and Compilation, ed. and trans. Peking, 1928.

Summaries of Leading Articles in the Chinese Press. London, 1932–37.

Sun Te-chung, ed. Ts'ai Yüan-p'ei hsien-sheng i-wen lei-ch'ao (A Topical Collection of the Bequeathed Writings of Mr. Ts'ai Yüan-p'ei). Taipei, 1961.

Survey of International Affairs. London, 1927–37.

Ta-chung chan-ch'i (Battle Flag of the Masses). Peiping, Feb. 1936. (HI.)

Ta-kung-pao hsi-an fen-kuan (Sian Branch Office of the *Ta-kung-pao* [*L'Impartial*]), ed. Ling-hsiu k'ang-chan chien-kuo wen-hsien ch'üan-chi (The Leader's Collected Writings on the War of Resistance and National Construction). Sian, 1939.

Tai Chi-t'ao. Ch'ing-nien chih lu (The Road of Youth). 1st ed., Shanghai, 1927; 2d ed., Chungking, 1942.

Thomson, James Claude, Jr. Americans as Reformers in Kuomintang China, 1928–37. Ph.D. thesis, Harvard University, 1961.

———. "Communist Policy and the United Front in China," *Papers on China*, vol. 11 (1957), pp. 99–148.

Timperley, H. J. "The North China Federation of Students," *School and Society*, vol. 43 (Jan. 11, 1936), p. 1098.

Ting Chih-p'in. Chung-kuo chin ch'i-shih nien lai chiao-yü chi-shih (Events in Chinese Education during the Last Seventy Years). Shanghai, 1935.

Tong, Hollington K. Chiang Kai-shek, Soldier and Statesman. 2 vols. Shanghai, 1937.

Tretiakov, S. A Chinese Testament: the Autobiography of Tan Shih-hua, as Told to S. Tretiakov. New York, 1934.

"Two National Universities Discontinued in Three Days," *The China Critic*, 5:17 (July 7, 1932), 677–78.

Tzu Fang. See Hsiao Wen-lan.

Van Slyke, Lyman P. Friends and Enemies: The United Front and Its Place in Chinese Communist History. Ph.D. thesis, University of California at Berkeley, 1964.

Varg, Paul A. Missionaries, Chinese, and Diplomats: The American Protestant Missionary Movement in China, 1890–1952. Princeton, N.J., 1958.

Voice of the Chinese People Regarding the Sino-Japanese Questions. Shanghai, 1928. (WL.)

Wales, Nym. See Helen F. Snow.

Walker, Richard L. "Students, Intellectuals and 'The Chinese Revolution.'" In Jeane J. Kirkpatrick, ed., *The Strategy of Deception: A Study in World-wide Communist Tactics*. New York, 1963.

Wang Chien-hsing, ed. Hsüeh-sheng yü cheng-tang (Students and Political Parties). Shanghai, 1927. (TB.)

Wang Nien-k'un. Hsüeh-sheng yün-tung shih-yao chiang-hua (A Discussion of the Basic History of the Student Movement). Shanghai, 1951.

———. Wo-kuo hsüeh-sheng yün-tung shih hua (Some Words on the History of Our Country's Student Movement). Hankow, 1954.

Wang Tao-yü, Chin Chia-hsün, and Shang Hsi-fan, eds. Min-chung yün-tung yü hsün-lien (Mass Movements and Training). Peiping, 1928.

Wang, Y. Chu. "The Intelligentsia in Changing China," *Foreign Affairs*, 36:2 (Jan. 1958), 315–29.

———. "Intellectuals and Society in China, 1860–1949," *Comparative Studies in Society and History*, 3:4 (July 1961), 395–426.

Wen-hua (Culture). Shanghai, 1934–35.

Wilbur, C. Martin, and Julie Lien-ying How. Documents on Communism, Nationalism, and Soviet Advisors in China, 1918–1927. New York, 1956.

Wu Ching-hsien. "I-chiu san-erh nien chih chung-kuo hsüeh-ch'ao" (China's Student Tides in 1932), *Hsüeh-feng* (School Spirit), 3:1–2 (Mar. 1933), 13–23. (TB.)

Wu-hsien-tien (Radio), no. 1004. ?Sian, Jan. 24, 1937. (HI.)

Wu Jung-chih, ed. Min-chung t'uan-t'i tsu-chih fa (Organizational Laws for Mass Organizations). Shanghai, 1927. (SC.)

Yang Chia-ming. Min-kuo shih-wu nien chung-kuo hsüeh-sheng yün-tung kai-k'uang (A General Survey of the Chinese Student Movement in 1926). Shanghai, 1927. (HY.)

Yang Chün-ch'en. "I-erh chiu yün-tung ti hui-i" (Reminiscence of the December Ninth Movement), *Chieh-fang jih-pao* (*Giefang Rhbao*; Liberation Daily), Dec. 9, 1944. (HI.)

Yang Shu. See Hsiao Wen-lan.

Yang Yeh. Chung-kuo hsüeh-sheng yün-tung ti ku-shih (The Story of the Chinese Student Movement). Nanking, 1957.

Yao I-lin. "Chi-nien i-erh chiu" (Commemorating December Ninth), *Chieh-fang jih-pao* (*Giefang Rhbao*; Liberation Daily), Dec. 13, 1945. (HI.)

Yeh Sheng-t'ao (under pseud. Yeh Shao-chün). Han-chia ti i-t'ien (A Day in Winter Vacation). Peking, 1957.

Yen-ching hsin-wen—The Yenching News. Peiping, scattered issues, 1934–35. (HY.)

Yen-ching ta-hsüeh ch'ing-pao (Yenching University Intelligence Report). Peiping, 1935. (HI.)

Yen-ching ta-hsüeh hsiao-k'an (Yenching University Weekly). Peiping, Feb. 19 and 26, 1932; Mar. 4 and June 8, 1934. (HY.)

Yen-ching ta-hsüeh hsüeh-sheng tzu-chih-hui (Yenching University Student Self-governing Association), ed. Shih-erh chiu chou-nien chi-nien t'e-k'an (Special Memorial Issue on the Anniversary of December Ninth). Peiping, 1936. (HI.)

Yen-ching ta-hsüeh hsüeh-sheng tzu-chih hui ch'u-pan wei-yüan-hui (Yenching University Student Self-governing Association Publications Committee), ed. San i-pa chi-nien t'e-k'an (March Eighteenth Special Memorial Issue). Peiping, Mar. 17, 1936. (HI.)

The Yenching Gazette. See P'ing-hsi-pao.

Yen-ta chou-k'an (*Ianda Zhoukan*; Yenching University Weekly). Peiping, 1935–36. (HI.)

The Young Chinese. See Chiu-kuo k'ang-jih yüeh-k'an.

Yü-chou-feng (Cosmic Wind). Shanghai, 1936.

Yü I-ning. "Chi-nien 'i-erh chiu' yün-tung shih-liu chou-nien" (In Commemoration of the Sixteenth Anniversary of the December Ninth Movement), *Li-shih chiao-hsüeh* (Historical Pedagogy), no. 12 (Dec. 1951), pp. 185–86.

Yü-kuan k'ang-jih chan shih (The History of the War to Resist Japan at Shanhaikuan). Shanghai, 1934. (HY.)

Yü Ta-fu. "Hsüeh-sheng yün-tung tsai chung-kuo" (The Student Movement in China). In *Ta-fu ch'üan-chi* (Complete Works of Yü Ta-fu), vol. 7 (Shanghai, 1933), pp. 53–61.

Index

Index